The Failure of the Criminal Procedure Revolution

The Failure of the Criminal Procedure Revolution

Craig M. Bradley

To Kent,

Best wishes

Craig Bradley

UNIVERSITY OF PENNSYLVANIA PRESS　　Philadelphia

Library of Congress Cataloging-in-Publication Data

Bradley, Craig M.
    The failure of the criminal procedure revolution / Craig M.
Bradley.
        p.   cm.
    Includes bibliographical references (p.   ) and index.
    ISBN 0-8122-3200-3
    1. Criminal procedure—United States.   2. Criminal justice,
Administration of—United States.   I. Title.
KF9223.B7   1993
345.73′05—dc20
[347.3055]   92-42021
                                                        CIP

To Cindy, Derek, and Kathleen

Contents

.

Acknowledgments

Many people have assisted me in the preparation of this manuscript. I hope that I have remembered all of them. Some of these people may not even realize that they were helping with the book, since their comments were on the article in the *Journal of Criminal Law and Criminology* in which I first introduced the proposal that forms the basis of this book. In alphabetical order, these people are Prof. Francis Allen of the University of Florida, Prof. Ronald Allen of Northwestern University, Prof. Joshua Dressler of Wayne State University, Prof. John Garvey of the University of Kentucky, Prof. Yale Kamisar of the University of Michigan, Prof. Michael Klarman of the Univesity of Virginia, Krystie Herndon, Secretary, Indiana University, Prof. Joseph Hoffmann of Indiana University, Prof. Lauren Robel of Indiana University, Prof. George Rutherglen of the University of Virginia, Moira Squier, Student Research Assistant, Indiana University, and Prof. Robert Weisberg of Stanford University.

Chapter 5, the comparative chapter, required more extensive assistance from the following people: (Australia) Peter Waight, Senior Lecturer in Law, Australian National University; (England) David Feldman, Reader in Law, University of Bristol; (France) Richard Frase, Professor of Law, University of Minnesota; (Germany) Thomas Weigand, Professor of Law, University of Cologne; Volker Röben, Fellow, Institute for International Law, Kiel; Antje Petersen, Student Research Assistant, Indiana University; (Italy) Lawrence Fassler, Attorney, Shearman and Sterling, New York.

Finally, two people whose assistance went far beyond the call of duty: Professor William Stuntz of the University of Virginia and Professor Gerard Lynch of Columbia University.

Portions of this book have previously appeared, generally in somewhat different form, in the following law review articles: "The Exclusionary Rule in Germany," *Harvard Law Review* 96 (1983):

1032–1066; "Two Models of the Fourth Amendment," *Michigan Law Review* 83 (1985): 1468–1501; "The Uncertainty Principle in the Supreme Court," *Duke Law Journal* (1986): 1–64; "Criminal Procedure in the Land of Oz: Lessons for America," *Journal of Criminal Law and Criminology* 81 (Spring 1990): 99–135.

Finally, I wish to thank the American Bar Association for permission to use the Table in Chapter 3 and Her Majesty's Stationery Office for permission to reprint portions of the Police and Criminal Evidence Act and the Home Office Codes of Practice in the Appendix.

Introduction

"Criminal procedure" means the entire range of activities associated with bringing a criminal defendant to trial. It begins with investigation by the police, including searches of houses, cars, and so on, and lineups and photo displays of potential suspects; it proceeds through arrest, interrogation, arraignment, preliminary hearing, indictment by grand jury, trial, sentencing, appeal, and collateral challenges to conviction. The "criminal procedure revolution" refers to a series of constitutional decisions by the United States Supreme Court during the 1960s that "revolutionized" the criminal procedures of the states. For example, the Court required that unconstitutionally seized evidence must be excluded from state criminal trials, that police must warn criminal suspects of their constitutional rights before interrogating them (the *Miranda* warnings), and that indigent defendants must be given free counsel at any criminal trial that might lead to a prison sentence.

At the time these requirements were imposed, criticism of the Court's rulings was vehement. Many complained that the courts were "handcuffing the police." A rising crime rate was blamed on the Court's rulings, and Richard Nixon made the appointment of "law and order" Supreme Court Justices a major issue in his successful 1968 presidential campaign.

After Nixon had appointed four Justices, the pendulum swung in the opposite direction. Liberal critics of the "Burger Court" complained that constitutional guarantees of civil liberties were being "gutted" and that a reemergence of "police state" tactics by law enforcement authorities was imminent.

The dire predictions of both extremes have proved inaccurate. For example, the police have been able to adapt to giving the *Miranda* warnings to suspects without a major diminution in confessions. And, contrary to early expectations, the Burger Court did not overrule

Miranda, though it did not extend it so much as its liberal critics would have liked. Both sides seem to agree that representation of all criminal defendants by counsel at trial and on at least one appeal is a good thing and should be provided free of charge to indigent defendants. Of the three most significant innovations of the Warren Court, only the "exclusionary rule," forbidding the use of illegally seized evidence at trial, remains the subject of serious controversy.

Despite this agreement, nobody thinks that the criminal procedure system is working well. Police, prosecutors, judges (including the Supreme Court Justices themselves), crime victims, and academic commentators, both liberal and conservative, condemn the system as seriously flawed—as, indeed, a failure. The title of a 1988 report by the American Bar Association (ABA), *Criminal Justice in Crisis*,[1] captures this feeling. To some extent, these criticisms are unavoidable. Policies that appeal to one faction will not appeal to another. The failure of politicians to provide adequate funding to police departments to catch criminals, to courts to try them, and to prisons to hold them must also accept a major share of the blame. Naturally, people directly involved in the system will feel that it deserves more resources than will the average taxpayer, but so does every group that competes for limited governmental funding.

This book argues that the American criminal procedure system is flawed in a way that goes beyond ideological criticisms and lack of resources. To put it another way, no shift in ideology; no commitment of resources, no matter how large; no refinement of Supreme Court jurisprudence, no matter how skilled; would solve the problems that are the subject of this book. Because of a unique constitutional system, America has developed its "rules" of criminal procedure piecemeal, on a case-by-case basis, rather than through a code of criminal procedure. Every other major country in the world uses a legislatively enacted code of criminal procedure. Only the United States expects its police to follow a set of rules so cumbersome, and so complex, that one area of criminal procedure law alone—search and seizure—requires a four-volume treatise to explicate it.

As we will see, there are historical reasons why this deeply flawed system developed as it did. In brief, in the nineteenth and early twentieth centuries, the belief grew that the federal government should step in to remedy the widespread abuses by state and local police of the rights of criminal suspects, particularly black criminal suspects. But it was not clear whether the federal government, being one of limited powers, had the authority to do so. Eventually, through a long process, beginning with the watershed case of *Brown v. Mississippi* in 1936, the Supreme Court began to interpret the due process clause of the post-Civil War fourteenth amendment as giving it power to deter abuses of the most fundamental rights of criminal suspects by the states, and to ensure fair trials, by reversing the convictions of those abused. That is, the Court held that someone who had been convicted on the basis of an unreasonable search or an involuntary confession had been deprived of his or her liberty without "due process of law."

Over the ensuing years, the Court expanded its view of what rights were "fundamental" to include virtually all the guarantees (previously applicable only to the federal government) in the Bill of Rights. Thus the Bill of Rights prohibitions against unreasonable searches and seizures and self-incrimination and its requirements of trial by an impartial jury and right to counsel were applied to the states to the same extent as to the federal government. Gradually, the Court decided so many cases in the criminal procedure area that courts and lawyers looked to it as, essentially, the only authoritative source of law on the subject. Today, one can look in vain through a law school criminal procedure book for any serious discussion of state cases and statutes. Law students are taught, essentially correctly, that the only source of law that matters in this area is Supreme Court cases (though some states do have fairly detailed codes).

However, these Supreme Court cases, because of their nature, are inherently flawed as a method of declaring rules, particularly rules for non-lawyers (i.e., police), which must be easy to understand, internalize, and obey. Few of the criticisms of the exclusionary rule stem from any disagreement that fundamental law violations by the police should be deterred by evidentiary exclusion. Rather they reflect a belief that, because of the complexity and incompleteness of the "rules," the police violations do not seem "fundamental." To expect the police to discern how to act in a given situation from a series of thirty-page Supreme Court cases rendered over, perhaps, a twenty-year period is unrealistic. No wonder, as recent studies have shown, that neither state and local police nor state courts are able consistently to understand and apply the criminal procedure "rules" declared by the Supreme Court.[2]

Until recently, all I could propose was that the Court should recognize the problems that inhered in its efforts to declare rules of criminal procedure case by case, and to try, as best it could, to simplify those rules so that the police could follow them more readily.[3] While, as discussed in Chapter 7, I still believe that this would be a useful reform, it does not avoid the two problems that inhere in using cases as a means of developing rules of criminal procedure: uncertainty and incompleteness. As will be developed in detail in Chapter 4, uncertainty as to the precise limits of the rule being declared arises because of the fact-bound, precedent-bound nature of case law. Moreover, since cases can only deal with the issue presented, cannot anticipate variations on that issue, and are driven by the exclusionary rule, case law is necessarily incomplete. It can take, and has taken, twenty years or more for the Supreme Court to resolve issues that could have been settled in advance by a statute. Many other such issues remain unsettled today and show no prospect of being resolved at any time soon.

The problem has been that the only legislative body capable of promulgating nationally applicable rules of criminal procedure is Congress, or a rulemaking body established by Congress. Congress has been thought to lack jurisdiction to do this, but, as I argued in a 1990 article in the *Journal of Criminal Law and Criminology*,[4] once the Supreme Court incorporated the Bill of Rights into the due process clause of the fourteenth amendment it automatically gave Congress the power to legislate to enforce these rights as well. Section 5 of the fourteenth amendment provides that "Congress shall have power to enforce, by appropriate legislation, the provisions of this article." Indeed, the Supreme Court has repeatedly made it clear that Congress has greater authority under the fourteenth amendment, because of the explicit grant of authority in section 5, than the Court itself. Accordingly this book proposes that Congress, acting through a rule-making body appointed by it such as the current Advisory Committee on the Federal Rules of Criminal Procedure, should enact a national code of criminal procedure. The pros and cons of this proposal are discussed in detail in Chapter 6.

Chapter 1 of this book discusses the history of criminal procedural law in the United States prior to the 1960s. Chapter 2 discusses the "criminal procedure revolution" that occurred in that decade. Chapter 3 details how that revolution has failed and Chapter 4 explains why. Chapter 5 discusses the criminal procedure systems in six foreign countries: Australia, Canada, France, Germany, England, and Italy. Chapter 6 discusses why a national code of criminal procedure is possible, and why it is the best solution to the problem. Chapter 7 discusses three alternative approaches.

While many will regard this as a radical proposal, it is radical only in the sense that it shifts primary authority for developing rules of criminal procedure from the Supreme Court to Congress. It does not deprive the Supreme Court of its ultimate authority to determine the constitutionality of the rules of criminal procedure just as the Court does now, though no doubt the Court would be more hesitant to exercise that power than it is today if such exercise entailed overruling congressional legislation.

This proposal also does not strike a blow against federalism or "states' rights" in any meaningful way. While neither the Supreme Court nor the states like to admit it, the fact is that the Court has already completely coopted state authority in the area of criminal procedure. While it is true that there are gaps in the Court's jurisprudence, no one seriously believes that these gaps are a result of a lack of Supreme Court (i.e., federal) jurisdiction. Rather they exist simply because the Supreme Court, for a variety of reasons discussed in Chapter 4, has not gotten around to filling them and because the process of filling one gap tends to create others. As long ago as 1969, Edmund W. Kitch titled an article in the *Supreme Court Review*, "The Supreme Court's Code of Criminal Procedure: 1958–1969 Edition." This book simply proposes to make concrete and systematic what has existed in a de facto and disorganized way for many years. Just as it was time, in the early part of the century, for courts to admit that they made law rather than "finding" it, so it is time to admit that the declaration of the rules of criminal procedure has become a national matter and to proceed to develop a rational and comprehensive set of rules to govern criminal procedure nationwide.

This book is not about the failure of the criminal justice *system*. Most people would agree with the ABA study that the system is in crisis because of increased crime, particularly drug-related crime, and lack of adequate resources. These much-discussed problems are not treated here. Rather this book is about the failure (partial failure—many of the Warren Court innovations continue to dominate) of the criminal procedure *revolution*. It contends that the legal structure created by the Supreme Court is deeply flawed but can be improved relatively easily compared to the other problems of the system. The overall effect of this improvement cannot be guaranteed, but as a lawyer who has worked in and studied the criminal law for twenty years I believe it would be substantial.

Finally, though this book is written to be accessible to the general reader, extensive chapter endnotes are provided for those who want to delve more deeply into the matters discussed.

Notes

1. American Bar Association, *Criminal Justice in Crisis*.
2. William Heffernan and Richard Lovely, "Evaluating the Fourth Amendment Exclusionary Rule"; Craig Bradley, "Are State Courts Enforcing the Fourth Amendment?"
3. Craig Bradley, "Two Models of the Fourth Amendment."
4. Craig Bradley, "Criminal Procedure in the Land of Oz."

Chapter 1
Before the Revolution

Until the 1960s, the concept of "criminal procedure" did not have the same meaning that it does today. There was no law school course by that name; at best, some observations about the topic were tacked onto a course in criminal law. "Criminal procedure" generally meant the formal, legal procedure of the criminal justice system from arrest through sentencing. Thus, if one looks to rules of "criminal procedure" such as the American Law Institute's model rules adopted in 1930, one finds no mention of searches, interrogations, or police identification procedures.[1] What we think of as the very essence of the subject today was completely ignored. Because these matters took place outside the formal system of justice, lawyers and judges were oblivious to them. The common law rule was that "it matters not how you get [evidence]; if you steal it even, it would be admissible in [court]."[2] This non-exclusionary policy divorced the courts from the evidence gathering process. "Criminal procedure" was a matter for the courts. "Evidence gathering" was a matter for the police.

The problem with this policy of apartheid was that it was difficult to reconcile with federal and state constitutional provisions forbidding unreasonable searches and seizures and requiring that criminal defendants be accorded "equal protection" and "due process of law."* These constitutional guarantees caused the Supreme Court to make its first tentative explorations of what had heretofore been the constitutional terra incognita of police procedures. But before the Court

---

*The fourteenth amendment to the United States Constitution provides, in pertinent part: "[No State shall] deprive any person of life, liberty, or property without due process of law; nor deny to any person within its jurisdiction the equal protection of laws."

turned to issues surrounding the investigation of crimes, it concerned itself with what went on during the trial.

In *Strauder v. West Virginia*,[3] decided in 1879, the Court reversed the state criminal conviction of a Negro on the ground that a state statute barred Negroes from jury service, thus denying the defendant equal protection of the laws, in violation of the fourteenth amendment. More generally, the Court recognized that

Due process of law, guaranteed by the Fourteenth Amendment does not require the state to adopt a particular form of procedure, so long as it appears that the accused has had sufficient notice of the accusation and an adequate opportunity to defend himself in the prosecution.[4]

However, despite this open-ended statement of the requirements of due process, and hence of its own authority to reverse state court criminal convictions on due process grounds, the Court did not avail itself of this power in the nineteenth century, other than in a handful of cases involving statutory exclusion of Negroes from jury service.[5] Still, notice had been served that the Court had the power, if not yet the inclination, to demand that criminal procedural law at both the federal and state levels conform to certain standards, at least insofar as the conduct of trials was concerned.

In the late nineteenth and early twentieth centuries the Court went much further in its regulation of federal proceedings, concerning itself with the investigatory process. In *Boyd v. United States*,[6] decided in 1886, it struck down the forfeiture of goods that had been confiscated after Boyd was compelled to produce certain invoices. While this was not a criminal case, the Court's holding that private papers could not be subject to search or seizure (or subpoena) by the government and its implied holding that, if they were, they must be excluded from evidence were to have a major impact on the future development of criminal procedure law.

In the 1906 case of *Hale v. Henkel*[7] the Court held that federal subpoenas for corporate papers might run afoul of the fourth amendment if they were overbroad. More importantly, in 1914, in *Weeks v. United States*,[8] the Court held explicitly that any evidence obtained by federal authorities in violation of the fourth amendment* (that is, by way of an "unreasonable" search or seizure) must be excluded from

---

*The fourth amendment to the United States Constitution provides that "The right of the people to be secure in their persons, houses, papers, and effects, against unreasonable searches and seizures, shall not be violated, and no Warrants shall issue, but upon probable cause, supported by Oath or affirmation, and particularly describing the place to be searched, and the persons or things to be seized."

the defendant's criminal trial in federal court. The Court held that if illegally seized material can thus be "used in evidence against a citizen accused of an offense, the protection of the Fourth Amendment declaring his right to be secure against searches and seizures is of no value, and . . . might as well be stricken from the Constitution."[9]

This declaration of what came to be known as the "exclusionary rule" meant that the Court was prepared not just to regulate the formal, legal proceedings—what had heretofore been regarded as "criminal procedure"—but to extend its supervision to police practices as well. However, because federal law enforcement was much more limited then than it is today, *Weeks* did not have enough impact on the development of the law to change the popular conception among lawyers that "criminal procedure" law did not include police practices.

Still, once *Weeks* had declared that unreasonably seized evidence must be excluded from federal trials, it was natural, indeed, virtually unavoidable, for federal trial judges, and eventually for the Supreme Court itself, to attempt to define just what police investigative activity was "reasonable" and what was "unreasonable." Otherwise, decisions to exclude or admit evidence would be perceived as irrational and law enforcement officials would not know what to do. Thus it was that the Court, without really admitting to itself that it had taken on this task, began attempting to declare the "rules" of criminal procedure—that is, to give the police guidance as to what searches would, and what would not, be considered "reasonable."

The effort started slowly. In *Silverthorne Lumber Co. v. United States*,[10] decided six years after *Weeks*, the Court held that a corporation was entitled to fourth amendment protection and that the arrest of the defendant at his home gave no right to search the corporate offices. Consequently, the books and papers seized from the offices not only could "not be used before the Court" but could "not be used at all."[11] (That is, they could not be used as leads for finding other evidence.) Thus, the "fruit of the poisonous tree" doctrine was born.

In the 1921 case of *Gouled v. United States*[12] the Court struck a major, albeit ill-advised, blow for criminal defendants, holding that only fruits or instrumentalities of the crime, not "mere evidence," could be subject to search or seizure at all. Thus, if a suspect maintained a list of "murders I have committed," because this was his list and was not "stolen or forged"[13] it was not subject to seizure and, if seized, must be excluded from evidence. This distinction, based on outmoded common law property notions, caused constant confusion in fourth amendment law until it was abandoned by the Supreme Court in 1967.[14] Over the next decade, the court established the "warrant requirement" for searches of, at least, houses,[15] and required that the probable cause in those warrants be based on more than just the officer's statement of his or her belief that contraband was to be found at the place to be searched.[16] And, in a series of cases it recognized consent, automobile, and incident to arrest searches as exceptions to the warrant requirement.[17] Similarly, in the spirit of its fourth amendment exclusionary rule, the Court had long held that coerced confessions, including those induced by threats and promises, as well as by brutality, were inadmissible in federal trials because they violated the fifth amendment* prohibition against compulsory self-incrimination.[18]

But if the Court had made some strides at controlling the activities of federal law enforcement authorities, it had made little effort to regulate state proceedings, and such effort as it had made was limited to the conduct of trials. Police practices were ignored altogether. Charles Nutting, discussing this topic in a 1935 article in the *University of Chicago Law Review*, summarized the "restricted scope" of Supreme Court intervention in state procedures:

Race discrimination in the selection of juries has been the concern of the bulk of the cases. Aside from this, such rudimentary requirements of due process as the lack of pecuniary interest of a magistrate, freedom from mob domination, the right to representation by counsel (in a capital case), the existence of some evidence to connect the accused person with the violation of the statute, and, possibly, the requirement that one shall not be convicted on the basis of perjured testimony consciously used by the prosecuting attorney have been insisted on.[19]

While the states were thus put on notice that "elementary decencies must be observed" in their trial courts, their police felt free to treat criminal suspects with barbarity. The situation was so bad that it aroused President Herbert Hoover, while complaining that "our law enforcement mechanism . . . unduly favors the criminal,"[20] grudgingly to appoint a National Commission on Law Observance and Enforcement (commonly known as the Wickersham Commission, after its chairman) to report on enforcement of the prohibition laws as well as on lawlessness in law enforcement. This body conducted an extensive investigation of police interrogation practices and concluded that

the third degree—that is the use of physical brutality, or other forms of cruelty, to obtain involuntary confessions or admissions— is widespread. Protracted questioning of prisoners is commonly employed. Threats and methods of intimidation, adjusted to the age or mentality of the victim, are frequently used, either by themselves or in combination with some of the

---

*The fifth amendment to the United States Constitution provides in pertinent part: "No person . . . shall be compelled in any criminal case to be a witness against himself. . . ."

other practices mentioned. Physical brutality, illegal detention, and refusal to allow access of counsel to the prisoner is common. Even where the law requires prompt production of a prisoner before a magistrate, the police not infrequently delay doing so and employ the time in efforts to compel confession. . . . Brutality and violence in making an arrest are also employed . . . in order to put [the prisoner] in a frame of mind that makes him more amenable to questioning afterwards.[21]

The Commission proceeded to detail numerous instances of truly reprehensible police misconduct. It also found that "searches or seizures without warrants required by law" were "habitual" in certain regions of the country.[22]

By contrast, in a study of unfairness at trial, the Commission found that, while abuses did exist, they were "sporadic"—"the fault of the individual trial judge or individual prosecutor"—rather than the result of official policy.[23] Moreover, the Commission found that there was little evidence of the practice of the third degree among federal authorities.[24]

While the best explanation for the observance of law by trial personnel and federal agents compared to state and local police surely related to professionalism, the Supreme Court probably noticed that in the areas where it had attempted to improve procedures—federal law enforcement and state trials—improved procedures seemed to have occurred. By contrast, the area that it had left untouched—state police practices—was a national disgrace.

Whether inspired by the findings in the Wickersham report, which it was to rely on in *Miranda v. Arizona*,[25] concerned about racism affecting even-handed law enforcement,[26] or simply disgusted by the facts of the cases coming before it, the Court soon changed its policy. The circumstances under which the confessions of the defendants in *Brown v. Mississippi* (1936)[27] were obtained by the police are set out in the opinion of Chief Justice Charles Evans Hughes:

The crime with which these defendants, all ignorant negroes, are charged, was discovered about one o'clock p.m. on Friday, March 30, 1934. On that night one Dial, a deputy sheriff, accompanied by others, came to the home of Ellington, one of the defendants, and requested him to accompany them to the house of the deceased, and there a number of white men were gathered, who began to accuse the defendant of the crime. Upon his denial they seized him, and with the participation of the deputy they hanged him by a rope to the limb of a tree, and having let him down, they hung him again, and when he was let down the second time, and he still protested his innocence, he was tied to a tree and whipped, and still declining to accede to the demands that he confess, he was finally released and he returned with some difficulty to his home, suffering intense pain and agony. The record of the testimony shows that the signs of the rope on his neck were plainly visible during the so-called trial. A day or two thereafter the said deputy, accompanied by another, returned to the home of the said defendant and arrested him, and departed with the prisoner towards the jail in an adjoining county, but went by a route which led into the State of Alabama; and while on the way, in that State, the deputy stopped and again severely whipped the defendant, declaring that he would continue the whipping until he confessed, and the defendant then agreed to confess to such a statement as the deputy would dictate, and he did so, after which he was delivered to jail.

The other two defendants, Ed Brown and Henry Shields, were also arrested and taken to the same jail. On Sunday night, April 1, 1934, the same deputy, accompanied by a number of white men, one of whom was also an officer, and by the jailer, came to the jail, and the two last named defendants were made to strip and they were laid over chairs and their backs were cut to pieces with a leather strap with buckles on it, and they were likewise made by the said deputy definitely to understand that the whipping would be continued unless and until they confessed, and not only confessed, but confessed in every matter of detail as demanded by those present; and in this manner the defendants confessed the crime, and as the whippings progressed and were repeated, they changed or adjusted their confession in all particulars of detail so as to conform to the demands of their torturers. When the confessions had been obtained in the exact form and contents as desired by the mob, they left with the parting admonition and warning that, if the defendants changed their story at any time in any respect from that last stated, the perpetrators of the outrage would administer the same or equally effective treatment.

Further details of the brutal treatment to which these helpless prisoners were subjected need not be pursued. It is sufficient to say that in pertinent respects the transcript reads more like pages torn from some medieval account, than a record made within the confines of a modern civilization which aspires to an enlightened constitutional government.

Nevertheless, the Supreme Court of Mississippi upheld the admissibility of the confessions and the convictions.

Although *Brown* obviously involved compulsory self-incrimination, contrary to the fifth amendment, the Court in *Brown* reiterated the 1908 holding of *Twining v. New Jersey*[28] that the privilege against self-incrimination did not apply to the states. But "Compulsion by torture to extort a confession is a different matter. The State is free to regulate the procedure of its courts in accordance with its own conceptions of policy unless in so doing it 'offends some principle of justice so rooted in the traditions and conscience of our people as to be ranked as fundamental.'"[29] Because the conduct of the police in this case did offend such a principle, it violated fourteenth amendment "due process," and the convictions were reversed on that ground.

Having opened the Pandora's box of police interrogation procedures, the Court was to find that it could never close it. Four years after *Brown* it decided *Chambers v. Florida*.[30] In that case, after the murder of a white man, twenty-five to forty Negroes were rounded up without warrants, detained for five days without charge, questioned repeatedly, and threatened with mob violence until one of them "broke." After declaring that "abhorrence of illegal confinement, torture and extortion of confessions" was at the very heart of due process of law,[31] the Court reversed the convictions. In doing so, the Court noted that

the due process provision of the Fourteenth Amendment—just as that in the Fifth—has led few to doubt that it was intended to guarantee procedural safeguards adequate and appropriate, then and thereafter, to protect, at all times, people charged with or suspected of crime by those holding positions of power and authority. Tyrannical governments had immemorially utilized dictatorial criminal procedure and punishment to make scapegoats of the weak, *or of helpless political, religious or racial minorities.* . . . Under our constitutional system, courts stand against any winds that blow as havens of refuge for those who might otherwise suffer because they are helpless, weak, outnumbered, or because they are nonconforming victims of prejudice and public excitement.[32]

To the same effect were *White v. Texas*[33] and *Canty v. Alabama*,[34] both decided during the same Term and both involving extended interrogations of unschooled Negro defendants.

Throughout these early cases the Court deplored the police interrogation tactics, causing some to believe that the reason that the confessions were ordered excluded was to deter the use of such tactics in the future. But in the 1941 case of *Lisenba v. California*[35] the Court held that that was not the purpose of the exclusionary rule in these cases. Rather the purpose was to promote a "fair trial in court." The use of a coerced confession, which is likely to be unreliable, interferes with the "fair trial" goal. By contrast, in *Lisenba* the defendant had been detained in violation of state statutes requiring that he be brought before a magistrate and had not been allowed to consult with his counsel prior to the final period of interrogation. Finding that neither of these state law violations rendered the confession unreliable or the trial otherwise unfair, the Court affirmed the conviction. The test, according to *Lisenba*, was whether the state practice in question deprived the defendant of "that fundamental fairness essential to the very concept of justice."*

---

*This "due process" test in *Lisenba*, elsewhere referrred to by the Court as the "conscience shocking" test, must not be confused with the test for whether a provision of the Bill of Rights should be incorporated into the fourteenth amendment for all cases. This position was stated by Justice Cardozo in *Palko v. Connecticut* 320 U.S. 319 (1937): whether the right in question was "implicit in the concept of ordered liberty." Not until 1964, in *Malloy v. Hogan* 378 U.S. 1, was the Court to agree that the fifth amendment was incorporated in the fourteenth, and consequently that all violations of the right against self-incrimination, however non-shocking, would result in evidentiary exclusion in state courts.

In a series of cases decided in the 1940s,[36] however, the Court went beyond *Lisenba*, recognizing that illegal police practices could, in particular cases, deprive the defendant of fundamental fairness, even if the trial was not thereby rendered unfair. In a 1954 article in the *Stanford Law Review* Monrad Paulsen summarized the Court's position:

The federal confessions rule would be used to discourage illegal police practices and not simply to guard against erroneous convictions. But none of the opinions had precisely defined the interrogation practices which were forbidden.[37]

For example, as Justice Jackson pointed out, dissenting in *Ashcraft v. Tennessee* (1944), if, as the Court held in that case, thirty-six hours of questioning are to be considered "inherently coercive," what of thirty-five, or thirty? What indignities other than removal of clothing, as in *Malinski v. New York* (1945), are prohibited? What acts are "subversive of the accusatorial system" and destroy the right of the accused to remain silent?[38] The Court, excluding evidence case by case resulting from illegal police practices, was simultaneously aware both that it was not a rulemaking body and that it must be.

The problem was (and is) that it was generally believed that no institution other than the Supreme Court had the power, much less the inclination, to declare such rules at the national level. The only hope was that the states, prodded by the Supreme Court rulings of the thirties and forties, would draft their own codes of criminal procedure and train and discipline their own police to eliminate the widespread abuses that the Wickersham Commission and the Court had been discovering.

But this was not to be. Indeed, even today, most states have no code provisions governing police interrogations. By 1946, Charles McCormick reported in the *Texas Law Review* that

it seems probable that third degree practices are still prevalent in many parts of the country. They constitute a betrayal and a mockery of those principles of respect for the worth of the individual citizen upon which our religious ideas, our constitution, and our philosophy of government rest.[39]

Nor did the passage of another decade change matters. In his treatise on criminal procedure published in 1959, Roy Moreland reported that

Much has been written about the third degree.* The most obvious thing to one who has any familiarity with criminal practice is the general inconsistency

---

*Moreland claims that the term "third degree" comes from Russian police procedures: "The Russian police rules had three degrees: 1st, cross examination; 2d, confrontation; 3d, severe physical duress." However, *Brewer's Dictionary of Phrase and Fable* contends that the term relates to Masonic ritual.

between the pious imprecations against the practice and recurring unlawful pressures put upon prisoners by law officers in their efforts to obtain confessions or evidence of crime. The usual approach to the problem—both by judges and legal writers—is to condemn the practice, to say that it is barbaric, that it is contrary to law, that it should not be permitted—and then to wink at the fact that it occurs repeatedly and was practiced in the case under discussion—unless the circumstances of the particular occasion were so sensational as to be particularly revolting.[40]

The Court continued its efforts. In the federal courts it held that the sixth amendment required that lawyers be appointed for indigent defendants in all criminal cases.[41] And, in a further effort to discourage the employment of third degree tactics by federal officials, it held in 1943 that an otherwise voluntary confession must be excluded from a federal trial if obtained during a prolonged delay between arrest and arraignment.[42]

The Court's endeavor to regulate the states during the late forties and the fifties was more mixed. In *Wolf v. Colorado* (1949)[43] it extended fourth amendment protections to the states, but refused to apply the *Weeks* exclusionary rule to state trials, thus inviting the states to ignore Supreme Court fourth amendment decisions, which many did. In *Rochin v. California*,[44] decided just three years after the *Wolf* refusal to extend the exclusionary rule, the Court nevertheless ordered evidence seized in a particularly brutal and offensive search excluded. The reason was that the police behavior in this case "shock[ed] the conscience." The evidence was excluded, not because the search was "unreasonable" in fourth amendment terms, but because "due process" required that "convictions cannot be brought about by methods that 'offend a sense of justice.'" But just when many commentators were beginning to feel that the states might be bound by essentially the same standards as federal authorities, the Court reaffirmed the double standard in *Irvine v. California*,[45] decided in 1954, where the police action in breaking into the suspect's house to install secret microphones was described as flagrant and deliberate misconduct (i.e., a violation of the fourth amendment), but the Court refused to exclude the evidence because the "conscience shocking" standard of *Rochin* had not been exceeded.

In the confessions area, the Court worked hard after *Brown v. Mississippi* to eliminate the use of the third degree by state authorities. The test developed by the Court depended on whether the confession could be deemed "voluntary" or not. The results of these numerous cases are summarized by Wayne LaFave and Jerold Israel:

In the course of suppressing confessions, the Court . . . condemned such practices as whipping or slapping the suspect, depriving him of food or water or sleep, keeping him in a naked state or in a small cell, holding a gun to his head or threatening him with mob violence.

Another very important consideration is whether the defendant was subject to extended periods of incommunicado interrogation (and how extended and intensive that interrogation was).[46]

The problem with the voluntariness test was that it was standardless. It did not tell the police what they could or could not do, nor did it inform trial courts as to when they should suppress confessions. Was the confession of a suspect held for eight hours of incommunicado questioning valid? It depended on the suspect's education level and health, what was said by the police, and myriad other factors. But certainly the issue of whether a confession was "voluntary" did seem to go to the heart of the issue: whether there was *compulsory* self-incrimination as prohibited by the fifth amendment. Moreover, "voluntariness" would seem to be no more difficult to determine than is "reasonableness" in the fourth amendment context. As will be seen, in the 1960s the Court chose to jump to the opposite extreme, giving the police a clear rule to follow but largely losing track of the issue of whether a confession was obtained by means that might be deemed to constitute compulsion.

By 1960 the Court had declared its authority fully to govern the conduct of federal law enforcement authorities and to back up its dictates with the exclusionary remedy. As to the states, while it had declared the fourth amendment prohibition of unreasonable searches and seizures to be applicable to the states through the due process clause of the fourteenth amendment, the Court's refusal to apply the exclusionary remedy except in "conscience shocking" cases meant that, for all practical purposes, the Court was not regulating searches and seizures by state and local police. By contrast, the Court had made extensive efforts to ensure that only voluntarily given confessions be used in state courts, acting under the due process clause of the fourteenth amendment, even though it had not recognized the fifth amendment itself to be incorporated within the fourteenth. Police identification procedures, such as lineups, had not been subjected to Supreme Court scrutiny. The states were only required to provide counsel to capital defendants and were not required to afford convicted defendants an appeal, though *Griffin v. Illinois*[47] had held, in 1956, that if appeals were allowed, indigent defendants must be furnished with a free trial transcript.

But if the Court had done a lot, it was believed by many, including a majority of the Court itself, that it had not done enough. The attitude of Chief Justice Earl Warren is summarized by his biographer, John D. Weaver:

Twenty-five years [after *Brown v. Mississippi*] many state courts were still cheerfully ignoring constitutional dictates in regard to unreasonable searches and seizures, self incrimination and the right to counsel. The Bill of Rights sheltered well-to-do suspects, including Mafia murderers, but not the poor, the uneducated, and the mentally handicapped, all of whom generally stood most in need of these ancient guarantees.[48]

Notes

1. American Law Institute, *Code of Criminal Procedure*.
2. *R. v. Leathan* 8 Cox C.C. 498, 501 (1861).
3. 100 U.S. 303 (1879).
4. *Rogers v. Peck* 199 U.S. 425, 435 (1905).
5. See discussion in Charles Nutting, "The Supreme Court, the Fourteenth Amendment and State Criminal Cases." In *Neal v. Delaware* 103 U.S. 370 (1880) the Court reversed a conviction on due process/equal protection grounds because Negroes were excluded by law from grand jury service.
6. 116 U.S. 616. (1886)
7. 201 U.S. 43 (1906).
8. 232 U.S. 383.
9. Id. at 393.
10. 251 U.S. 385 (1920).
11. Id. at 392.
12. 255 U.S. 298 (1921).
13. Id. at 309.
14. *Warden v. Hayden* 387 U.S. 294 (1967).
15. *Agnello v. United States* 269 U.S. 20 (1925).
16. *Byars v. United States* 273 U.S. 28 (1927).
17. E.g., *Amos v. United States* 255 U.S. 313 (1925); *Carroll v. United States* 267 U.S. 132 (1925); *Marron v. United States* 275 U.S. 192 (1927).
18. E.g., *Bram v. United States* 168 U.S. 532 (1897); *Wan v. United States* 266 U.S. 1 (1924). See, generally, Otis H. Stephens, *The Supreme Court and Confessions of Guilt*.
19. Nutting, supra note 5 at 259 (citations omitted).
20. Quoted in National Commission on Law Observance and Enforcement, Report No. 8, *Criminal Procedure*, 1.
21. National Commission on Law Observance and Enforcement, Report No. 11, *Report on Lawlessness in Law Enforcement*.
22. Id. at 340.
23. Id.
24. Id. at 4.
25. 384 U.S. 436, 445 (1966).
26. See, e.g., Louis Lusky, "Minority Rights and the Public Interest," 26–30, discussing the extent to which concerns about racial discrimination may have influenced the Court's early criminal procedure decisions. Cf., Herbert Packer, "The Courts, the Police, and the Rest of Us," 238, 240 to the same effect as to the decisions of the Warren Court.
27. 297 U.S. 278 (1936).
28. 211 U.S. 78, 114 (1908).
29. 297 U.S. at 285.

30. 309 U.S. 227 (1940).

31. Id. at 236.

32. 309 U.S. 227, 235–36, 241 (emphasis added).

33. 310 U.S. 530 (1940).

34. 309 U.S. 629 (1940).

35. 314 U.S. 219 (1941).

36. *Ashcraft v. Tennessee* 322 U.S. 143 (1944); *Malinski v. New York* 324 U.S. 401 (1945); *Haley v. Ohio* 332 U.S. 596; *Watts v. Indiana* 338 U.S. 49 (1949).

37. Monrad Paulsen, "The Fourteenth Amendment and the Third Degree," 420–21.

38. Justice Jackson's opinion is summarized in id. at 421.

39. Charles McCormick, "Some Problems and Developments in the Admissibility of Confessions," 244.

40. Roy Moreland, *Modern Criminal Procedure*, 91.

41. *Johnson v. Zerbst* 304 U.S. 458 (1938).

42. *McNabb v. United States* 318 U.S. 332 (1943); reaffirmed in *Mallory v. United States* 354 U.S. 449 (1957).

43. 338 U.S. 25 (1949).

44. 342 U.S. 165 (1952).

45. 347 U.S. 128 (1954).

46. Wayne LaFave and Jerold Israel, *Criminal Procedure* I, 444–45.

47. 351 U.S. 12 (1956).

48. John D. Weaver, *Warren: The Man, the Court, the Era*, p. 221.

Chapter 2
The Criminal Procedure Revolution

It is now apparent, on the basis of the material presented in Chapter 1, that the so-called "criminal procedure revolution" of the 1960s was more an acceleration of an evolutionary process that had begun in the 1930s than a true revolution. The fourth amendment had already been applied to the states, and numerous state convictions had been reversed by the Supreme Court because police interrogation procedures had violated the Court's concept of "due process." The Court had also intruded on the state criminal trial, striking down convictions in a variety of cases where it felt that the defendant had not received a fair trial. Up until the 1960s, however, the Court had been content to base its decisions reversing state convictions on the general concept of "due process" as expressed in the fourteenth amendment. In *Adamson v. California*,[1] decided in 1947, it had specifically refused to hold that the concept of "due process" necessarily incorporated the entire body of the Bill of Rights. But in a series of cases decided in the 1920s, 30s, and 40s, it had decided that the first amendment protections of speech, press, and religion were all applicable to the states[2] and, as discussed, it had applied the fourth amendment to the states in 1949 (but had never used it as the basis for reversing a state conviction.)

The stage was thus set to apply to the states those other provisions of the Bill of Rights that the Court deemed "fundamental." In the short period from 1961 to 1969 the Court's conception of what was fundamental was expanded to include all the significant provisions of the Bill of Rights. The process began with the landmark case of *Mapp v. Ohio*.[3] In *Mapp* the Court was confronted with the case of a black woman whose house had been searched by the police looking for a bombing suspect. When Mapp refused the police entrance without a search warrant, they broke into the house and ran "roughshod" over Mapp. They did not find their bombing suspect, but they did find some obscene books and photographs. Mapp was prosecuted for possession of these items.

In striking down Mapp's conviction, the Supreme Court ignored the issue briefed and argued by the parties: whether one had a first amendment right to possess obscene materials in the privacy of one's own home. Instead, they took this opportunity to reconsider the holding of *Wolf v. Colorado* that the exclusionary rule would not be applied to the states under the fourth and fourteenth amendments. In doing so, the Court noted that use of the exclusionary rule against federal authorities had prevented the fourth amendment from being "reduced to a 'form of words.'" By contrast, states such as California that had had no exclusionary rule at the time of *Wolf* had since been forced to adopt one. The California Supreme Court had felt "compelled" to adopt the exclusionary remedy "because other remedies have completely failed to secure compliance with the constitutional provisions."[4] Noting that "nothing can destroy a government more quickly than its failure to observe its own law," the Court held that evidence seized in violation of the fourth amendment must be excluded from state as well as federal trials. That is, applying the fourth amendment to the states was an "empty promise" if it did not include the exclusionary remedy.

In the ensuing years the Court applied the Bill of Rights criminal provisions to the states through the fourteenth amendment virtually in its entirety:

Fifth Amendment

No person shall . . . be subject for the same offense to be twice put in jeopardy of life and limb . . . (*Benton v. Maryland* 1969)
. . . nor shall be compelled in any criminal case to be a witness against himself . . . (*Malloy v. Hogan* 1964)

Sixth Amendment

In all criminal prosecutions the accused shall enjoy the right to a speedy and public trial . . . (*Klopfer v. North Carolina* 1967)
. . . by an impartial jury . . . (*Duncan v. Louisiana* 1968)
. . . to be confronted with the witnesses against him . . . (*Pointer v. Texas* 1965)
. . . to have compulsory process for obtaining witnesses in his favor . . . (*Washington v. Texas* 1967)
. . . and to have the assistance of counsel for his defense (*Gideon v. Wainwright* 1963).

EIGHTH AMENDMENT

. . . nor shall cruel and unusual punishments [be] inflicted (*Robinson v. California* 1962).

By the end of the Warren Court era, only the fifth amendment requirement of indictment by grand jury and the eighth amendment prohibition against excessive bail had not been applied to the states; they have not been applied to this day, though the Court has said that the latter right "has been assumed to have applications to the States through the Fourteenth Amendment."[5]

This application of the various Bill of Rights provisions to the states may have seemed to be more important from a symbolic than from a practical viewpoint because, as we have seen, the Court had already been striking down state convictions on the ground that police tactics in an individual case offended due process. However, application of the Bill of Rights, and particularly the exclusionary rule, to the states did make a difference. By "incorporating" a particular provision of the Bill of Rights into the fourteenth amendment, the Court also "incorporated" the body of law that it had attached to that provision through years of cases involving federal officials. Thus a case such as *Irvine v. California*, which had given state officials more leeway than federal agents in applying the exclusionary rule, was implicitly overruled by *Mapp*, which applied the "same constitutional standards prohibiting 'unreasonable searches and seizures'" to the states as to the federal government.[6] By the same token, the series of federal cases that had developed the law of search incident to arrest, for example, became automatically applicable to the states after *Mapp*. Therefore, as each constitutional provision was applied to the states, a sometimes extensive body of Supreme Court case law was applied to them as well.

This new body of law placed much more powerful weapons in the hands of lower federal judges, many of whom were activists recently appointed by the Kennedy and Johnson administrations, than had been available under the vague and limited mandates of the "fundamental fairness" approach. The Supreme Court thus ensured that its new rulings would be enforced by giving the lower federal courts a ready-made body of law to apply to the states, and by greatly expanding the jurisdiction of those courts to review state convictions by means of federal writs of habeas corpus* in the 1963 case of *Fay v. Noia*.[7]

---

*The Habeas Corpus Act of 1867 provided that the federal courts "shall have power to grant writs of habeas corpus in all cases where any person may be restrained of his

Naturally, having been ordered by the Supreme Court to "follow the Bill of Rights," police, state courts, and lower federal courts all looked to the Court for further advice on just what the rights against compulsory self-incrimination or unreasonable searches, for example, meant in particular factual contexts. The Supreme Court obliged them, proceeding to decide roughly twenty cases per year in all areas of criminal procedure—search and seizure, interrogation, confrontation, cruel and unusual punishment, and so on—throughout the 1960s, 70s, and 80s.[8]

However, the Court was, and continues to be, ambivalent about its role. In the 1963 case of *Ker v. California*,[9] eight Justices agreed that the states should be bound by the same standards as the federal government. Only Justice John Harlan would have held them to a lesser, fundamental fairness, standard because to apply the federal cases to the states would place them "in an atmosphere of uncertainty since this Court's decisions in the realm of search and seizure are hardly notable for their predictability."[10] The four Justice plurality was sympathetic to Harlan's concerns, declaring that "*Mapp* did not attempt the impossible task of laying down a 'fixed formula' for the application in specific cases of the constitutional prohibition against unreasonable searches and seizures." Rather searches were simply to be judged according to their "reasonableness"—a question to be answered "in the first instance [by the] trial court." The plurality continued:

> The States are not thereby precluded from developing workable rules governing arrests, searches and seizures to meet 'the practical demands of effective criminal investigation . . . provided that those rules do not violate the constitutional proscription of unreasonable searches and seizures.'[11]

It sounded as if the Court was prepared to give the states considerable leeway, providing few specific instructions and only ordering the exclusion of evidence in state cases when the search was truly "unreasonable" in some fundamental sense. If the Court had stuck with this position, then the change in the law from the 1956 "conscience shocking" standard of *Rochin v. California* to a new "reasonableness" standard would have been relatively slight, and the Court would have

---

or her liberty in violation of the constitution . . . or law of the United States." In *Noia* the Court held that federal jurisdiction under this statute was not limited to the question of whether the state court had jurisdiction, as had previously been thought, but rather extended to "give the federal courts superintending control so as to ensure that there would be full recognition of federal rights" at state criminal trials. Wayne LaFave and Jerold Israel, *Criminal Procedure*, 1016.

largely stayed out of the troublesome business of attempting to declare the rules of criminal procedure case by case. Indeed, the plurality's statement in *Ker* that it found no "offensiveness"[12] in a warrantless, "no-knock" entry to arrest supports the impression that a regime that left the creation of specific rules to the states was exactly what the plurality had in mind.

A much more activist view of the Court's role was advanced by the dissenters in *Ker*, Justices Brennan, Douglas, Goldberg, and Chief Justice Warren, who would have set forth a "clear rule" that

the Fourth Amendment is violated by an unannounced police intrusion into a private home, with or without an arrest warrant, except (1) where the persons within already know of the officer's authority and purpose, or (2) where the officers are justified in the belief that persons within are in imminent peril of bodily harm, or (3) where those within, made aware of the presence of someone outside (because, for example, there has been a knock at the door), are then engaged in activity which justifies the officers in the belief that an escape or the destruction of evidence is being attempted.[13]

The dissenters stated that "we have no occasion here to decide how many of the situations in which, by the exercise of our supervisory power over the conduct of federal officers, we would exclude evidence, are also situations which would require the exclusion of evidence from state criminal proceedings under . . . *Mapp.*" Still, it was clear that they believed that, in many cases, the states would require much more specific instructions from the Supreme Court than a mere admonition to act "reasonably" or "not offensively" would provide.

The very next Term, the *Ker* dissenters won out. In *Aguilar v. Texas*[14] they picked up the vote of Justice Harlan, who declared that, having lost in *Ker*, he must now accede to the adoption of tough and specific rules governing state procedures because otherwise federal standards would be weakened by lenient decisions in state cases. (Justice White also switched to the liberal side, without explanation.)

In *Aguilar* the Court was faced with a search warrant, issued on the affidavit of a policeman, which stated no more than that he had "received reliable information from a credible person . . . that [narcotics] are being kept at the above described premises. . . ." The Court reviewed a long line of prior federal cases and struck down the warrant. In doing so, it endeavored to provide guidelines as to what would constitute an adequate affidavit in the future, namely that such a warrant must satisfy a "two-prong" test—establishing both the reliability and veracity of the informant. The dissenters complained that "the Court has substituted a rigid academic formula for the unrigid standards of reasonableness. . . ." But the die was cast. In *Stoner v. Califor-*

nia,[15] decided the same year as *Aguilar*, the Court held that a hotel room was entitled to the same constitutional protection as a house. In *Preston v. United States*[16] it set limits on how long the right to search "incident to the arrest" continued after the arrest was completed. In *Clinton v. Virginia*[17] it declared the use of a spiked microphone stuck in a wall to be an unreasonable search.

The next Term the Court attempted (without much success) to define "probable cause,"[18] held that hearsay information could be used in a search warrant,[19] and struck down an arrest as not being based on probable cause.[20] By the 1968 Term, the Court found itself attempting to define the precise limits of a search incident to arrest[21] and striking down, in *Spinelli v. United States*, a search warrant under the "two-prong test" that was much less obviously deficient than the warrant struck down in *Aguilar*.[22] (Indeed, in the view of dissenting Justice Black, *Spinelli* changed the standard for obtaining a search warrant to proof beyond a reasonable doubt.) The Court had also created, or reaffirmed, a variety of exceptions to the so-called "warrant requirement" such as administrative searches,[23] auto searches,[24] "hot pursuit,"[25] and so on. In other words, despite the disclaimers in *Ker* that such a task was "impossible," the Court was attempting to provide "fixed formulas" to govern various aspects of the search process rather than confining itself to striking down an occasional, particularly offensive, state search as "unreasonable."

This situation illustrates the perpetual dilemma in which the Court finds itself. On the one hand, sensitive to concerns about federalism, it does not feel comfortable issuing a "code of criminal procedure." "Police powers" are, after all, generally acknowledged to be a state function under the Constitution. Furthermore, such formulas are generally thought to be the province of legislatures, not courts. The former are to declare rules to govern future behavior, the latter simply to decide the cases before them. Finally, the Court has recognized the need to respond flexibly to individual fact patterns. As soon as the Court declares that "warrants are always required" in a given situation, a case will arise where the failure to obtain a warrant seems reasonable and the Court is forced either to reach an unjust result or to create an exception to its rule.

On the other hand, it simply will not do for the Court to reverse state convictions with a curt declaration that "the search in this case was unreasonable" unless the behavior of the police was blatantly wrong. Not only would it seem an arrogant exercise of naked power, but it would leave police in the dark about how to avoid this outcome in the future. Nor can individual state legislatures offer any meaningful guidance to police as to these matters of federal constitutional policy. Consequently the Court is impelled to explain just what the police did wrong in this case and how they can avoid these problems in the future. That is, it is forced to endeavor to declare "clear rules" for the police to follow. Despite continued lip service to the "limited authority" view of *Ker*, the Court, throughout the Warren, Burger, and even the Rehnquist eras, has generally given in to the temptation to attempt to adumbrate "clear rules," though this end has proved no more attainable than it was when Justice Harlan dissented in *Ker* in 1963. The Court's inherent inability to formulate such "clear rules" effectively is the subject of Chapter 3.

If the Court was reluctant to engage in rulemaking in the search and seizure area, it was no less reluctant to do so in the area of confessions. In both areas it recognized that to exclude evidence because of police misconduct in a given case meant that a convicted criminal would not only have his or her conviction reversed but would likely go free because the illegally obtained evidence was frequently the cornerstone of the prosecution's case. The problem was that, just as with searches, the police continued to commit unacceptable violations of the rights of suspects and the state courts continued to ignore this misconduct.

The Supreme Court dealt at length with its concerns about the use of abusive interrogation tactics by the police in three cases in the 1960 Term (the same Term in which *Mapp* was decided). In light of subsequent events, these cases may be seen as a last plea by the Court to the states to put their houses in order if they were to avoid serious intrusions into their sovereignty by a Supreme Court determined to ensure that rich or poor, black or white, criminal suspects were treated with fundamental fairness not only at the trial but at the investigatory stage.

The first case was *Rogers v. Richmond*.[26] Here the Supreme Court made explicit what had become generally understood: that involuntary confessions were to be excluded not only because they might be untrue but "because the methods used to extract them offend an underlying principle in the enforcement of our criminal law; that ours is an accusatorial and not an inquisitorial system—a system in which the state must establish guilt by evidence independently and freely secured and may not by coercion prove its charge against an accused out of his own mouth." In other words, the exclusionary rule was to be employed not just to ensure a fair trial but to deter police misconduct.

In the second case, *Reck v. Pate*,[27] the Court struck down by a 7–2 vote a murder conviction based on the use of confessions obtained from a nineteen-year-old of subnormal intelligence who had been held incommunicado for eight days and interrogated extensively despite an illness that required hospitalization. In *Reck* the Court admitted that

> this case lacks the physical brutality present in *Brown v. Mississippi*, the threat of mob violence apparent in *Payne v. Arkansas*, the thirty-six hours of consecutive questioning found in *Ashcraft v. Tennessee*, the threats against defendant's family used in *Harris v. South Carolina*, or the deception employed in *Spano v. New York*. Nor was Reck's mentality apparently so irrational as that of the petitioner in *Blackburn v. Alabama*. However it is equally true that Reck's youth, his subnormal intelligence, and his lack of previous experience with the police (coupled with the factors noted above) . . . presents a totality of coercive circumstances far more aggravated than those that dictated our [affirmance of the conviction] in *Turner v. Pennsylvania*.[28]

Finally, the Court distinguished *Stein v. New York*,[29] noting that, in that case, where the use of the confession had been upheld, the petitioners were not "young, soft, ignorant or timid," "inexperienced in the ways of crime or its detection," or "dumb as to their rights."[30] Thus *Reck* suggested that the Court was willing to probe the circumstances of confessions much more closely than in the past, and to inquire into factors that had not heretofore been deemed relevant to the "voluntariness" inquiry. In hindsight, the Court's concern with defendants' knowledge of their rights must be regarded as especially portentous.

In the third case, *Culombe v. Connecticut*,[31] Justice Frankfurter, who had also written *Rogers*, engaged in a lengthy discussion in a plurality opinion that reversed the conviction of a mentally defective prisoner who had been subjected to incommunicado questioning by the New Britain, Connecticut police for five days. Frankfurter began by recognizing the problem:

> Since under the procedures of Anglo-American criminal justice [suspects] cannot be constrained by legal process to give answers which incriminate them, the police have resorted to other means to unbend their reluctance, lest criminal investigation founder. Kindness, cajolery, entreaty, deception, persistent cross-questioning, even physical brutality have been used to this end. In the United States, "interrogation" has become a police technique, and detention for purposes of interrogation a common, although generally unlawful practice. . . .
>
> This practice has its manifest evils and dangers. Persons subjected to it are torn from the reliances of their daily existence and held at the mercy of those whose job it is . . . to prosecute them. They are deprived of freedom without a proper judicial tribunal having found them guilty, without [even] having found that there is probable cause to believe that they may be guilty. What actually happens to them behind the closed door of the interrogation roof is difficult if not impossible to ascertain. Certainly, if through excess of zeal or aggressive impatience or flaring up of temper in the face of obstinate silence a prisoner is abused, he is faced with the task of overcoming, by his lone

testimony, solemn official denials. The prisoner knows this—knows that no friendly or disinterested witness is present—and the knowledge itself may induce fear. But, in any case, the risk is great that the police will accomplish behind their closed door precisely what the demands of our legal order forbid: make a suspect the unwilling collaborator in establishing his guilt.[32]

Frankfurter was not necessarily a liberal in these matters. He went on to recognize that "questioning suspects is indispensable to law enforcement," that "prolongation of the interrogation period [often] will be essential" and that "Legal counsel for the suspect will generally prove a thorough obstruction to the investigation. Indeed, even to inform the suspect of his legal right to keep silent often will prove an obstruction." But "the terrible engine of the criminal law is not to be used to overreach individuals who stand helpless against it. . . . a prisoner is not to be made the deluded instrument of his own conviction."[33] Frankfurter, in common with many other Americans, had come to this country to escape just such tactics by European police.

He also recognized that state legislatures had enacted statutes "designed to curb the worst excesses . . . of the police" but that

it is the courts which are charged, in the ultimate, both with the enforcement of the criminal law and with safeguarding the criminal defendant's rights. . . . Under our federal system this task . . . is, of course, primarily the responsibility of the state courts. *The Fourteenth Amendment, however, limits their freedom in this regard. It subjects their broad powers to a limited, but searching, federal review and places upon this Court the obligation . . . to adjudicate what due process of law requires by way of restricting the state courts in their use of the products of police interrogation.*[34]

Frankfurter then went on to suggest that the voluntariness inquiry should involve a "three-phased process": (1) finding the "historical facts," (2) finding the "psychological facts" (what impact the police practices had had on the suspect), and (3) applying the rules of law to these findings. After applying this analysis to the case, Frankfurter concluded that certain of Culombe's confessions should have been excluded, reversed the convictions, and ordered that any retrial not make use of those confessions.

Only Justice Stewart joined the Frankfurter opinion. Four other Justices, Chief Justice Warren and Justices Black, Douglas, and Brennan, concurred in the result, believing that *all* the defendant's confessions should have been suppressed, not just some of them. Justices Douglas and Black would have suppressed the confessions on the ground that Culombe's request to see a lawyer was denied by the police. Justice Brennan and the Chief Justice simply believed that all the confessions were "coerced." Even the dissenting Justices (Harlan, Clark, and Whittaker) agreed with Frankfurter's "delineation of the general principles governing police interrogation" but disagreed that on these facts Culombe's confessions were coerced.

Of particular interest is Chief Justice Warren's concurrence:

> [Frankfurter's] opinion is in the nature of an advisory opinion, for it attempts to resolve with finality many difficult problems which are at best only tangentially involved here. The opinion was unquestionably written with the intention of clarifying these problems and of establishing a set of principles which could be easily applied in any coerced-confession situation. . . . However, I would prefer not to write on many of the difficult questions which the opinion discusses until the facts of a particular case make such writing necessary. In my view, the reasons which have compelled the Court to develop the law on a case-by-case approach, to declare legal principles only in the context of specific factual situations, and to avoid expounding more than is necessary for the decision of a particular case are persuasive.[35]

But the states did not take the hint. Only five years after he had penned this paean to judicial restraint and case-by-case decision making, Chief Justice Warren was to author, in *Miranda v. Arizona*, the most dramatic example of Supreme Court "legislating" that had occurred in the nation's history.

It was a change in the Court's makeup that would make such sweeping changes possible. In *Culombe* Justice Frankfurter had adopted a middle-of-the-road position, striking down some of the defendant's confessions while allowing others to be used and generally recognizing the importance of interrogations and confessions, and the obstructiveness of constitutional warnings and defense lawyers, to effective police work. Four Justices would have gone much further. In 1962 Frankfurter resigned, replaced by the activist liberal Arthur Goldberg, who joined the four concurring Justices in *Culombe* to provide the majority necessary to drive the criminal procedure revolution to new heights (or depths, depending on one's perspective).*

The newly constituted Court first held, in *Gideon v. Wainwright* (1963),[36] that every felony defendant was entitled to be represented by counsel at trial (provided free of charge to indigents). Then it applied the fifth amendment to the states in *Malloy v. Hogan* (1964).[37] In *Escobedo v. Illinois* (1964)[38] it held, by a 5–4 vote, that the right to counsel extended to police interrogation of suspects, at least where the suspect requested a lawyer. Thus for the first time the Court reversed a conviction not because the confession was involuntary

---

*Goldberg was replaced in 1965 by Abe Fortas, who held similar ideas about criminal procedure reform.

(broadly interpreted to include police misconduct) but because the police had violated another constitutional provision, not heretofore thought applicable to the interrogation room—the right to counsel. Fred Inbau, a leading pro-law enforcement authority on police procedures, termed *Escobedo* the "hardest body blow the court has struck yet against enforcement of law in this nation."[39]

Escobedo involved a suspect who actually *had* counsel. But what if he had not? And what if he had not requested to see his counsel? Did the police have to inform him of that right? And if they had to inform him of a right to counsel, did they also have to inform him of his right against self-incrimination (applied to the states in *Malloy*)? And what if, having been informed of his rights to counsel and against self-incrimination, he said that he did not want to answer any questions?

Fred Graham, the *New York Times* Supreme Court correspondent, summarized what happened next in his book, *The Self-Inflicted Wound*:

> The Supreme Court had been expected to let these and other questions simmer for years in the lower courts, where various solutions could be tested and modified. . . . But events forced another course. Appeals flooded the lower courts. Most of them stood pat on *Escobedo* and passed the cases up to the Supreme Court for further amplification. By the autumn of 1965 the Court had decided to answer all of the questions at once, to undertake a broad rule-making hearing unlike anything that had ever occurred before in a court of the United States . . . to frame broad legislative codes to cover future police conduct.[40]

Miranda v. Arizona[41] was actually five cases consolidated into one. The case of the named petitioner, Ernesto Miranda, is indicative of the kinds of cases the Court was dealing with and why the Court's 5–4 decision provoked such a strong reaction. Miranda was a mentally disturbed truck driver who had been convicted of kidnapping and raping an eighteen-year-old girl. After the victim identified him, he talked voluntarily to the police, giving a full confession within two hours. No brutality, threats, or tricks were used to induce his confession.

Nevertheless, the Court reversed his conviction, along with those of the other petitioners, finding that any statement obtained during "custodial interrogation" is inadmissable in court unless it was preceded by the now-familiar warnings as to the rights to silence and counsel and the suspect had "knowingly and intelligently" waived those rights.[42] "Unless adequate protective devices are employed to dispel the compulsion inherent in custodial surroundings, no statement obtained from the defendant can truly be the product of his free choice." Furthermore, if the suspect "indicates in any manner . . . that he wishes to remain silent, the interrogation must cease. . . . If the individual states that he wants an attorney, the interrogation must cease until an attorney is present."[43]

While *Miranda* essentially signaled that the Court had given up hope that the states would ever effectively control the police, the decision did contain a cryptic passage that exhorted both Congress and the states to further action:

We have already pointed out that the Constitution does not require any specific code of procedures for protecting the privilege against self-incrimination during custodial interrogation. Congress and the States are free to develop their own safeguards for the privilege, so long as they are fully as effective as those described above in informing accused persons of their right of silence and in affording a continuous opportunity to exercise it.[44]

Just what these "fully effective safeguards" might be, no one knew. And since *Miranda* no one has attempted to find out. The Supreme Court has coopted the field not only of interrogation law but of the entire body of criminal procedure. One can look in vain in a law school criminal procedure casebook for any discussion of state law. Many states, shell-shocked by the Supreme Court's blasts, have limited their participation in this area to attempting to decipher and apply Supreme Court law and, in some of the more liberal states, to using the state constitution to resist incursions by subsequent Courts on the rights established by the Warren Court.[45] Some states have, by contrast, attempted to develop rules in areas in which the Supreme Court has been silent.[46]

But immediately after *Miranda* the states, as represented by their Senators and Representatives in Washington, did not give in so easily. The reaction to the criminal procedure revolution in general, and to *Miranda* in particular, was vituperative. As Fred Graham has pointed out, the "criminal procedure revolution" could not have come at a worse time from a political standpoint:

During the period of the Warren Court's most active criminal law reform— from 1960 to 1968—the annual number of reported murders increased by 52 percent; reported rapes rose 84 percent; robbery, 144 percent; aggravated assault, 86 percent.[47]

While it is unlikely, or at least unproved, that the Supreme Court's decisions had anything to do with the crime increase, critics were quick to blame them. Senator McClellan introduced a bill to overrule *Miranda* and, during the debate, displayed a graph showing the rising crime rate. He declared:

The Supreme Court has set a low tone in law enforcement, and we are reaping the whirlwind today! Look at that chart! Look at it and weep for your country—crime spiraling upward and upward and upward. Apparently nobody is willing to put on the brakes.[48]

Senator Sam Ervin declared: "Enough has been done for those who murder and rape and rob! It is time to do something for those who do not wish to be murdered or raped or robbed."[49] An obscure court of appeals judge in Washington, DC, Warren Burger, also criticized the Supreme Court for "revising the code of criminal procedure and evidence piecemeal on a case-by-case basis, on inadequate records and incomplete factual data."[50] Richard Nixon made the Supreme Court the centerpiece of his presidential campaign, declaring that Court decisions had "weaken[ed] the peace forces as against the criminal forces in this country."[51]

In the end, the reaction to *Miranda* was far more significant than the decision itself which, studies found, did not substantially impede the process of obtaining confessions.[52] By contrast, the political impact of the decision was tremendous, as explained by Fred Graham:

In 1968 Congress voted overwhelmingly to include in the Omnibus Crime Control Act a provision that purported to reverse *Miranda* in the federal courts.* Abe Fortas was denied confirmation as Chief Justice, with the critics of the criminal law decisions leading the way. Richard Nixon won the Presidency after promising to appoint Justices to retract *Miranda* and other decisions. Finally, Earl Warren was replaced, upon his retirement, with Warren Burger, a judge who had criticized much that the due process revolution had produced.[53]

Still, while *Miranda* may have been the high water mark of the criminal procedure revolution, the reaction to that decision did not deter the Court from pressing ahead with signficant changes in criminal procedure law. In 1967, despite cries of protest from law enforcement officials, the Court placed tough restrictions on electronic eavesdropping,[54] required the presence of counsel at lineups,[55] and extended the speedy trial right to the states.[56] However, the decisions in that Term were not entirely one-sided as the Court frequently backed the government's position. For example, it abandoned the "mere evidence" rule, which had forbidden searches for other than fruits or instrumentalities of a crime,[57] allowed the recording of a conversation between a suspect and a government informant,[58] upheld the use of confidential informants as the basis for search warrants[59]

---

*The Department of Justice, by order of Attorney General Ramsey Clark, ignored this statute and ordered federal prosecutors to use only evidence obtained in compliance with *Miranda*.

and established the harmless error rule to allow convictions to be upheld despite relatively minor constitutional violations at trial.[60]

The following Term was similarly mixed. In *Katz v. United States*[61] the Court overruled an earlier precedent in holding that the electronic bugging of a phone booth was a "search" under the fourth amendment; physical intrusion was not required. It also upheld a taxpayer's refusal, on fifth amendment grounds, to disclose income from illegal activities,[62] extended the right to a jury trial to the states,[63] and held that the use of the confession of a non-testifying co-defendant violated the defendant's right to confront the witnesses against him.[64] However, in *Terry v. Ohio*,[65] an opinion that is considered by many to have spelled the end of the criminal procedure revolution,[66] the Court held that a brief detention on the street of a crime suspect, as well as a patdown of his clothing, would be allowed even in the absence of probable cause.

In writing *Terry* Chief Justice Warren recognized the limits of the exclusionary rule: it could not serve to regulate police where the police practice in question was not designed to uncover evidence. Police would stop and frisk suspects regardless of what the Supreme Court said, at least if they believed the person to be armed. However, the Court then proceeded to treat this as an ordinary exclusionary rule case, requiring a new evidentiary standard—reasonable suspicion—before such stops would be allowed (i.e., before the evidence obtained from such stops would be admissible in court). The Court was probably right on both counts. There are limits to what the exclusionary rule can accomplish, but since stops and frisks frequently do produce evidence, applying the exclusionary rule to the practice is just as likely to have a deterrent impact as applying it to any other evidence-gathering procedure.

Yale Kamisar has agreed with Fred Graham that *Terry* marked the end of the criminal procedure revolution, and has offered some observations about why that may have occurred:

The change in the Warren Court can hardly be attributed to a change in its personnel. Justice Goldberg (1962) and then Justice Fortas (1965) replaced the less adventurous Frankfurter; Justice Marshall (1967) succeeded the more prosecution-oriented Clark. The change does seem attributable to "the buffeting of rapid historical developments that incessantly place unprecedented strains upon the Court." The last years of the Warren Court's "criminal procedure 'revolution'" constituted a period of social upheaval, marked by urban riots, violence in the ghettos, and disorders on the campuses. The political assassinations and near-assassinations of the late 1960's, both Congress's and presidential candidate Richard Nixon's strong criticism of the Court, the "obviously retaliatory" provisions of the Crime Control Act of 1968, and the ever-soaring crime statistics and ever-spreading fears of the breakdown of public order "combined to create an atmosphere that, to say the least, was unfavorable to the continued vitality of the Warren Court's mission in criminal cases."[67]

Yet, despite the existence of these powerful societal pressures, there is little evidence that the Warren Court in the October Term 1968, the year after *Terry* and the final year of Earl Warren's tenure on the Court, had lost its zeal to continue its reformation of the law of criminal procedure. In that Term, the Court decided *Chimel v. California*,[68] which limited the scope of searches incident to arrest, and *Spinelli v. United States*,[69] which, as previously discussed, seemed to conservatives to impose utterly unrealistic limitations on the issuance of search warrants. It also struck down "investigatory arrests,"[70] expanded the discovery rights of persons subjected to electronic surveillance,[71] and extended one of the few remaining unincorporated provisions of the Bill of Rights—the fifth amendment's double jeopardy guarantee—to the states.[72] While, as in previous Terms, its record was mixed, still, until the retirement of Earl Warren, the criminal procedure revolution proceeded apace.

By the beginning of the 1969 Term, two of the five members of the *Miranda* majority, Fortas and Warren, had resigned and Warren Burger had taken over as Chief Justice. (Fortas's seat remained unfilled until late in the Term, when Harry Blackmun was confirmed as his replacement.) Two more Nixon appointees, William Rehnquist and Lewis Powell, joined the Court in January 1972, replacing Black and Harlan. Thus it would not seem necessary to delve any deeper than the identities and politics of the Court's members to ascertain why the criminal procedure revolution ground to a halt when it did.

It might seem that the revolution ended at this point simply because there was nothing more to be done. After all, the Court had extended all but two minor aspects of the Bill of Rights criminal process guarantees to the states. But the Court had not gone nearly as far as civil libertarians would have wished. *Miranda* is a good example of the tempering of activism with a degree of pragmatism that was characteristic of the Warren Court's decisions. As Kamisar has pointed out, "*Miranda* may fairly be viewed as a compromise between the old voluntariness—totality of the circumstances test . . . and extreme proposals that threatened (or promised) to 'kill' confessions."[73] *Miranda*, after all, did not forbid police questioning of suspects altogether or require that such questioning could occur only in the presence of counsel or before a judge. Such a holding would have been truly revolutionary, but it did not occur. And, as discussed, while the Warren

Court did expand the rights of suspects greatly, it also produced a number of decisions that were helpful to the police.

In its early years the Burger Court showed every sign of being prepared to dismantle many of the constitutional protections established during the Warren years. However, only in one area, pretrial identification procedures, did this occur. In 1967, in *United States v. Wade*,[74] the Court had required the presence of counsel at lineups. Furthermore, *Wade*, together with its companion cases *Gilbert v. California*[75] and *Stovall v. Denno*,[76] "seemed to require the presence of counsel at all pretrial identifications," absent exigent circumstances.[77] However, in *Kirby v. Illinois*[78] the Court, with all four Nixon appointees in place, held that the "right to counsel" only attached after "formal proceedings had begun" (i.e., after the defendant had been indicted or arraigned). Consequently, during the investigatory stage, when lineups, photo showups, and other identification procedures are usually held, counsel is not required. Only four Justices joined in this opinion. Justice Powell concurred only in the result, stating tersely that he "would not extend the *Wade-Gilbert* exclusionary rule." Thus Powell, joined by Stewart, White, and, later, Blackmun, staked out his position as a moderate who, while not prepared to join Brennan, Douglas, and Marshall in continuing the criminal procedure revolution, was also not necessarily ready to join Burger and Rehnquist in dismantling it.

The record of the Burger Court vis-à-vis the Warren Court in criminal procedure can thus best be described as putting an end to the revolution—refusing to extend, and sometimes narrowing, its major holdings—rather than as a counter-revolution that set the law back to where it had been prior to 1961. Indeed, by 1980 Chief Justice Burger, who, both before he joined the Court and in his early years as Chief Justice, had been such an outspoken critic of the Warren Court reforms, had clasped the despised *Miranda* opinion to his bosom:

The meaning of *Miranda* has become reasonably clear and law enforcement practices have adjusted to its strictures; I would neither overrule *Miranda*, disparage it, nor extend it at this late date.[79]

In sum, as Stephen Saltzburg observed in 1980,

The Warren Court decisions and the trends they set in motion, with a few exceptions, were more consistent with developed doctrines than many realized when Warren was Chief Justice but also . . . the constitutional protections that were established during the Warren era generally survived and often were strengthened during the 1970s. The Burger Court has reaffirmed, explicitly or implicitly, nearly all of these decisions. Although some recent decisions limit the possible reach of earlier cases and the Warren Court probably would have gone further in subsequent rulings than the current Court has gone, the differences between the Warren and the Burger decisions tend to be more at the margin than at the heart of the constitutional principles for which the Warren Court is remembered.[80]

Notes

1. 332 U.S. 46 (1947).
2. *Gitlow v. New York* 268 U.S. 652, 666 (1925); *Near v. Minnesota* 283 U.S. 697, 701 (1931); *Cantwell v. Connecticut* 310 US. 296 (1940) (free exercise of religion); *Everson v. Board of Education* 330 U.S. 1 (1947) (no establishment of religion by state).
3. 367 U.S. 643 (1961).
4. *People v. Cahan* 282 P.2d 905, 911 (Cal. 1955), quoted at 367 U.S. at 651.
5. *Schilb v. Kuebel* 404 U.S. 357, 365 (1971).
6. *Ker v. California* 374 U.S. 23, 30–31 (1963).
7. 372 U.S. 391 (1963).
8. These cases are summarized in Bureau of National Affairs, *The Criminal Law Revolution and Its Aftermath, 1960–1977.*
9. 374 U.S. 23 (1963).
10. Id. at 45.
11. Id. at 34.
12. Id. at 38.
13. Id. at 47.
14. 378 U.S. 108 (1964).
15. 376 U.S. 463 (1964).
16. 376 U.S. 364 (1964).
17. 377 U.S. 158 (1964).
18. *United States v. Ventresca* 380 U.S. 102 (1965).
19. Id.
20. *Beck v. Ohio* 379 U.S. 89 (1965).
21. *Chimel v. California* 395 U.S. 752 (1969).
22. *Spinelli v. United States* 393 U.S. 410 (1969).
23. *Camara v. Municipal Court* 387 U.S. 523 (1967). While the Court claimed to adhere to the warrant requirement in *Camara*, the "warrant" required did not have to set forth individualized probable cause and therefore did not conform to the fourth amendment requisites for a warrant.
24. *Chambers v. Maroney* 399 U.S. 42 (1970), reaffirming *Carroll v. United States* 267 U.S. 132 (1925).
25. *Warden v. Hayden* 387 U.S. 294 (1967).
26. 365 U.S. 534 (1961).
27. 367 U.S. 433 (1961).
28. Id. at 442 (citations omitted).
29. 346 U.S. 156 (1953).
30. 367 U.S. at 443.
31. 367 U.S. 568 (1961).
32. Id. at 572–73.
33. Id. at 581.

34. Id. at 587 (emphasis added).

35. Id. at 636.

36. 372 U.S. 335 (1963).

37. 378 U.S. 1 (1964).

38. 378 U.S. 478 (1964).

39. In Gowran, How Supreme Court Ruling Puts Straightjacket [sic] on Police," *Chicago Tribune*, Aug. 11, 1964, p. 27.

40. Fred Graham, *The Self-Inflicted Wound*, 155.

41. 384 U.S. 436 (1966).

42. Id. at 444.

43. Id. at 473–74.

44. Id. at 490.

45. See William Brennan, "State Constitutions and the Protection of Individual Rights," 90, encouraging this practice.

46. See Barry Latzer, *State Constitutions and Criminal Justice* for a detailed discussion of state action in this area. As Latzer observes, some states have amended their state constitutions to require that their courts go no further in excluding evidence than the United States Supreme Court requires (id. at 37).

47. Graham, supra note 40 at 11.

48. Id. at 12.

49. *New York Times*, July 23, 1966, p. 54.

50. Warren Burger, Speech to the Ohio Judicial Conference, 1968; quoted in Liva Baker, *Miranda: Crime, Law, and Politics*, 195.

51. Quoted in Graham, supra note 40 at 15.

52. See, e.g., Gerald Caplan, "Questioning Miranda," summarizing studies of the impact of *Miranda*.

53. Graham, supra note 40 at 9.

54. *Berger v. New York* 388 U.S. 41 (1967).

55. *United States v. Wade* 388 U.S. 218 (1967).

56. *Klopfer v. North Carolina* 386 U.S. 213 (1967).

57. *Warden v. Hayden* 387 U.S. 294 (1967).

58. *Osborn v. United States* 385 U.S. 323 (1967).

59. *McCray v. Illinois* 386 U.S. 300 (1967).

60. *Chapman v. California* 386 U.S. 18 (1967).

61. 389 U.S. 347 (1967).

62. *Marchetti v. United States* 390 U.S. 39 (1968).

63. *Duncan v. Louisiana* 391 U.S. 145 (1968).

64. *Bruton v. United States* 391 U.S. 123 (1968).

65. 392 U.S. 1 (1968).

66. E.g., Graham, supra note 40 at 144: "[In] *Terry v. Ohio*, Chief Justice Earl Warren capitulated so decisively to [the] practical arguments against the exclusionary rule that he erased in one stroke the long-standing assumption that evidence seized without probable cause can never be used." See also Yale Kamisar, "The Warren Court (Was It Really So Defense-Minded?), the Burger Court (Is It Really So Prosecution-Oriented?) and Police Investigatory Practices," 67.

67. Kamisar, supra note 66 at 67–68 (citations omitted).

68. 395 U.S. 752 (1969).

69. 393 U.S. 410 (1969).

70. *Davis v. Mississippi*, 394 U.S. 721 (1969).

71. *Alderman v. United States*, 394 U.S. 165 (1969).

72. *Benton v. Maryland*, 395 U.S. (1969).

73. Kamisar, supra note 66 at 66.

74. 388 U.S. 218 (1967).

75. 388 U.S. 263 (1967).

76. 388 U.S. 293 (1967).

77. Kamisar, supra note 66 at 69.

78. 406 U.S. 682 (1972).

79. *Rhode Island v. Innis* 446 U.S. 291, 304 (1980).

80. Saltzburg, "Foreword: The Flow and Ebb of Constitutional Criminal Procedure in the Warren and Burger Courts," 153.

Chapter 3
The Failure of the Criminal Procedure Revolution

The title of this chapter seems inconsistent with the discussion that has preceded it. The criminal procedure revolution, at least from the perspective of its instigators on the Warren Court, along with their supporters, would seem to have been a huge success. Criminal procedure law *was* revolutionized and, despite the political reaction to the Warren Court, those significant innovations largely survived subsequent changes in Supreme Court personnel. Moreover, despite the inevitable failure of law reforms to alter behavior in the field fully, there is substantial evidence that police respect for constitutional rights has increased considerably. Police and federal law enforcement officials receive training in criminal procedure law, prosecutors put pressure on police to follow that law, and trial judges, at least in most states, regularly exclude evidence because of, and in order to deter, constitutional violations by the police. The "third degree" seems to have largely disappeared from the American scene.

At trial, all defendants are generally afforded a speedy trial, are represented by at least reasonably competent counsel, and have a right to a jury. Moreover, all states afford convicted defendants at least one appeal with free counsel and a transcript given to those who cannot afford to pay. Finally, federal courts, exercising habeas corpus jurisdiction as to all but fourth amendment claims,[1] oversee this whole process to ensure that state courts are toeing the line.[2] Even many conservative critics of the Warren Court, while still adamantly opposed to extending the exclusionary rule to the states, have grudgingly conceded that *Miranda* was not so bad[3] and seem to have accepted that the reforms of the criminal trial were, by and large, a good idea.[4] I too agree with this list of achievements.

Despite this impressive list of substantive achievements, the criminal procedure revolution has failed because it does not provide adequate guidance to police as to what to do. That is, criminal procedure law, whatever one may think of its ideological content, is totally inadequate as a system of rules for police to follow. To understand why this is a major failing depends on recognizing the unique position of criminal procedure in the constitutional spectrum. Criminal procedure law, insofar as it concerns the investigatory stage of the criminal process, is written not primarily for lawyers and judges, who may contemplate and debate it at relative leisure, but for non-law-trained police, who must apply it rapidly on the street. If the Supreme Court decides, for example, that creches may or may not be displayed on public property, city attorneys will scrutinize that decision with care and, in due course, advise the city how to adjust its Christmas display to conform to Supreme Court pronouncements. Other lawyers will then examine that display, compare it to the Supreme Court decision, and, if they feel it does not pass muster, bring a lawsuit on behalf of their Buddhist, Hindu, or atheist clients. The issue will then be litigated through the courts, and possibly back to the Supreme Court again, until it is resolved. Other potential litigants may wait for the outcome of the first case before going to the expense and trouble of pressing their own claims.

Criminal procedure works differently. The day after a Supreme Court decision on searches incident to arrest, for example, a thousand arrestees around the country are searched by police who have not even heard of the Supreme Court opinion, much less received legal advice on how to implement it. The next day, a thousand more arrestees are searched. Moreover, it is in the nature of current Supreme Court law, now that the criminal procedure revolution is over, that that law is devoted to trimming and molding earlier cases, rather than declaring bold and memorable new rules. So, even if the police department has a legal advisor who circulates a memo explaining the case, the chance that the police in the field will be able to understand and internalize this latest nuance of the law of searches incident to arrest is nil. But, because all criminal defendants receive counsel, even if they cannot afford to pay, most of these searches that produce evidence will be litigated in a motion to suppress the evidence that was found.

Further, every defendant who goes to trial and is convicted will appeal the conviction, raising every issue that might lead to a reversal, regardless of the fact that the same issue is being raised in nine hundred and ninety-nine other cases around the country. After all, it does not cost indigent defendants anything to litigate, and their attorneys are duty-bound to raise any issue that may reasonably prove to be a winner. These attorneys cannot wait to see how other cases may come out as can the attorneys in the civic creche example. Finally, if the courts conclude that the police acted wrongly, that wrong cannot be undone in the same way that the city can simply alter its Christmas display. The exclusionary rule is an indirect remedy, aimed at deterring future police misconduct, rather than remedying the wrong that has occurred in this case. The court cannot "unsearch" the arrestee, and an innocent victim of an illegal search derives no benefit from the exclusionary rule at all. Rather the conviction is reversed and, if the evidence in question was essential to the prosecution's case, the defendant must be set free.

It is thus apparent that in the area of criminal procedure, unlike any other field of Supreme Court endeavor, the doctrine must be clear, it must be complete, and it must be stable. It is in these respects that criminal procedure law has failed. The usual leisurely manner of constitutional decision making where the Supreme Court announces a rule one year and then answers the questions to which that rule gives rise over the next fifteen or twenty years is inappropriate in this field, where the police need clear guidance and where the penalty for police mistakes is high.

Criticism from All Quarters

The Supreme Court's criminal procedure jurisprudence has attracted volumes of criticism. Most of this has been ideological: conservatives criticized the Warren Court; liberals criticized the Burger and Rehnquist Courts. The validity of these complaints depends on one's political stance. However, occasional commentators, or dissenting Supreme Court Justices, have addressed themselves to the pragmatic concerns that are the subject of this book, but among these commentators, regardless of their ideology, none, to my knowledge, has claimed that the current body of criminal procedure law is acceptable, or even marginally comprehensible.

For example, Stephen Saltzburg, after a comprehensive review of both the Warren and Burger Courts' criminal procedure decisions—a review that was generally well disposed toward the Warren Court innovations—concluded in a 1980 article that "failures of doctrinal exposition by both Courts have resulted in erratic decisions that have in turn confused law enforcement personnel."[5] Charles Whitebread made a similar observation in 1985 from the perspective of one who attempts to teach the rules of criminal procedure to state and local police at the FBI National Academy:

The Burger Court's jurisprudential preference for case-by-case analysis rather than announcing its decisions in criminal cases in rules may be its most dangerous characteristic. . . . This Court is reluctant to announce rules that the police, lower courts and other components of the criminal justice system can both understand and apply.[6]

Finally, Lloyd Weinreb, after comparing American and European systems, concluded that the American law of criminal investigation

does not make sense. Its fine distinctions elude understanding even in the quietude of the courtroom, to say nothing of the harried circumstances of police patrol.[7]

These criticisms of criminal procedure law under the Burger Court might be written off as the complaints of liberal academics disgruntled that the Warren Court innovations had not been carried through with vigor. But this is not the case. *Everyone* who has considered the question of the workability of the "rules" of criminal procedure has found them defective. Consider the comments of an attorney for the (conservative) Mountain States Legal Foundation concerning the Burger Court's efforts to help the police by creating exceptions to the exclusionary rule:

Police will increasingly err, often through no fault of their own, on the wrong side of the law. Evidence will be thrown out that could have been properly secured and our interest in punishing the guilty will drown in a heated sea of argument because of the Court's failure to draw clear rules. . . . Although it is a widely perceived myth that police officers detest the exclusionary rule, most I know have accepted the rule well—it enhances police training and has raised the level of professionalism. [But] in the absence of firm rules the police will err on the wrong side of the line.[8]

The police attitude toward the law of criminal procedure was summarized by a Chicago police lieutenant:

Of course there has to be an exclusionary rule. I don't want this to be a police state. There have to be guidelines. The problem is that the guidelines aren't clear. I believe that the Supreme Court is not making the law clear. They take a tough situation in which a police officer must act in an instant, they think about it for five months and come out seven to six. What kind of a system is that for making the law?[9]

From a prosecutor's perspective, the chief of the trial bureau of the Nassau County, New York district attorney's office, while agreeing that illegally seized evidence should be suppressed, wrote, in 1990:

The standards used by the courts to determine illegality have become so contradictory and confusing that few officers can understand what is required by the Constitution to effect a lawful arrest. . . . If the Chief Justice of the United States sat in the back of a squad car in Manhattan, I doubt he could counsel the officer, within a degree of legal certainty, on the constitutionality of a police action. Is it any wonder that the police are angry at the courts.[10]

Warren Burger, before he became Chief Justice, criticized the Supreme Court for "revising the code of criminal procedure piecemeal, on a case-by-case basis, on inadequate records and incomplete factual data."[11] But in 1982, twelve years after Burger had become Chief Justice and the "Nixon four" had been in control of the development of criminal procedure doctrine for a decade, Attorney General William French Smith declared:

Simply put, the law of the Fourth Amendment is so uncertain and so constantly changing that police officers cannot realistically be expected to know what judges themselves do not know.[12]

The Court itself occasionally recognizes the problem, usually when it purports to be solving it. For example, in *Oliver v. United States*[13] the Court excluded "open fields" from the coverage of the fourth amendment in order to have a "clear rule" and thus avoid the criticisms of its fourth amendment jurisprudence which Wayne LaFave, the leading expert in the field, had leveled at it:

Fourth Amendment doctrine . . . is primarily intended to regulate the police in their day-to-day activities and thus ought to be expressed in terms that are readily applicable by the police in the context of the law enforcement activities in which they are necessarily engaged. A highly sophisticated set of rules, qualified by all sorts of ifs, ands, and buts and requiring the drawing of subtle nuances and hairline distinctions, may be the sort of heady stuff upon which the facile minds of lawyers and judges eagerly feed, but they may be "literally impossible of application by the officer in the field." [underlined portion quoted by the Court][14]

Perhaps the best evidence of the complexity of criminal procedure law is that it takes LaFave four volumes (3,375 pages) to summarize the law of search and seizure alone.[15] Is it any wonder that the police are confused?

The Studies

Studies concerning the impact of the exclusionary rule are not very helpful in assessing the overall success of the Warren Court criminal procedure innovations. Suppose, for example, that a study shows that a high percentage of all arrests are dismissed because of exclusionary rule concerns. Does this mean that the exclusionary rule is a disaster

because it is causing a lot of criminals to be released, or a vital safe-
guard to civil liberties because the police are so lawless? By contrast,
if the percentage of lost cases is low (which most studies have found),
does this mean that the rule is working really well and at a low cost to
society, or that the state courts are not excluding evidence in many
cases where it should be excluded because they do not want to let
criminals go free because the constable blundered? Furthermore,
whatever the percentages, no study distinguishes between those evidentiary exclusions that are clearly justifiable because the police behavior in question is genuinely unreasonable, or where the police
could not have gotten the evidence at all but for the violation, and
those exclusions that are based on technicalities or understandable
police confusion about the rules. Finally, the success of exclusionary
rules in controlling police behavior is necessarily limited to those areas
in which the Supreme Court has declared rules. As will be discussed
in the next chapter, one of this book's principal criticisms of the Supreme Court's criminal procedure jurisprudence is that it is incomplete, leaving many areas of police procedure untouched, while
overregulating others. Consequently, the efficacy, or inefficacy, of the
exclusionary rule as an enforcement device is frequently irrelevant.[16]

  With these reservations in mind, let us briefly consider the studies.
The best source of information about the studies is Thomas Davies's
1983 review of them, summarized by the Supreme Court in *United
States v. Leon*,[17] stating that the exclusionary rule

results in nonprosecution of between 0.6% and 2.35% of individuals arrested
for felonies. . . . The estimates are higher for particular crimes, the prosecution of which depends heavily on physical evidence. Thus the cumulative
loss due to nonprosecution or nonconviction of individuals arrested on felony
drug charges is probably in the range of 2.8% to 7.1%. Davies' analysis of
California data suggests that screening by police and prosecutors results in
the release because of illegal searches or seizures of as many as 1.4% of all
felony arrestees, that 0.9% of all felony arrestees are released, because of
illegal searches and seizures, at the preliminary hearing or after trial, and that
roughly 0.5% of all felony arrestees benefit from reversals on appeal because
of illegal searches.

                    *   *   *   *

Many of these researchers have concluded that the impact of the exclusionary
rule is insubstantial, but the small percentages . . . mask a large absolute number of felons who are released because the cases against them were based in
part on illegal searches or seizures.[18]

  The American Bar Association also attempted to measure the impact of the exclusionary rule, and found that "most prosecutors

TABLE 1. The Perceived Impact of the Fourth and Fifth Amendments
            on Outcomes

Prosecutors
  Percentage of cases dismissed because of *Miranda* problems
              None   16%
              1–5 percent   71%
              6–10 percent   10%
              11 percent or more   3%   (N = 234)
  Percentage of cases dismissed because of search and seizure problems
              None   6%
              1–5 percent   68%
              6–10 percent   16%
              11 percent or more   10%   (N = 234)

Judges
  Percentage of outcome determinative motions to suppress evidence
              None   13%
              1–5 percent   34%
              6–10 percent   27%
              11 percent or more   34%   (N = 216)

Defense attorneys
  Percentage of cases in which motions to suppress evidence were granted
              None   12%
              1–5 percent   32%
              6–10 percent   25%
              11 percent or more   31%   (N = 94)

Source: Table 25 in an unpublished supplement to American Bar Association, Special Committee on Criminal Justice in a Free Society, *Criminal Justice in Crisis* (Washington, DC: ABA: 1988). Reprinted by permission.

perceive that 5 percent or less of all cases are dismissed because of the exclusionary rule. Similarly, roughly three quarters of the judges and defense lawyers polled claim that 10 percent or fewer of the suppression motions filed are successful." The study also found that "Eighty-seven percent of the 234 prosecutors surveyed believed that 5 percent or less of their cases were dismissed because of *Miranda* problems."[19] (See Table 1.)

These percentages do not sound too bad, but, as the Supreme Court has suggested, it is important to consider not just percentages but absolute numbers. In the United States in 1988 there were about two million arrests for "Index" crimes[20] and another million for drug and weapons violations.[21] If 5 percent of these cases were dismissed due to search problems, and another 5 percent due to *Miranda* problems, then 30,000 cases were dismissed nationwide in one year because of the exclusionary rule. Moreover, as both the ABA and the Supreme Court agree, the dismissal rate from evidentiary exclusion is particularly high in drug cases, which, unlike aggravated assaults, for example, invariably depend on physical evidence seized from defendants, their effects, or their premises. In those cases, one study found as many as 30 percent of arrests lost due to search problems.[22] The ABA agreed that more gun and drug cases than other types of cases are lost because of evidentiary exclusion—as many as 50 percent in one city—though it concluded that this was "a symptom of a drug problem that defies recognized means of control . . . and not an inherent failing of the Fourth Amendment or the exclusionary rule"[23] (i.e., police may know that they are breaking the rules when they arrest drug and weapons suspects, but do so to get the contraband off the street).[24]

Actually, the ABA study cited in Table 1 could be described as demonstrating, contrary to the ABA's own characterization of it, disturbingly high numbers of cases lost due to evidentiary exclusion. The study shows that a substantial majority of judges (61%) granted outcome determinative motions to suppress in at least 6 percent of their cases and that 34 percent of judges granted outcome determinative motions to suppress in at least 11 percent of their cases. Similarly, 58 percent of defense attorneys had motions to suppress granted in at least 6 percent of their cases. A 1987 study in Chicago by Peter Nardulli found that motions to suppress physical evidence were filed in about 9 percent of the over 4,000 cases studied, and were successful 63.8 percent of the time (mostly in drug cases).[25] While there is reason to believe that, in some of these cases, the granting of the motion to suppress may have simply been the vehicle for disposing of a weak case, still, a success rate of 63.8 percent suggests a system with serious problems. The most recent study in this area does provide some optimistic data—that in cases where the police have obtained a search warrant the chance that a motion to suppress will succeed is quite low. Moreover, presumably because of police awareness of this fact, warrant use appears to be on the upswing.[26] Still, it is generally agreed, and was my own experience as a prosecutor in Washington, D.C., that warrantless searches, with their greater potential for evidentiary loss, occur substantially more often than searches by warrant.[27]

In raw numbers, then, a substantial quantity of arrests are lost and, therefore, a substantial number of criminals released, particularly in drug and weapons cases, due to criminal procedure violations. There are no data as to what percentage of these are lost due to inadequacies in the rules as opposed to police failure to obey rules that a reasonable police officer could have followed. For this, we have only the uniformly held opinion among both criminal justice professionals and academic commentators, that the inability of the Supreme Court to declare clear rules for police to follow represents a major failing of the criminal justice system.

A recent study confirms the main point of this chapter: that the police do not understand the rules. In an article in the *University of Michigan Journal of Law Reform*, William Heffernan and Richard Lovely reported their study of police comprehension of the rules governing search and seizure.[28] They presented 547 police officers with six fact situations and asked them whether the searches undertaken by the police in the scenarios were proper or improper. In fact, though the police were not told this, the scenarios were lifted from actual Supreme Court cases; so it was already known that three of the searches were legal and three illegal. The mean score of the police was 3.4. That is, on average, they evaluated 3.4 of the scenarios correctly—just slightly better than if they had guessed randomly. (A group of lawyers scored 4.4.)[29] The authors' conclusion is a striking indictment of the state of, at least, fourth amendment law—that even if all police officers were disposed to adhere to the rules of search and seizure, there would nonetheless be substantial deviation from those rules as they are presently constituted because of police mistakes about what they require.[30]

Moreover, statistics such as these mask what may be an equally important problem with the law of criminal procedure: that it is not being consistently applied by the trial courts. If the trial courts are ignoring constitutional violations by the police, or, because of the complexity of the law, are not even able to recognize that such violations have occurred, then statistics showing a low percentage of cases lost because of the exclusionary rule take on a different significance. Now such statistics suggest that the only reason that the cost of the exclusionary rule is low is that constitutional violations are consistently being ignored by the courts.

No study has fully examined this issue. However, in 1988, I published a preliminary survey in the *Georgetown Law Journal* in which I examined the reported fourth amendment decisions of the appellate courts of nine states in 1986.[31] I found that 15.7 percent of the 223 cases studied resulted in convictions being reversed on appeal on fourth amendment grounds. (This is in addition to all the cases lost at or before trial, as described in the other studies.) Another 10.3 percent of cases should have been reversed but were not because the appellate court incorrectly applied fourth amendment law. It must be emphasized that this is only a study of reported cases. Many convictions are summarily affirmed (and, much less frequently, reversed) without a reported opinion, so that the actual percentage of convicted criminals who were or should have been affected by the exclusionary

TABLE 2. Apellate Court Fourth Amendment Decisions in Nine States, 1986

State (crime rate/100,000 population) (1986 population)[a]	Total cases[b]	Cases studied[c]	Decisions for the government[d]	Decisions for the defendant	Wrong cases for the government[e]	Consent searches	Percentage wrong cases for the government	Percentage decisions for the defendant
Georgia (5,455) (6,104,000)	57	57	55	2	10	11	17.5	3.5
Illinois (5,546) (11,553,000)	51	51	39	12	8	8	15.7	23.5
Idaho (4,207) (1,003,000)	13	13	9	4	0	1	0	30.7
South Carolina (5,137) (3,378,000)	3	3	2	1	0	1	f	f
Louisiana (6,078) (4,501,000)	66	42	38	4	5	10	11.9	9.5

Alabama (4,288) (4,053,000)	46	26	20	6	0	3[g]	0	23.0
Oklahoma (6,014) (3,305,000)	19	19	16	3	0	2	0	16.0
Arizona (7,321) (3,312,000)	4	4	3	1	0	1	[f]	[f]
Utah (5,478) (1,665,000)	8	8	6	2	0	0	0	25.0
Totals	267	223	118	35	23	37	10.3	15.7

[a] 1986 FBI Uniform Crime Statistics.

[b] Civil cases involving search and seizure issues not counted in total. Cases noted under both "arrest" and "search and seizure" counted only once. Only includes reported cases. Many states have substantial numbers of unreported decisions that are not broken down as to subject matter.

[c] Because of time constraints, a random selection of cases was studied for some states.

[d] This means the decision on the fourth amendment issue, not necessarily the whole case.

[e] "Wrong" subjectively determined by author.

[f] Sample too small to calculate percentages. Arizona and South Carolina data included in totals.

[g] Including one case decided for the defendant.

Source: Craig Bradley, "Are State Courts Enforcing the Fourth Amendment? A Preliminary Study." *Georgetown Law Journal* 77 (1988): 251–86.

rule is undoubtedly substantially less than the 26 percent (15.7% plus 10.3%) disclosed by this survey. (See Table 2, which summarizes the results.) On the other hand, there is no reason to believe that the courts got the fourth amendment issue right any more often in summary affirmance cases than they did in reported cases, and erroneous exclusions of evidence by trial courts will never reach the appellate court when defendants are acquitted.

In any case, it is a striking testament to the poor quality of fourth amendment law that, even after the most obvious violations have been weeded out by pretrial dismissals and motions to suppress before trial, and after the issues have been briefed and argued by the lawyers, fully one quarter of the reported appellate decisions from across the country (that is, cases in which the disputed evidence had already survived a challenge at the trial level) contained fourth amendment violations by the police, and at least 10 percent of the appellate decisions got the fourth amendment law wrong.* This suggests that studies finding that few cases are lost due to evidentiary exclusion may be missing a major aspect of the problem.

The other striking finding in this study was that in only a very few of these 223 cases was the police behavior clearly "wrong" in any obvious way. In all the others, at least as the facts were disclosed in the opinions, the police seemed to have acted in a way most people would have considered reasonable had they not known of the excruciatingly complex rules that the police are expected to follow.[32]

Thus there are two classes of "unreasonable" searches: searches that involve unreasonable police behavior in the ordinary sense of the word—oppressive behavior, or violations of clearcut rules—and searches that are called "unreasonable" by the courts because that is what the fourth amendment, on which the Supreme Court's rulemaking capacity depends, prohibits. It is provocative to realize, as discussed in Chapter 5, that, while the United States is in no way unique in having an exclusionary rule for police behavior that is "unreasonable" in the former sense, it *is* unique in having a (theoretically) mandatory rule for searches that are "unreasonable" only because they break the (often confusing) rules. As Table 2 shows, searches that are unreasonable only in the "rulebreaking" sense are subject to extraordinarily erratic decision making by courts at all levels when it comes to applying the exclusionary sanction. It is, in my view, a failure to distinguish between these two types of "unreasonable" searches that leads to much of the disagreement between liberals and conservatives

---

*I did not study how many appellate cases decided fourth amendment issues incorrectly in favor of defendants.

about the exclusionary rule.* It may also be that recognizing this important distinction will lead to the development of a more flexible approach to police violations of the rules. This issue is discussed at the end of this chapter and in Chapter 5.

Specific Areas

Search and Seizure Law

It seems to be generally agreed that, of the various aspects of criminal procedure, the law governing searches and seizures is the most complex and confusing. The fourth amendment, as I observed in a 1985 *University of Michigan Law Review* article, is "the Supreme Court's tar-baby: a mass of contradictions and obscurities that has ensnared the Court in such a way that every effort to extract itself only leaves it more profoundly stuck."[33] In 1971 Justice Harlan called for "an over-hauling" of fourth amendment law,[34] but this has not occurred. In the early 1970s, Lloyd Weinreb cited the fact that in the preceding five Terms (1968–69 to 1972–73) the Court had rendered sixteen major opinions interpreting the fourth amendment, illustrating that the "body of [fourth amendment] doctrine . . . is unstable and unconvincing."[35] But in the first five years of the eighties the Court decided *thirty-five* cases involving the fourth amendment. In seven of these there was no majority opinion. In the seventeen cases decided in the 1982–83 and 1983–84 Terms the Court never reached the same result as all lower courts and usually reversed the highest court below, rendering a total of sixty-one separate opinions in the process.†

Consider the Supreme Court's discussion, in a case involving the search of a paper bag and a leather pouch found in an automobile (*United States v. Ross*), of the efforts of the judges in the court below (the D.C. Circuit) to decipher an earlier Supreme Court decision:

> Judge Tamm, the author of the original panel opinion, reiterated the view that *Sanders* prohibited the warrantless search of the leather pouch but not the search of the paper bag. Judge Robb agreed that this result was compelled

---

*Conservatives are upset that mere rule-breaking searches led to exclusion; liberals fear that without the rule gross violations by the police will go unpunished.

†Matters continue to deteriorate. Between 1985 and 1990, the Court decided 43 fourth amendment cases, reversing the court below in 85 percent of cases that were decided in the government's favor. Phyllis Bookspan, "Reworking the Warrant Requirement: Resuscitating the Fourth Amendment," 474 n. 4. However, in the October Term 1991 the Court, for the first time in memory, decided no fourth amendment cases. Unfortunately, the law by now is such a mess that simply refraining from making a greater mess is not an adequate solution.

by *Sanders*, although he stated that in his opinion "the right to search an automobile should include the right to open any container found within the automobile, just as the right to search a lawfully arrested prisoner carries with it the right to examine the contents of his wallet and any envelope found in his pocket. . . ." Judge MacKinnon concurred with Judge Tamm that *Sanders* did not prohibit the warrantless search of the paper bag. Concerning the leather pouch, he agreed with Judge Wilkey, who dissented on the ground that *Sanders* should not be applied retroactively.[36]

Amazingly, all this disagreement was just among the dissenting judges, whose views obviously all differed from that of the majority as well.

The Supreme Court Justices themselves have frequently condemned the Court's efforts in this area. For example, in *Florida v. Royer*[37] a 5–4 majority struck down, as an "arrest" without probable cause, the fifteen-minute detention of an airline passenger at an airport by narcotics agents. Justice Rehnquist, dissenting, argued that

Analyzed simply in terms of its "reasonableness", as that term is used in the Fourth Amendment, the conduct of the investigating officers toward Royer would pass muster with virtually all thoughtful civilized persons not overly steeped in the mysteries of this Court's Fourth Amendment jurisprudence.

Shortly after his retirement, Justice Stewart, a major figure in the criminal procedure revolution, described the Court's search and seizure doctrine as "as complex a delineation of rules, exceptions and refinements as exists in any field of jurisprudence."[38] He continued:

Looking back, the exclusionary rule seems a bit jerry-built—like a roller coaster track constructed while the roller coaster sped along. Each new piece of track was attached hastily and imperfectly to the one before it, just in time to prevent the roller coaster from crashing, but without the opportunity to measure the curves and dips preceding it or to contemplate the twists and turns that inevitably lay ahead. With the wisdom of hindsight, it is certainly possible to criticize opinions dealing with the exclusionary rule for misapplying or misconstruing prior precedents and for failing to consider how a given decision would affect the future developments of the law.[39]

Similarly, for automobile searches, Justice Powell once observed that

the law of search and seizure with respect to automobiles is intolerably confusing. The Court apparently cannot agree even on what it has held previously, let alone on how these cases should be decided.[40]

Perhaps the most striking, albeit tacit, admission by a Supreme Court majority of the poor quality of the Court's fourth amendment law is the decision in *United States v. Leon*.[41] In *Leon* the Court held that evidence would not be excluded, despite the fact that it was obtained in violation of the fourth amendment, if the police acted in "reasonable good faith" reliance on a search warrant issued by a neutral and detached magistrate. As Justice Stevens pointed out in dissent, this holding seems inconsistent with the fourth amendment itself. Before a fourth amendment violation is found in the first place, a search must be "unreasonable." How then can the police activity be "unreasonable" and "reasonable" at the same time? *Illinois v. Gates*,[42] decided the previous Term, had already redefined probable cause in a "practical nontechnical" way to avoid warrants being overturned on technicalities.

While the majority did not respond to Stevens's point, the honest answer would have been: "Because our rules (that is, our definitions of what conduct is 'reasonable') are so complex, incomplete, and incoherent, it happens every day that police, despite acting in a manner that most would consider 'reasonable,' nevertheless break the rules. In cases where they get a warrant first, we are willing to wink at that violation." Indeed, the logic of *Leon*, that you cannot deter the police from breaking the rules when they do not realize that they are breaking them, would apply equally to warrantless searches, but the Court has not yet gone that far. *Leon* is, essentially, a confession of failure by the Court. If its fourth amendment rules were more straightforward, it would not be necessary to excuse certain violations of those rules because such violations are "reasonable."*

Confessions Law

The area of confessions law is somewhat clearer simply because, in *Miranda*, the Court engaged in legislative-type rulemaking. It announced a clear requirement that police must inform suspects of certain constitutional rights in every custodial interrogation and that, once the suspect invokes these rights, interrogation must cease. After *Miranda*, however, the Court's flirtation with legislative-type rules ended, and it went back to resolving interrogation issues case by case, leading the Court, in 1985, to describe the law on such issues as when "custody" begins and "whether a given unwarned statement will ultimately be held admissible" as "murky and difficult."[43] Other unre-

---

*Note that the *Leon* exception to the exclusionary rule is not based on the premise that certain fourth amendment rules are sufficiently minor in nature that their breach should not lead to exclusion, as is suggested at the end of this chapter. See *United States v. Caceres* 440 U.S. 741 (1979), where the Court refused, under its supervisory power, to exclude evidence due to the failure of an IRS agent to follow IRS electronic surveillance regulations.

solved questions in this area concern how the police are to proceed when the suspect indicates that he or she wants to remain silent (*Miranda*'s holding that questioning "must cease" in such a case was deemed unclear by the Court in *Michigan v. Mosley*),[44] what constitutes an "initiation" by the suspect such that questioning may resume after an assertion of the right to counsel, and how long interrogations may last and what may go on after the warnings have been given.

Some Hypothetical Examples

It is all very well to muster statements by critics and (admittedly inconclusive) statistics to show that the criminal procedure revolution has been a failure. Others might be able to muster a similar array of statistics and opinions to show that it has been a success (though no one experienced in the system would want to do such a thing). Perhaps the most telling criticism of the system is that leveled by Judge Friendly twenty-five years ago when he gave an example of a completely unremarkable fact situation involving a clearly culpable defendant and no obvious misbehavior by the police that, on careful examination by one "steeped in the mysteries" of Supreme Court law, was found to be shot through with reversible error. Judge Friendly's conclusion was that a legislatively enacted code was the only way to develop criminal procedure law properly.[45] What follows is an updated version of that fact situation, but no updating of his conclusion is required:

Officers A and B see a man, X, emerging from a building carrying a brown paper bag in a "high narcotics area." They recognize the man as an addict. They approach him, saying "hold it!" but before they reach him he drops the bag and puts his hands in the air. Officer B grabs X. Officer A opens the bag, which contains a glassine envelope containing a white powder. The officer opens the envelope and tastes the powder, which, his training leads him to believe, is heroin. X is searched by the police, who uncover a bloody knife in his belt (later established to be the weapon used in an unsolved murder) and a tinfoil packet containing a white powder in his shirt pocket. B gives X the *Miranda* warnings and then asks him, "Where'd you get this packet?" X replies, "I got it four hours ago from Y. He's selling out of 123 Queen Street around the corner."

Officers A and B go to 123 Queen Street and knock on the door, announcing, "Police, open up!" They hear scuffling inside and, after about five seconds, open the unlocked door. A shot rings out, killing Officer A. Just then, Officers C and D arrive and the three officers burst into the apartment. Inside are two men, Y and Z. It later turns out that this is Z's apartment; Y has spent the night there, but the police know nothing of this at the time. The police see a quantity of white powder sitting on a table. They tell both men they are under arrest, cuff their hands behind their backs, and search their clothing, finding a glassine envelope containing white powder in Y's pocket and a recently fired pistol in Z's pocket. They fully search the room, finding more white powder in a cabinet fifteen feet from where Y and Z are arrested. They also look in the kitchen, finding still more white powder in the refrigerator. They look in the bedroom, finding Z's wife hiding in the closet. A frisk of her produces five marijuana cigarettes. A large box on the closet floor produces twenty kilos of cocaine. Officer B says to Y, "Got any more?" Y replies, "You forgot to look in the oven." They do this and find another bag of cocaine.

A squad car arrives, and the suspects are put in the back. Officer E, the driver, recognizes Y from a previous narcotics arrest. "How you doin'?" says E in a jocular fashion. "Done a lot of business lately?" "Yeah," replies Y, "I sold a whole kilo yesterday." At the station, during routine booking procedures, Officer E, wanting to know if Y will affirm that he still lives at an address where a body was recently found, asks Y, "Do you still live at 496 Elm Street?" Y replies, "Yeah."

Believe it or not, *none* of the evidence obtained in this seemingly ordinary and straightforward case—statements, guns, drugs, the lot— would, in my opinion, be admissible under current Supreme Court law. For those who are interested, my reasoning is spelled out in Appendix 3-A at the end of this chapter.

The above example was designed to curl the hair of conservatives: bloody murder weapons suppressed; murderers and drug dealers going free because of what seems to be essentially appropriate, or at least not seriously bad, conduct by the police. However, a counter-example can be given showing how the police can misuse current law to their benefit. In fact, Albert Alschuler has already created such an example as to the Court's interrogation law.

[A] police training manual authored by Justice Holmes' "bad man of the law" might now offer the following advice:

Upon arresting a suspect, do not give him the *Miranda* warnings. When the public safety requires it, you may question this suspect without advising him of his rights, and his answers will be admissible. In the absence of a special public need, however, you should not question an arrested, unwarned suspect. If the suspect does make a statement, it will be a "volunteered" statement of the sort that *Miranda* makes admissible. Moreover, if the suspect remains silent, his silence may be used to impeach any defense that he offers at trial.

After an hour or two (during which your suspect will have provided either a statement or a potentially useful period of silence) you should advise him of his rights. If the suspect waives these rights, his statement will be admissible. If he indicates that he wishes to remain silent or to consult an attorney, however, *continue to interrogate him without a lawyer.* Although the prosecutor will be unable to introduce as part of the state's case-in-chief any statement that the suspect makes, the suspect's statement will become admissible to impeach his testimony if he later takes the witness stand to say something different from what he told you. . . . Do not place too much pressure on the suspect, however. If a court holds his confession involuntary under pre-*Miranda* standards, it will be inadmissible for any purpose. The Supreme Court has said that pre-*Miranda* voluntariness standards are part of the "real" Constitution. *Miranda* is part of the Court's "just pretend" Constitution.[44] (Emphasis in original.)

I might add the following suggestions to Alschuler's hypothetical officer on the law of search and seizure:

If you're not sure whether you have a probable cause that contraband will be found in a building, or whether you need a warrant, search anyway, without a warrant. If you find evidence, claim that a "reliable informant" (your partner is "reliable," right?) told you it would be there, and go for a warrant after the fact. If you have no prospect of obtaining probable cause, go ahead and search anyway. If you don't find anything, there's no evidence to suppress. (Just make sure you don't search the houses of innocent people who are likely to sue.) If you do find something, the evidence can be used to impeach, and that's better than nothing. When you arrest the defendant inside his home, don't cuff him right away. This restricts the "area within his immediate control." Instead search the room in which he's arrested, then cuff and remove him from the room. If he wants to go into another room (e.g., to get his shoes), let him, and search that room too.

If you see someone walking down the street with a suitcase that you have probable cause to believe contains contraband, wait and see if he's going to put it in a car. That way you don't need a warrant to search the suitcase, and you can take a look around the car for other contraband in plain view. If you have an arrest warrant for someone, wait until he goes into his home to arrest him. That way you can search the room incident to the arrest (see above) and may also be able to perform a "protective sweep" of the whole house that may uncover other contraband. Also, be sure that your department has drawn up broad "routine procedures" for inventorying automobiles and items seized from arrestees.

See Appendix 3-B for a discussion of the cases that support Alschuler's and my views of the current state of the law.

Many Supreme Court Justices might be surprised to learn that the Court's doctrines had become so shot full of holes. "But each decision was reasonable!" they would protest. (But see Justice Stewart's "wisdom of hindsight" comments above.) The problems described by Judge Friendly, Alschuler, and myself have arisen, not primarily because any of the fact-specific cases decided by the Court were intrinsically unreasonable (though some of them surely were) or because the Justices cynically set out to cut the heart out of the *Miranda* rule or the warrant requirement (though some may have) or to confuse the police. Rather, this doctrine that the Justices themselves now describe as "steeped in mysteries" and "murky and difficult" has simply been eroded by the natural forces of the case method wearing it away over time. The Court is never, by its nature, able to sit back and decide, apart from the cases before it, what the entire body of confession or search law should be like or to examine comprehensively what police behavior, in terms of arrest, booking, interrogation, identification procedures, and so on, is reasonable and what is not. A case-specific system necessarily leads to a patchwork system and to resulting confusion on the part of everyone involved in the process. Until some body undertakes the task of examining the entire system, criminal procedure law will only become more and more murky and difficult as police and courts try to wade through an ever-growing body of complex precedent looking in vain for ever-more-elusive answers to everyday questions.

It must be emphasized that abolishing the exclusionary rule is not the solution to the problems of the criminal procedure system. It was only the creation of that rule, and its application to the states, that caused anyone to care about police lawlessness in the first place.[47] Abolishing the rule would allow everyone to pretend, ostrichlike, that a continuing problem does not exist. The exclusionary rule is hated because it forces society to pay a continuing price for police violations of constitutional rights.[48] But most people would agree that excluding evidence because the police cannot understand the rules they are supposed to follow advances neither the cause of law enforcement nor that of civil rights. As Yale Kamisar has pointed out, "if the law of search and seizure is too technical, this is an attack on the *content* of the law, not the remedy for effectuating it. If the law . . . is too unrealistic or unprincipled, it ought to be changed, not defied or disregarded."[49] It is just such a change that this book seeks to lay out.

If, as proposed in this book, a more detailed code of procedure is developed, it may be the case that the exclusionary rule should play a less sweeping role than it currently does. While the *Leon* decision seemed to be based on police inability to be fully informed as to the Court's fourth amendment rules, it could also be read as endorsing the view that some of the technical rules developed by the Court for search warrant affidavits, particularly such technicalities as the "two-prong" requirement of *Spinelli*, were not important enough to be backed up by the exclusionary remedy.

As noted in the study of state court exclusionary rule decisions quoted above, there are two kinds of "unreasonable searches." In the first category are searches that are "unreasonable" in ordinary parlance because the police engaged in conduct that is offensive, or that obviously violates a clear rule. By contrast are searches deemed "unreasonable" by the Court, such as the searches in *Leon* and *Spinelli*, that do not qualify under the above standard but nevertheless break rules the Court has deemed important. Because the fourth amendment only prohibits "unreasonable" searches, these searches have also been given that label, even though, as Justice Rehnquist noted in his *Royer* dissent quoted above, they would not seem to warrant it and, since *Leon*, they may not lead to evidentiary exclusion in cases where a warrant was obtained.

To the extent that a code expands the range of criminal procedure law, such as prescribing the criteria for night searches, search warrant returns, or the length and conduct of interrogations, it may be appropriate to specify which rule violations do, and which do not, warrant the exclusionary remedy, or to allow some flexibility in applying the exclusionary rule in other ways.* Otherwise conservatives who would agree that the police could use more guidance will be reluctant to make a new code more comprehensive than the current system. Indeed, the mandatory exclusionary rule for all constitutional violations (subject to the *Leon* exception) surely has much to do with the Supreme Court's failure to close the gaps in the current law. If a more flexible approach to remedies for police violations were adopted, the United States would move closer to the European and Canadian models discussed in Chapter 5.

As recent English experience has demonstrated, when the *rules* that the police are expected to follow are clearly set forth in a code then courts, even courts with no exclusionary tradition, as in England, are willing to exclude evidence to deter police violations of that code on a discretionary basis. Consequently, the uniquely American mandatory exclusionary rule may not be necessary to ensure judicial enforcement of rules in a regime where the rules are clearer. Whether a new American code should leave all exclusionary decisions in the hands of the trial judge,† or adopt a hybrid system where some police violations are subject to mandatory and some to discretionary exclusion, is a matter that will have to be worked out.

---

*The Supreme Court has already recognized that police adherence to a statute later determined to be unconstitutional should not lead to evidentiary exclusion. *Illinois v. Krull* 480 U.S. 340 (1987).

†Except for coerced confessions, which all countries agree must be mandatorily excluded.

Appendix 3-A

This Appendix relates to the hypothetical case discussed on pp. 52–53.

1. In regard to dropping the bag, *California v. Hodari D.* 59 LW 4335, 4336 (1991) holds: "an arrest requires *either* physical force . . . or, where that is absent, submission to the assertion of authority." Consequently, this appears to be an "arrest" without probable cause and the seizure of the bag is illegal.

2. Even if we assume that the seizure of the bag is legal (if this was not an arrest), nothing about the bag suggests that its contents are illegal. *Texas v. Brown* 460 U.S. 730 (1983). Consequently, the police are not entitled to look in the bag. *Arizona v. Hicks* 480 U.S. 321 (1987).

3. Even if they are entitled to look in the bag, it is not clear that they are entitled to open the glassine envelope and taste the contents. Arguably, this is a further search, for which they need a warrant. See *Arizona v. Hicks*, supra #2.

4. If the arrest were valid the search of X would be a legitimate search incident to arrest. However, the probable cause to arrest was illegally obtained (see #1). Therefore the arrest is the fruit of the poisonous tree and the search incident to the arrest is no good. Neither the knife nor the packet may be used against X.

5. The questioning of X is also a fruit of the illegal arrest. X's answers cannot be used against him, despite the *Miranda* warnings. *Brown v. Illinois* 422 U.S. 590 (1975). However, they could be used to impeach X (as could the knife and the packet in #4) if he testified at trial and they can be used against Y, who lacks standing to protest these violations of X's rights.

6. Arguably, the information provided by X, who apparently has no record as a "reliable informant," is insufficient to provide probable cause to search 123 Queen Street. However, most courts would probably conclude that, given all the circumstances, it is at least reasonably likely that X's information is accurate.

7. In any event, there is no justification here for a warrantless search. The information is already four hours old. It will not clearly imperil the finding of the evidence to take another hour or so to go for a warrant. Nor are the police entitled to enter a dwelling to arrest someone without a warrant. Consequently, everything subsequently found in the apartment is a fruit of this illegal entry.

8. Since Y has spent the night, both he and Z have standing to protest this illegal entry. Moreover, even if the police had gotten an arrest

warrant for Y, this entry would have been illegal. What is required is a search warrant to search Z's apartment either for Y or for drugs. *Steagald v. United States* 451 U.S. 204 (1981).

9. Forget the details of the search of the apartment. *Nothing* found in it is admissible, including the gun, because of the warrantless entry.

10. Aside from #9, the searches of Y and Z would be appropriate as searches incident to arrest. However, the search of a cabinet fifteen feet away would not seem to be the area "within the immediate control" of the suspects. *Chimel v. California* 395 U.S. 752 (1969). However, the cabinet would fall within the scope of the search for narcotics which was the original purpose of the police entry.

11. The search of the refrigerator would also not be justified incident to arrest, nor under a "protective sweep" theory. However, if the initial entry to the apartment were upheld as based on probable cause and exigent circumstances, these areas could legitimately be searched because they are areas in which narcotics could have been secreted.

12. The search of the bedroom would be appropriate as a protective sweep if the original entry were appropriate. *Maryland v. Buie* 110 S.Ct. 1093 (1990). Given the shooting of Officer A, the frisk of Mrs. Z would also be OK. However, that frisk must be for weapons. *Terry v. Ohio* 392 U.S. 1 (1968). Five marijuana cigarettes could not feel like a weapon. Arguably, however, the marijuana and the cocaine in the box would be admissible based on the original probable cause to search for narcotics, but for the illegal entry—#9 above.

13. Any statements obtained from the suspects are fruits of the illegal arrest and inadmissible. *Brown v. Illinois*, #5.

14. Aside from #13, the statement by Y, "You forgot to look in the oven," would also be inadmissible as a *Miranda* violation. However, the cocaine in the oven would be admissible, because the "fruit of the poisonous tree" doctrine does not apply to *Miranda* violations. *Oregon v. Elstad* 470 U.S. 298 (1985).

15. Aside from #13, the statement in the squad car to Officer E is inadmissible as a *Miranda* violation—custodial interrogation, likely to elicit a response. *Rhode Island v. Innis* 446 U.S. 291 (1980).

16. While *Pennsylvania v. Muniz* 110 S.Ct. 2638 (1990) has now indicated that routine booking questions are probably an exception to *Miranda*, it is unclear from that case whether a seemingly routine question, asked with intent to incriminate, falls within the "booking question exception."

Appendix 3-B

This Appendix relates to the hypothetical "police training manual" discussed at pp. 53–54.

Murray v. United States 108 S.Ct. 2529 (1988) upheld the admission of narcotics that were first found during an illegal, warrantless search and then seized pursuant to a subsequently obtained warrant that was not based on the illegally obtained information. In *"Murray v. United States*: The Bell Tolls for the Search Warrant Requirement," at 917 I opined that *"Murray* positively encourages [a policeman] to proceed with illegal search[es]. If he finds nothing he simply shrugs his shoulders and walks away. If he finds evidence, he leaves his partner to watch over it, repairs to the magistrate, and reports that 'an anonymous reliable informant . . . called to tell me that he had just seen bales of marijuana stored at a warehouse at 123 Elm Street.'"

In *United States v. Havens* 446 U.S. 620 (1980) the Court held that evidence seized in violation of the fourth amendment may be used to impeach.

In *Chimel v. California* 395 U.S. 752 (1969) the Court held that searches incident to arrest were limited to the area "within the immediate control" of the suspect.

In *California v. Acevedo* 111 S.Ct. 1982 (1991) the Court held that the police do not need a search warrant to search a suitcase or other container that has been placed in a car. However, they *do* still need a warrant if such a container has *not* been placed in a car.

See *Chimel v. California,* supra. *Payton v. New York* 445 U.S. 573 (1980) held that an arrest warrant was sufficient justification to enter someone's home for the arrest. *Maryland v. Buie* 110 S.Ct. 1093 (1990) upheld "protective sweeps" incident to arrests in a home.

In *Florida v. Wells* 110 S.Ct. 1632 (1990) the Court made it clear that it would grant considerable leeway to police departments that had broad "routine procedures" for inventorying seized vehicles and other property.

See Albert Alschuler, "Failed Pragmatism: Reflections on the Burger Court," 1442–43 for Alschuler's sources.

Notes

1. This was withdrawn in *Stone v. Powell* 428 U.S. 465 (1976).

2. At the time of this writing, however, the Court is in the process of seriously restricting the access of state prisoners to federal courts via the habeas corpus remedy. See, e.g., Linda Greenhouse, "High Court Votes to Further Limit Prisoner Appeals," 1, discussing *Keeney v. Tamayo-Reyes* 112 S.Ct. 1715 (1992).

3. E.g., Yale Kamisar, remarks at Constitutional Law Conference sponsored by United States Law Week, September 12, 1987, Washington, D.C.: "Overturning *Miranda* seems to be an idea whose time has come and gone." But see Joseph Grano, "The Changed and Changing World of Constitutional

Criminal Procedure: The Contribution of the Department of Justice's Office of Legal Policy," 397–409 and sources cited therein for a summary of the continuing conservative opposition to *Miranda.*

4. E.g., Grano, supra note 3 at 396, approving of *Gideon v. Wainwright.* But see U.S. Dept. of Justice, Office of Legal Policy, "Report to the Attorney General on the Law of Pre-Trial Interrogation," Part I.B.2.b, 480–81.

5. Stephen Saltzburg, "Foreword: The Flow and Ebb of Constitutional Criminal Procedure in the Warren and Burger Courts," 158.

6. Charles Whitebread, "The Burger Court's Counter-Revolution in Criminal Procedure: The Recent Criminal Decisions of the United States Supreme Court," 473.

7. Lloyd Weinreb, *Denial of Justice,* 14.

8. K. Preston Oade, The High Court Sows Confusion," 18, col. 4.

9. Lieutenant Karczewski, quoted in Myron Orfield, "The Exclusionary Rule and Deterrence: An Empirical Study of Chicago Narcotics Officers," 1052.

10. *New York Times,* February 2, 1990, p. A14.

11. Quoted in Liva Baker, *Miranda: Crime, Law, and Politics,* 195.

12. *L.A. Daily Journal,* Oct. 14, 1982, p. 4, col. 3.

13. 12.466 U.S. 170 (1984).

14. Wayne LaFave, "'Case-by-Case Adjudication' Versus Standardized Procedures: The Robinson Dilemma," 141.

15. Wayne R. LaFave, *Search and Seizure: A Treatise on the Fourth Amendment.*

16. Richard Frase has lodged a similar criticism against criminal procedure law. "Criminal Procedure in a Conservative Age: A Time to Rediscover the Critical Nonconstitutional Issues," 83.

17. Thomas Davies, "A Hard Look at What We Know (and Still Need to Learn) About the Costs of the Exclusionary Rule: The NIJ Study and Other Studies of Lost Arrests," 621.

18. 468 U.S. 897, 907 n. 6 (1984) (citations omitted).

19. American Bar Association, *Criminal Justice in Crisis,* pp. 17, 33.

20. Murder, forcible rape, robbery, aggravated assault, burglary, larceny-theft, motor vehicle theft, and arson.

21. U.S. Dept. of Justice, FBI, *Uniform Crime Reports* (1988), 169.

22. U.S. Dept. of Justice, National Institute of Justice, *Criminal Research Report—The Effects of the Exclusionary Rule: A Study of California,* 18.

23. ABA, supra note 19 at 18.

24. Id. at 45.

25. Peter Nardulli, "The Societal Costs of the Exclusionary Rule Revisited," 230.

26. Craig Uchida and Timothy Bynum, "Search Warrants, Motions to Suppress and "Lost Cases": The Effects of the Exclusionary Rule in Seven Jurisdictions," 1061.

27. E.g., American Law Institute, *Model Code of Pre-Arraignment Procedure,* § SS 230, commentary at 521, and sources cited therein.

28. William Heffernan and Richard Lovely, "Evaluating the Fourth Amendment Exclusionary Rule: The Problem of Police Compliance with the Law."

29. Id. at 332–33.

30. Id. at 339.

31. Craig Bradley, "Are State Courts Enforcing the Fourth Amendment? A Preliminary Study."

32. Id. at 283.

33. Craig Bradley, "Two Models of the Fourth Amendment."

34. *Coolidge v. New Hampshire* 403 U.S. 443, 490–91 (1971) (Harlan, J., concurring in the judgment).

35. Weinreb, "Generalities of the Fourth Amendment," 49.

36. *United States v. Ross* 456 U.S. 798, 803 n. 3 (1982).

37. 460 U.S. 491 (1983).

38. Potter Stewart, "The Road to *Mapp v. Ohio* and Beyond: The Origins, Development and Future of the Exclusionary Rule in Search and Seizure Cases."

39. Id. at 1366.

40. *Robbins v. California* 453 U.S. 420, 430 (1981) (Powell, J., concurring).

41. 468 U.S. 897 (1984).

42. 462 U.S. 213 (1983).

43. *Oregon v. Elstad* 470 U.S. 298, 316 (1985).

44. 423 U.S. 96, 101–3 (1975).

45. Henry Friendly, "The Bill of Rights as a Code of Criminal Procedure," 930.

46. Albert Alschuler, "Failed Pragmatism: Reflections on the Burger Court," 1442–43 (emphasis added, citations omitted).

47. For a summary and discussion of the variety of evidence suggesting that the exclusionary rule does in fact deter police violations of constitutional rights, see Donald Dripps, "Beyond the Warren Court and Its Conservative Critics: Toward a Unified Theory of Constitutional Criminal Procedure," 627–630 and n. 154.

48. As Dripps has observed, "one is left with the uncomfortable belief that conservatives favor alternatives to the exclusionary rule because [those alternatives] do not deter." Id. at 629.

49. Yale Kamisar, "Remembering the 'Old World' of Criminal Procedure: A Reply to Professor Grano," 553.

Chapter 4
Reasons for Failure

As detailed in the last chapter, the Court has failed to produce adequate doctrine. However, contrary to most commentators who operate, as does the Court, on a case-by-case basis, I do not attribute the failings of the system to a series of poorly decided cases by the Supreme Court. Rather it is the thesis of this book that, because of the nature of the judicial process, no Supreme Court, no matter how competent and regardless of its political leanings, could have done much better. The only blame that should attach to the Court is for failing to realize its limitations. Why is the Supreme Court incapable of declaring adequate criminal procedure doctrine? There are two reasons, uncertainty and incompleteness.

The Uncertainty Principle

There is an uncertainty principle* that operates on Supreme Court decisions such that any attempt to resolve an issue of constitutional law will tend to create more uncertainty than it resolves. The process of rendering a decision will tend to distort the issue decided as well as the precedents upon which that decision is based.[1]

Justice Brennan recognized how the majority was doing this in his dissenting opinion in *Oregon v. Elstad*:[2]

---

*This term is borrowed from quantum physics, where the uncertainty principle, developed by the German physicist Werner Heisenberg, holds that it is impossible to ascertain with complete accuracy both the position and the velocity of a particle because the process of measuring one characteristic introduces uncertainty in the measurement of the other.

The Court's decision says much about the way the Court currently goes about implementing its agenda. In imposing its new rule . . . the Court mischaracterizes our precedents, obfuscates the central issues, and altogether ignores the practical realities of custodial interrogation that have led nearly every lower court to reject its simplistic reasoning. Moreover, the Court adopts startling and unprecedented methods of construing constitutional guarantees. Finally the Court reaches out once again to address issues not before us.

Justice Brennan was right about the Court's opinion in *Elstad*, but he failed to recognize that such distortion of issues and precedents occurs in virtually every Supreme Court decision, including those written by Justice Brennan himself. It is instructive to understand why this is so. There are at least seven reasons why Supreme Court opinions tend to create more uncertainty than they resolve.

The Lawyer Mentality

While the Justices of the Supreme Court may come from diverse backgrounds, they all share one characteristic: they are all lawyers who have practiced their profession for at least twenty years or so before joining the Court. As such they are professional advocates who have learned to marshal all reasonable arguments in favor of the position they are advocating. Thus it is an almost invariable aspect of a Supreme Court decision that the position advanced by the majority will be backed up by more than one stated reason. One might argue that this is sensible, creating confidence in the soundness of the result, or, at worst, unnecessary. However, it creates considerable problems when cases are used as a vehicle for rulemaking. For example, in *Michigan v. Mosley*[3] the Court endeavored to answer one of the many questions that had been raised by *Miranda*: what should the police do if the suspect, after being warned of his or her rights, says that he or she does not want to answer any questions?

Miranda had said that, in that event, "the interrogation must cease."[4] While this seemed clear enough, a majority of the *Mosley* Court, now dominated by Nixon appointees, professed uncertainty as to "under what circumstances, if any, a resumption of questioning is permissible." In *Mosley* the suspect had been arrested for robbery and advised of his rights; he stated that he did not want to answer any questions. The police stopped the interrogation and placed him in a cell. Two hours later, a homicide detective rewarned him and, after Mosley agreed to talk, questioned him about an unrelated murder case. During this interrogation, Mosley made incriminating statements about the murder. In approving the homicide interrogation the Court held that:

> This is not a case . . . where the police failed to honor a decision of a person in custody to cut off questioning, either by refusing to discontinue the interrogation upon request or by persisting in repeated efforts to wear down his resistance and make him change his mind. In contrast to such practices, the police here immediately ceased the interrogation, resumed questioning only after the passage of a significant period of time and the provision of a fresh set of warnings, and restricted the second interrogation to a crime that had not been a subject of the earlier interrogation.[5]

Elsewhere in the opinion, the Court points out that Mosley "was questioned by another police officer, at another location about an unrelated holdup murder." Thus the Court pointed to six different reasons why the requestioning of Mosley was allowable: immediate cessation of questioning, passage of time, new warnings, different crime, different interrogator, different location of second interrogation. This reasoning sounds just like the sort of argument a good lawyer would make: "Your honor, there are six reasons why you should decide this case for my client." But when the Supreme Court does it, uncertainty results. What if the homicide detective had questioned Mosley about the homicide immediately after the robbery detectives ceased their interrogation? Would the result have been the same? Or, what if the robbery detectives had gone to Mosley two hours later to ask if he would like to reconsider his refusal to talk about the robbery?

It is unclear in *Mosley*, and remains unclear fifteen years later, which of the various factors cited by the Court is critical to the outcome and which is not. Consequently, while *Mosley* offers a variety of reasons to support the Court's conclusion in that particular case, it offers virtually no guidance for future cases where the facts may differ (i.e., virtually all future cases).[6] This is not to suggest that *Mosley* was, necessarily, a poor opinion. It is perfectly reasonable judicial behavior for the Court to advance as many reasons as possible to explain why it is refusing to follow the apparently applicable *Miranda* precedent. Rather, since such lawyerlike behavior is naturally to be expected from a group of lawyers, this analysis points to the difficulties that inhere in using judicial opinions as a mode of criminal procedure rulemaking. Legislatively declared rules, by contrast, do not include a list of reasons why the rule was promulgated. Consequently, the absence of one or more of such reasons in the next case does not cast doubt on whether the rule should be applied.

The Committee Problem

Anthony Amsterdam once recognized the applicability to the Supreme Court of the joke that a camel is a horse designed by a committee.[7] The drafting of a Supreme Court opinion is a committee process, even though the final result may bear the name of a single Justice as the author. Consider *Mosley* again. Suppose that Justice Stewart, who wrote the majority opinion, was initially of the view that, when a suspect invoked the right to silence, the only obligation on the part of the police was to stop the interrogation for at least an hour, at which point it would be appropriate to return to the suspect and inquire if he had changed his mind and would now like to talk. Because in *Mosley* two hours passed before the suspect was requestioned, Stewart could have written a brief opinion affirming the conviction that would have given clear guidance to the police in future cases. Suppose further that he drafted such an opinion and circulated it to the other seven Justices (Justice Douglas had retired before *Mosley* was decided). Presumably Justice Rehnquist and Chief Justice Burger, who disliked *Miranda*, would have agreed to join such an opinion. But this would still leave Stewart two votes short of a majority.

Justice Powell comes to see Stewart and argues that merely allowing an hour to pass is inconsistent with *Miranda*'s requirement that interrogation must cease. Powell, however, is prepared to affirm the conviction because Mosley was questioned about a *different* crime than the one as to which he had asserted his right to silence. He would join an opinion that relied on that fact. Stewart has little choice. Unless the case is to have no majority opinion, which would give even less guidance to police, he must change the opinion. He issues a second draft, which relies on both the fact that the second interrogation occurred two hours after the first *and* that Mosley was questioned about a different crime in the second interrogation. Now Justice Blackmun sends Stewart a memo stating that, for him, the important facts in *Mosley* were that not only was there a two-hour delay and questioning about a different crime but Mosley was questioned by a different detective and received a new set of *Miranda* warnings. While Stewart does not agree that these factors are significant, he needs Blackmun's vote, so he includes these factors in the third draft of his opinion.

Justice White now attacks the opinion from the opposite direction, saying that Stewart has made it too difficult for the police to question defendants once they have asserted the right to silence. In White's view, the defendant can make a voluntary and intelligent waiver of this right *at any time*, regardless whether he or she has asserted the right to silence. However, White, seeing that he lacks the votes to prevail with this position, tells Stewart that he will join the majority if Stewart will include a footnote indicating that the result might be different if Mosley had asserted his right to counsel rather than to silence. Though Stewart does not agree with this distinction, he agrees to put in a footnote to that effect. While he does not need White's vote to have a majority, still a 6–2 opinion is better than a 5–3 one and one footnote seems a small price to pay.

As a result of this compromise, White joins the opinion, and writes a separate concurrence, rather than merely concurring in the result. Six years later he uses the footnote that Stewart put in (footnote 7) as the basis for his opinion in *Edwards v. Arizona*,[8] which held that if a suspect asserts the right to *counsel* (as opposed to silence), questioning must cease until an attorney is present[9]—a distinction of *Mosley* that many critics have deemed nonsensical.[10] Thus the fact that a committee participated in the drafting of this decision, while it may have led to a good result, clearly detracted from the opinion's clarity.*

The Committee Problem is particularly acute when the writing Justice is unwilling to make the changes demanded by other Justices and ends up with an opinion that does not command a majority of the Court. In this case, it becomes necessary for one who wants to know the holding of the case to pore over not only the main (plurality) opinion but also the opinions of other Justices to try to discern what points a majority of the Court agrees on.

A striking example of the problems caused by plurality opinions can be found in the 1990 case of *Pennsylvania v. Muniz*.[11] The Court apparently granted certiorari in *Muniz* to answer the question of whether *Miranda* warnings must be given to a suspect before police can ask routine booking questions such as name, address, or age. However, *Muniz* was an unusual case in that the police videotaped the booking process and attempted to use Muniz's slurred responses to these questions to show that Muniz was drunk at the time of booking, the better to prove the drunk driving case against him. Five Justices (the plurality of four, Justice Brennan writing, plus Justice Marshall, concurring in part and dissenting in part) agreed that "booking questions" were "custodial interrogation" and that therefore *Miranda*'s strictures would seem to be applicable. However, the plurality concluded that there was a "booking question exception" to *Miranda* that

*The above discussion is purely hypothetical and does not reflect any inside knowledge of the decisional process in this particular case. However, in my experience as a Supreme Court law clerk, this is the way such cases are frequently decided, and is a possible explanation of the actual result in *Mosley*.

exempted these kinds of questions from the warning requirement.[12] Justice Marshall did not subscribe to this portion of the plurality opinion, arguing that the warnings should be given prior to any custodial interrogation, including booking questions.

Chief Justice Rehnquist, writing for the other four Justices, also did not subscribe to the "booking question exception" because, in his view, "Muniz's responses to the videotaped 'booking' questions were not testimonial and do not warrant application of the privilege against self-incrimination. Thus, it is unnecessary to determine whether the questions fall within the 'routine booking question' exception to *Miranda* Justice Brennan recognizes."[13] One thing that may have bothered the Chief Justice was the plurality's footnote observing that the booking exception does not apply to "questions, even during booking, that are designed to elicit incriminatory admissions."[14] Thus following *Muniz* we are left in the dark as to whether there is a "booking questions" exception to *Miranda*, with four Justices saying there is, one saying that there is not, and four refusing to decide because the case at hand does not properly present the issue.

Besides not deciding the issue it was granted to resolve, the case leaves another question as well. What if the suspect's admission that he stays at his girlfriend's house at 123 Elm Street would be potentially incriminatory because a body had just been discovered at that address? Does it matter if the police ask this question with the intent to elicit incriminating information (as the footnote quoted above suggests), or, as the plurality had earlier observed, is "the perception of the suspect" that this is merely a routine booking question, "rather than the intent of the police,"[15] the significant factor? All this confusion occurs in a case where a careful reading of the opinions suggests that eight of the nine Justices agree that there should be a "booking questions" exception to *Miranda*, if only they could decide when it was applicable. As argued in this book, Supreme Court opinions do not provide adequate guidance as to the rules of criminal procedure. But plurality opinions are worse than no guidance at all because they usually, as in *Muniz*, provide contradictory advice. It is easy to see that a statute could resolve the booking question issue either way in one or two lines.

The Tyranny of the Majority Opinion

When a Supreme Court Justice joins an opinion, the most he or she can expect is to agree with the result and the broad outlines of that opinion. Sometimes, as discussed above, a Justice may feel sufficiently strongly about a point to make its inclusion in the majority opinion the price of his or her vote. More commonly, however, it will be impolitic or impossible to quibble with every point made by the author, even though the joining Justice almost invariably will not agree with all of them. In a number of dissenting opinions, for example, Justice Rehnquist has expressed the view that a case-by-case "reasonableness" approach would be the best way to deal with fourth amendment cases.[16] Yet in the case of *Oliver v. United States* he joined an opinion that contained a paragraph vigorously condemning such an approach.[17] Presumably he liked the majority decision better than the dissent and was unable, or unwilling, or did not have time, to convince the author to leave out the paragraph in question.

Consequently, though a majority opinion purports to "speak for" five or more Justices, particular statements made in the opinion may not represent the opinion of all of them. When one of the joining Justices has an opportunity to address the issue in another case, that Justice will probably slant it somewhat toward his or her own viewpoint, never conceding that this represents a departure from the previous decision. And, for the same reasons previously discussed, the author of the original opinion is likely to acquiesce in this distortion provided it is not too severe. Obviously, the potential for uncertainty in this process is great.

In his book *The Supreme Court: How It Was, How It Is* Justice Rehnquist discusses his observations of this phenomenon from his perspective as a law clerk to Justice Jackson, in connection with the Steel Seizure Case:

When one reads the separate opinions written by Justices Jackson, Frankfurter, Douglas and Burton, it is apparent that they, too, did not fully subscribe to the view set forth in (the majority) opinion, but they nonetheless joined it. There simply does not seem to have been enough time for the negotiation that often goes on in order to enable those who disagree with minor parts of a proposed Court opinion, but not with the result, to effect some sort of compromise that will enable them to join the principal opinion.[18]

My own observation, as a law clerk to Justice Rehnquist, largely squares with his. Usually a Justice who cares enough about a point in the majority opinion to write separately will first try to negotiate a change in that opinion, as Justice Rehnquist suggests (leading to the Committee Problem, discussed above). However, there are many matters, about which a joining Justice does not feel that strongly, or does not notice, or has failed in attempts to change, that go (unlike the Steel Seizure Case) uncommented upon, but not fully agreed with, into the majority opinion.

Cases or Controversies

The case-or-controversy limitation is a constitutional one, stemming from article III, which states that "the judicial power shall extend" to a variety of "cases" and "controversies." As R. Lea Brilmayer has observed, "The wording [of article III] has traditionally been understood to include the power to resolve abstract legal issues, including constitutional issues, but only as a necessary byproduct of the resolution of particular disputes between individuals."[19] The Court claims to have "followed a policy of strict necessity in disposing of constitutional issues"[20] (i.e., it will only decide such issues if such a decision is strictly necessary to resolve the dispute between the parties).

This is an extraordinary limitation, given that the stated purpose of the certiorari grant, as the Court has observed, is specifically *not* to resolve disputes between parties but to decide "an important question of federal law which has not been, but should be, settled by . . . [the Supreme] Court."[21] The purpose in granting certiorari is, in other words, essentially to legislate—to declare broad policy that will be applicable nationwide. As Robert Dahl has observed, "The Supreme Court is . . . a political institution, an institution, that is to say, for arriving at decisions on controversial questions of national policy."[22] Thus the Court, which considers itself principally a policy making body, can only make policy as a by-product of a dispute between parties. It must sit and wait and hope that two parties will bring it the issue that it wants to decide.[23] Resolving such a case does not readily lend itself to establishing a general principle; the statement of the general principle is limited by the bounds of the individual case. This limitation leads to several possible results.

First, there may be fudging of the case-or-controversy doctrine as the Court reaches out to decide issues that are not presented by the case. For example, in *United States v. Leon*[24] and *Massachusetts v. Sheppard*,[25] the Court held that it is inappropriate to exclude evidence obtained from an unconstitutional search when the police error was made in "good faith." Yet dissenting Justice Stevens noted that the search, at least in *Leon*,[26] actually *was* constitutional under the test announced the previous term in *Illinois v. Gates*.[27] Thus there was no need to decide whether certain *illegal* searches fell under the "good faith exception," because the search in question was legal. The Court, charged Stevens, was "reach[ing] out to decide what is undoubtedly a profound question concerning the administration of criminal justice [without] assuring itself that this question is actually and of necessity presented by the concrete facts before the Court." In doing this, the

Court necessarily creates uncertainty not only about the scope of the "case or controversy" limitation but also about what types of searches the new exception covers.

In addition to deciding issues that are not presented, the Court may distort the issue in order to find the case justiciable. *Taylor v. Louisiana*,[28] for example, involved a challenge by Taylor, a man, to the exclusion of women from the jury venire. In order to find that Taylor had standing, the Court had to define the sixth amendment right to a jury trial as a right to a jury drawn from a "representative cross-section of the community" (which Taylor clearly did not get) rather than to an unbiased and impartial jury (which Taylor apparently did get), a definition that was highly disputable, as Justice Rehnquist pointed out in dissent.[29]

By deciding issues that are not presented, or by misstating the issue presented in order to avoid the case-or-controversy limitation, the Court sows confusion about what has been decided and increases the probability that a future decision will interpret the issue differently than the first Court intended. After *Leon* and *Sheppard*, for example, it is not clear what constitutes a "good faith" mistake. Is it only a mistake that arguably was not a violation at all (as in these cases), or does the concept include more obvious examples of police misconduct? If a future Court wanted to limit these cases, it would be easy to say that the definition of a good faith mistake is very narrow, though that does not seem to be the intent of the opinions in *Leon* and *Sheppard*.

Finally, the Court may refuse to decide issues that need resolution simply because the issue is not presented by the parties, because the issue is moot, or because the parties lack standing. For example, in *DeFunis v. Odegaard*[30] the Court declined to decide whether a law school's preferential admissions policy for blacks constituted an equal protection violation of the rights of whites. The Court decided instead that the plaintiff's claim was moot because he had been admitted to, and was about to graduate from, law school. It took four more years for the Court to get a case on this topic that it considered justiciable.[31] In other cases, such as *Michigan v. Mosley* discussed above, the Court is forced by the facts of the case before it to decide a narrow issue when it might have liked to resolve a broader one. In *Mosley* the Court dealt with a suspect who had asserted his right to silence after receiving *Miranda* warnings. He was then questioned, two hours later and after another *Miranda* warning, by another detective about another crime. The Court approved this questioning, but in doing so it failed to resolve the much more common issue that it had, presumably, granted certiorari to decide: whether police can requestion the suspect about the same crime after an assertion of the right to silence.

Twenty-five years after *Miranda* this fundamental issue in interrogation law remains unresolved by the Supreme Court.

The necessity to decide issues that are not presented, as in *Sheppard* and *Leon*, to sidestep justiciability issues, as in *Taylor*, or to forbear from deciding a case or an issue because of justiciability problems, as in *DeFunis* and *Mosley*, affects the Court's ability to resolve disputes on important questions of federal law. The worst problem with the case method, however, is that it is not forward looking. It does not allow that Court, as an ordinary rulemaking body would, to anticipate future cases and to craft its rules, and the exceptions to those rules, with such cases in mind. Thus the Court is invariably left in the position of declaring a partial rule, such as the rule of *Miranda* and *Mosley* about when questioning must cease upon a suspect's invocation of the right to silence, that fails to deal adequately with the majority of subsequent cases that present related issues. Compounding this problem is that, because the Court has other things to do than to resolve the problems of criminal procedure law, it may be decades before it returns to an issue for further consideration.

Stare Decisis

When a legislature wishes to declare a new law, or to change an old one, it simply does so. There is no need to account for the new law in terms of similar laws that have been passed, or to explain why this new law is consistent with its predecessors. Not so with the Supreme Court. When it makes law, the doctrine of *stare decisis et non quieta movere* governs the process. Stare decisis is seen as a doctrine that lends stability and legitimacy to the judicial process, as Justice Cardozo once observed: "[T]he labor of judges would be increased almost to the breaking point if every past decision could be reopened in every case, and one could not lay one's own course of bricks on the secure foundation of the courses laid by others who had gone before him."[32] Of course, judges and lawyers know that stare decisis is honored as much in the breach as in the observance, but, as Justice Goldberg once condescendingly pointed out, it at least "fosters public confidence in the judiciary and public acceptance of individual decisions by giving the appearance of impersonal, consistent, and reasoned opinions."[33]

Whatever the necessity or value of stare decisis, it unquestionably interferes with the Supreme Court's stated goal of settling important questions of federal law. This is particularly true in constitutional decisions, where the Court must consider the intent of the framers as well as, in some cases, two hundred years of precedent. As the Court adds to the pile of precedents, the problem gets worse. Particularly in the criminal procedure area, where clearly settled law is of the utmost importance, stare decisis makes such clear settlement virtually impossible. Justice Stevens noted that as "the body of precedent continues to grow year after year, the likelihood that doctrinal inconsistency may force the Court to reject one precedent in favor of another must likewise increase."[34]

Yet the problem is more acute than Justice Stevens recognized. Not only may doctrinal inconsistency force the Court to reject one precedent in favor of another; it may also make it impossible to establish any clear rules. Because a "new" rule must be phrased in terms of unclear and often conflicting precedents, it will be imprecise at its inception. These factors exacerbate the already difficult task of drafting a clear rule.

Consider the *Miranda* line of cases discussed earlier. It is probably fair to say, as the *Miranda* dissenters did, that "The proposition that the privilege against self-incrimination forbids in-custody interrogation without the warnings specified in the majority opinion . . . has no significant support in the history of the privilege or in the language of the Fifth Amendment."[35] Nevertheless, the majority based its decision on a series of earlier cases.[36] According to the Court's opinion, *Miranda* "is not an innovation in our jurisprudence, but is an application of principles long recognized and applied in other settings."[37] The Court then rounded up the usual precedents—the English Bill of Rights, *Cohens v. Virginia*, and selected passages from more recent cases—to support its position that *Miranda* was a simple, almost inevitable, outgrowth of earlier cases. The dissents cited an equally impressive array of cases to show that this case was a radical departure from what had gone before.

A few years after *Miranda* had been decided, the composition of the Court changed and a majority disagreed with the *Miranda* holding. Had they not been precluded by stare decisis, they presumably would have overruled it. This did not occur, for reasons discussed by Geoffrey Stone:

> The task of a court confronted with a precedent that a majority of its members believe to be seriously misguided or worse is never an easy one. And the difficulty is exacerbated when that precedent is recent, highly controversial, and deeply embedded in the public consciousness. In such a context, the expedient of direct overruling may seem unattractive, for such action would inescapably raise strong doubts about the integrity and the stability of the judicial process. Faced with this problem, a court may attempt to avoid or to postpone a direct overruling of the disfavored precedent. The very existence of the conflict, however, is likely to exert considerable strain on the court in

its efforts to deal forthrightly with issues posed by the precedent. This seems to be the current plight of the Burger Court with respect to *Miranda v. Arizona*.[38]

Thus instead of overruling *Miranda* the Court in a series of cases "interpreted" it narrowly. In *Harris v. New York*,[39] it held, despite clear language in *Miranda* to the contrary,[40] that a statement made by the defendant without a proper warning could be used to impeach his or her testimony at trial. Contrary statements in *Miranda* were written off as dictum.[41] The *Harris* Court, however, was forced by stare decisis to concede that "*Miranda* barred the prosecution from making its case [in chief] with statements of an accused made while in custody prior to having or effectively waiving counsel."[42] In *Michigan v. Tucker*[43] the Court found, contrary to the express holding of *Miranda*, that a failure to give the required warnings did not violate the fifth amendment but only the "prophylactic rule developed to protect that right." The Court's opinion makes it clear that this holding was not based on any misunderstanding of *Miranda* but rather on the Court's view of the fifth amendment and of the pre-*Miranda* cases.

How did stare decisis cause uncertainty in the post-*Miranda* cases? *Harris* was a short opinion that relied essentially on two earlier cases, *Miranda* and *Walder v. United States*.[44] To reach its result in *Harris* the Court found it necessary to dismiss a portion of *Miranda* as dictum. This raises questions as to what other parts of that broad opinion, or of other opinions, are dicta. These questions go to the heart not only of the issue presented but of the scope of stare decisis itself. If such a critical aspect of the *Miranda* opinion as the Court's statement that the "requirement of warnings is a fundamental with respect to the fifth amendment"[45] can be written off as dictum, then one wonders what is left of the "holding."[46] Thus, stare decisis has raised a series of superfluous and endlessly debatable issues about stare decisis itself.

Recognizing, as good lawyers, that an argument should be grounded on more than one footing (see the section on "The Lawyer Mentality" above), the *Harris* Court also discussed *Walder*. *Walder* had held that although a defendant's general denial of culpability could not be impeached by use of illegally seized evidence, an affirmative lie by the defendant could be. Because Harris had not gone beyond a mere denial of guilt in his direct testimony, it would appear that the *Walder* exception was inapplicable and that Harris's statement could not be used. In reaching the opposite conclusion the Court, in effect, "construed *Walder* as holding that unconstitutionally obtained evidence may always be used to impeach," as Dean Stone observed.[47] *Harris* ignored the contrary rule of *Agnello v. United States*,[48] to which *Walder* was a narrow exception.

Because *Harris* was limited to the fact situation then before the Court, and because precedential support was needed for a decision that, in fact, was a naked attempt to cut back *Miranda*, the Court in *Harris* raised questions about the scope of stare decisis and about the meaning of *Miranda*, *Agnello*, and *Walder*. When the additional statements of the *Harris* Court itself are added to the constitutional soup, it is obvious that a future Court will be unable to say precisely what *Harris* means. By purporting to rely on, rather than overrule, *Miranda*, *Agnello*, and *Walder*, the Court rendered a decision in *Harris* that was unclear. Indeed, time has shown that *Harris*, far from "resolving" problems raised by *Miranda*, gave rise to a whole series of new cases about the scope of *Harris* itself. What kind of testimony (direct or cross, outright lies or general denials) may be impeached by what type of evidence (illegally seized evidence, involuntary statements, or silence) obtained during what phase of the interrogation (prior to or after the warnings)? In the years since *Harris* the Court has decided nine cases that attempt to answer the various questions raised by *Harris*.[49] Naturally, these cases have given rise to further questions.

The opinion in *Tucker*, written by Justice Rehnquist, was much more complex than the opinion in *Harris* and consequently raised many more questions. To enumerate all of them would be too tedious, but recognizing even a few will make the impact of stare decisis clear. The *Tucker* Court, after discussing the early cases and the intent of the framers, observed that *Miranda* was the first case to find that a defendant's voluntary statement might be excluded at trial. Why is this relevant? Certainly it does not bear on what the holding in *Miranda* may have been. Whether *Miranda* was the first or twelfth case to so hold has nothing to do with whether the *Tucker* Court should follow it. Clearly, this observation in *Tucker* was homage to stare decisis. The Court was saying, in effect, "we may cut back on *Miranda* because it, not this decision, is out of sync with precedent." This attitude was perhaps justified by the claim of the *Miranda* majority that their decision did follow from the precedents.

After finding, contrary to *Miranda*, that the warnings were not constitutionally compelled, the Court in *Tucker* held that the "fruit of the poisonous tree" doctrine would not bar testimony of a witness who was discovered only as a result of a *Miranda* violation. However, the Court based its holding in part on the fact that the interrogation in *Tucker* had occurred before *Miranda* was decided. Thus *Tucker* did not settle the "poisonous tree" issue for post-*Miranda* cases. Obviously, the police could not have followed the specific requirements of *Miranda* in this pre-*Miranda* interrogation. Discussing the deterrent effect of the exclusionary rule, the Court observed that "Where the official action was pursued in complete *good faith* . . . the deterrence rationale loses much of its force."⁵⁰ Nevertheless the Court noted that the defendant's own statement (as opposed to the witness's testimony) must be excluded because *Miranda* had been declared retroactive in *Johnson v. New Jersey*.⁵¹ Justice Brennan, concurring in the judgment in *Tucker*, argued that the ruling in *Johnson*—that *Miranda* was applicable to trials beginning after *Miranda*—was "unnecessary to our decision" (i.e., dictum) and should not apply to "fruit of the poisonous tree" cases because it would place too great a burden on law enforcement.

Why did the conservative Justice Rehnquist accede to a broad reading of *Johnson*, which rendered the *Miranda* holding more potent, whereas the liberal Justice Brennan argued that *Miranda* should be cut back as a burden on law enforcement? The reason was stare decisis, not the backward-looking "accounting for precedent" of most cases, such as *Harris*, but a forward-looking "establishing of precedent." Justice Rehnquist undoubtedly recognized that by 1974, when *Tucker* was decided, a case finding the 1966 *Miranda* holding retroactive (but then denying the defendant relief) would be unimportant because it was unlikely that many additional pre-*Miranda* cases would come along. On the other hand, *Tucker* was a perfect opportunity to establish a precedential beachhead for later modification of Warren Court criminal procedure rules. Thus *Tucker* held that *Miranda* was not a constitutional holding but merely a set of prophylactic rules. This did not stop the Court from finding that *Miranda* operated to suppress the defendant's improperly warned statements; but in depriving *Miranda* of its constitutional basis, the Court "seems certainly to have laid the groundwork to overrule *Miranda*"⁵² (though as it turned out this did not occur).

At a minimum *Tucker* laid a foundation for finding that the collateral consequences of a *Miranda* violation would be slight. Perhaps just as important, the statement in *Tucker* that good faith violations by the police should not be the basis for evidentiary exclusion was reiterated and expanded by the Court in *United States v. Peltier*.⁵³ The *Peltier* decision, in turn, provided a strong precedential basis for the Court's holding, ten years later, in *United States v. Leon*.⁵⁴ *Leon*, as previously discussed, held that there is an exception to the exclusionary rule where illegal searches are conducted in "good faith" pursuant to a warrant. All this laying of groundwork in *Tucker* would be possible only if the Court found a *Miranda* violation in the first place—hence the seemingly incongruous positions taken by Justice Rehnquist and Brennan.

Although Justice Rehnquist established in *Tucker* that he could play stare decisis like a stringed instrument, he did nothing to clarify the

Miranda doctrine. Rather, the adherence to stare decisis, as well as the expectation of adherence in later cases, caused the Court to distort its purpose: to overturn *Miranda*. It also caused the Court to distort the cases on which it relied, leading to a pyramiding of confusion in the next case.

As in the nineteenth century, when courts purported to "find" the "true meaning" of unclear precedents and constitutional provisions, the Court is actually manipulating precedents to suit its purposes. This mystical process creates just as much cynicism and confusion today as it did in 1938, when the Court, in *Erie Railroad v. Tompkins*, purported to have abandoned the claim that law could be "found" and admitted to "making" law. Now the Court admits to making law, but claims to do so on the basis of precedents that are just as manipulable as the old concept of law. The upshot is that people trying in good faith to discover the legally prescribed course of conduct have the illusion of being able to do so by consulting, or hiring a lawyer to consult, Supreme Court cases and finding cases that support the legality of the course of action they wish to take. But they rely on former cases at their peril. As generations of State Supreme Court and United States Court of Appeals Judges, as well as Supreme Court litigants, have found, the fact that precedent is on one's side is of little value when a case is decided by the Supreme Court. The Court uses precedent not as a beacon to light the way but as a smokescreen to obscure the political basis of the decision. But, as discussed above, the process of paying homage to stare decisis, while virtually never determining the outcome of a case, may have a significant impact on the details of the opinion, as in *Harris v. New York*, where the Court neither followed nor overruled *Miranda*.

I do not necessarily decry this trend. Clearly the Court cannot be totally bound by precedent or the law would never change, and the claim that careful consultation of the constitutional text can, by itself, provide answers to the myriad problems that the Supreme Court is faced with is fatuous. Personally, I would prefer that the Court be more forthright and admit when it is not following precedent. Contrary to Justice Goldberg, I believe that the Court is fooling no one when it pretends just to apply the Constitution and the precedents to reach the result in each case. But, however that may be, as long as the Court continues in the vein that it has always mined, of purporting to follow precedent whether it actually does so or not, then uncertainty will be an inevitable side effect of its decisions. While such uncertainty may be desirable in certain constitutional areas in that it stirs up litigation and debate, it is highly undesirable in criminal procedure, where it causes individual rights to be violated, cases to be lost, and criminals to be released.

Clear Rules/Flexible Responses

In addition to resolution of disputes on major issues, another frequently stated or implied goal of the Supreme Court is clarity in the law. If the Court could set down clear rules for the police to follow, then there would be fewer violations by the police and also fewer complaints when evidence was excluded due to police violations of the rules. As previously discussed, it is impossible for the Court to establish clear rules to govern all future cases because of the case-or-controversy and stare decisis limitations, as well as the obvious problem that any "clear rule" will have unclear boundaries. Nevertheless, cases that are definitely governed by a prior holding frequently arise. One might suppose that these cases would pose no problems, but that is not invariably true. Applying the clear rule to an unforeseen factual situation sometimes leads to unjust results.

The Supreme Court discovered this in the civil context when, years ago, it endeavored to establish a standard "once and for all" regarding "reasonable" conduct of an automobile driver approaching an unmarked railroad crossing—the "stop, look, and listen rule."[55] The endeavor failed because the rule led to unjust results when applied to varying factual situations. After eight years of cases in which "stopping, looking, and listening" would have added nothing to the driver's safety, the Court abandoned the attempt.[56] It emphasized the "need for caution in framing standards of behavior that amount to rules of law. . . . Extraordinary situations may not wisely or fairly be subjected to tests or regulations that are fitting for the common-place or normal."[57] William Lloyd Prosser has elaborated on the problem:

> A decision of an appellate court that under certain circumstances a particular type of conduct is clearly negligent, or that it clearly is not negligent, . . . establishes a precedent for other cases where the facts are identical, or substantially the same. To that extent it may define the standard of reasonable conduct which the community requires. Unfortunately the inevitable tendency [is] to crystallize the law into mechanical rules . . . of universal application. Almost invariably the rule has broken down in the face of the obvious necessity of basing the standard upon the particular circumstances, the apparent risk and the actor's opportunity to deal with it.[58]

As discussed, in criminal procedure, the desire to formulate "clear rules" is particularly acute because of the need to give the police guidelines as to how to behave. Consider the Court's paean to clear rules in *United States v. Oliver*,[59] which involved a search of a fenced and posted field, over a mile from his farmhouse, where the defendant was growing marijuana. The defendant argued that there should be no fixed "open field doctrine," which always exempts fields from the coverage of the fourth amendment, but that the suspect's reasonable expectations of privacy should be analyzed in each individual case. The Court replied that:

> a case-by-case approach [would not] provide a workable accommodation between the needs of law enforcement and the interests protected by the Fourth Amendment. Under this approach, police officers would have to guess before every search whether landowners had erected fences sufficiently high, posted a sufficient number of warning signs, or located contraband in an area sufficiently secluded to establish a right of privacy. The lawfulness of each search would depend on a "highly sophisticated set of rules, qualified by all sorts of ifs, ands and buts and requiring the drawing of subtle nuances and hairline distinctions."[60]

Similarly, in *Dunaway v. New York*, the Court averred:

> A single familiar standard is essential to guide police officers, who have only limited time and expertise to reflect on and balance the social and individual interests involved in the specific circumstances they confront.[61]

The Court has not always taken this view. Prior to the criminal procedure revolution, as discussed in Chapter 2, it often stressed that "there is no formula for the determination of reasonableness. Each case is to be decided on its own facts and circumstances."[62] However, as we have discussed, once it had declared that evidence obtained in violation of the Constitution was to be excluded from state trials, the pressure to be more specific about just what constituted a "violation" caused a change of approach.

The most fundamental "clear rule" in criminal procedure is the search warrant requirement:

> The Fourth Amendment proscribes all unreasonable searches and seizures, and it is a cardinal principle that "searches conducted outside the judicial process, without prior approval by a judge or magistrate, are *per se* unreasonable," subject to a few specifically established and well delineated exceptions.[63]

The "few specifically established and well-delineated exceptions" to the fourth amendment's warrant requirement have expanded to a total of about twenty-three.[64] The reason for this is simple: The "clear rule" that warrants are always required could never work; exceptions had to be recognized from the beginning. Originally, the only exception involved circumstances where it would be impracticable to obtain a warrant.[65] This general exception came to be "codified" into a series of more particular exceptions, such as the automobile exception, the search-incident-to-arrest exception, and the hot pursuit exception. Once the boundaries of these exceptions were set forth, fact situations arose that fell outside these exceptions but in which, in the Court's view, it would have been unjust to suppress evidence. Such cases led to the creation of new exceptions, such as the "stop and frisk" exception and the enlarged automobile exception.

As Stephen Saltzburg has observed:

Because courts cannot determine with certainty what effect judicial decisions regarding the admission of evidence have on the behavior of government officials and because overturning a conviction has high social costs, appellate judges naturally may strain, often subconsciously, to preserve a conviction. . . . [T]his straining . . . tends to produce precedents that uphold police activity at the outer margin of permissibility. Often, the approval takes the form of poorly reasoned opinions. Law enforcement officials rely on the cases that stretch constitutional principles to their limits and in subsequent cases ask that these principles be stretched still further.[66]

The automobile cases are paradigmatic of this trend. In *Carroll v. United States*,[67] the Court upheld a warrantless search of a car that Prohibition agents had stopped with probable cause sixteen miles outside of Grand Rapids, Michigan in the middle of the night. The Court recognized that the mobility of a vehicle, in contradistinction to a house or store, made it impracticable "to secure a warrant because the vehicle can be quickly moved out of the locality or jurisdiction in which the warrant must be sought."[68] However, the Court added that "In cases where the securing of a warrant is reasonably practicable, it must be used."[69] Thus a fair reading of *Carroll* would lead to the conclusion that if the car had been stopped in downtown Grand Rapids in the middle of the day, such that one of the agents could have easily gone for a warrant while the other watched the car, this would have been the required course of action.

In *Chambers v. Maroney*[70] the Court dealt with a case in which a car had been seized by the police, its occupants arrested, and the car driven to the police station, where it was searched without a warrant. While on the facts of *Chambers* it certainly would have been "practicable" to obtain a warrant, the Court obviously considered the police activity reasonable anyway. It therefore relied on the "cars are different from houses" language in *Carroll*, ignoring the "reasonably practicable" limitation, to posit an exception to the warrant requirement in cases involving automobile searches.[71] Thus the "auto exception" grew to accommodate police behavior that, though violative of both the general warrant requirement and the express "practicability" holding of *Carroll*, seemed reasonable to the Court. Indeed, a contrary holding would have brought down a rain of criticism on the Court for suppressing evidence due to technicalities. Several other cases followed in which the court, in approving what seemed like reasonable behavior by the police, extended the automobile exception to the taking of paint scrapings from the outside of a car,[72] the search of a car at the station when no exigent circumstances had prevented an immediate search on the street (unlike *Chambers*),[73] and the full inventory search of a car being towed for parking violations.[74]

In 1982 in *United States v. Ross*[75] the Court expanded the automobile exception even more by holding not only that an automobile may be searched on probable cause without a warrant regardless whether it would have been practicable to obtain one,[76] but also that containers found therein, including locked suitcases, may be searched as well. In so holding, the Court overruled or modified previous cases that had granted suitcases, as repositories of personal effects, the same protection as houses, even when they were found in cars.[77]

Thus the Court must constantly tinker with its rules as it is faced with the choice of either excluding evidence due to "technicalities" or upholding police behavior that fails to conform to the rules. In *Ross* the Court hit upon a solution to this dilemma: create another exception to the warrant requirement. But such a partial effort poses two problems. First, *Ross* left many questions unanswered that threatened to suck the Court back into the morass. For example, is a recreational vehicle, which has the privacy aspects of a house and the mobility of a car, subject to the automobile exception?[78] Is the scope of a search incident to arrest greater when one is arrested in an automobile than at home?[79] And what is the scope of "less than probable cause" searches of automobiles, such as inventory searches?[80] The Court has had to grant a series of new cases in the years since *Ross* to answer these questions.

The second problem with *Ross* is that, in abandoning the warrant requirement, the Court adopted a new rule that would lead to injustices in other cases. In *United States v. Chadwick* the Court recognized that "No less than one who locks the doors of his home against intruders, one who [locks his possessions in a footlocker] is due the protection of the Fourth Amendment Warrant Clause."[81] The fact that such a suitcase or footlocker was found in a car did not diminish its privacy protection.[82] Now every such container found in a car will be subject to a search,[83] notwithstanding *Chadwick*'s recognition that such warrantless intrusions constitute serious invasions of personal privacy, because the Court felt that clear rules were necessary in this area, even at the expense of "reasonable expectations of privacy," which had previously been the (troublesomely flexible) basis of fourth amendment protections.

Thus the automobile exception, which was originally developed to allow a flexible response to the mechanistic warrant requirement when the police behavior seemed reasonable, has developed a life of its own as a mechanistic rule. Even if, in a particular case, it would not seem reasonable to search a car and its contents without a warrant, the automobile exception has created a new rule that can be applied mechanically to render patently unreasonable behavior "reasonable" under the fourth amendment.[84] Suppose the police suspect A of committing a crime on a particular date. They have probable cause to believe that a suitcase belonging to B, which is locked in the trunk of B's car, which is parked in front of B's house, contains B's locked diary, which has references to A's whereabouts on that date.[85] Under the automobile exception, the police, having only probable cause, may conduct a warrantless search of the car for the suitcase and the suitcase for the diary even though they have no reason to believe that the car is about to be moved.[86] Yet there are few instances in which one would have a greater expectation of privacy than when one's locked diary rests in a locked suitcase in the locked trunk of one's own car parked in front of one's own house.[87]

Of course this problem—that clear rules may lead to injustices in unforeseen cases that may induce the courts to modify the rules, or not to modify them and accept an unjust result—will arise with legislatively created rules as well as judicially created ones. However, the legislature has a distinct advantage over courts in formulating the rules in the first place. The legislative process is forward looking in a way that the judicial process, which deals with a preexisting case, is not. The legislature can think about hypothetical cases in advance and draft its rule to accommodate them. Interested parties can comment on the proposed rule and urge the rulemaker to modify it. By contrast, Supreme Court "rules" are promulgated by a Justice and a law clerk, neither of whom has, generally, any experience in the criminal justice system. The rules are not subjected to public or expert scrutiny, and are heir to the slings and arrows of the uncertainty principle previously discussed.

The Conservatives' Dilemma

Heretofore, all the factors that tend to create uncertainty in Supreme Court decisions have been endemic: they would operate on any Supreme Court, regardless of its ideological makeup. There is a last factor that has peculiarly afflicted the Burger and Rehnquist Courts because of their ideological bent. This is the "Conservatives' Dilemma." A conservative, by definition, seeks to conserve that which has gone before—to resist changes in doctrine. A conservative Justice, therefore, is particularly likely to feel bound by stare decisis. The dilemma that has faced the conservative majority on the Court since the four Nixon appointees joined it in the early 1970s is how to cut back on the Warren Court innovations in criminal procedure while still cleaving to the principle of stare decisis—that settled law should not generally be disturbed. Thus, in addition to the difficulties posed by the need to rely on precedents (i.e., stare decisis), the Justices of the post-Warren Court era are faced with the additional problems caused by wanting not to rely on precedents. One possible approach would be simply to swallow hard and live with, but not extend, the Warren Court innovations. As Yale Kamisar has pointed out, such an approach has indeed characterized much of the Burger Court's criminal procedure law.[88] But the conservative Justices have not all been satisfied with merely doing that. Justice Rehnquist, for example, once told an interviewer that one of his principal goals when he came on the Court was to reverse what he saw as the pro-defendant bias in criminal procedure.[89]

The cases previously discussed provide examples of how the new conservative majority of the 1970s dealt with the Warren Court precedents. In *Harris v. New York*,[90] for example, in deciding that statements obtained in violation of *Miranda* could be used to impeach the defendant's testimony at trial, the majority simply wrote off language to the contrary in *Miranda* as "dictum." And in *Michigan v. Tucker*[91] the majority held that a violation of *Miranda* was not a constitutional violation at all, but merely a breach of "prophylactic rules." Finally, in *Kirby v. Illinois*[92] the majority relied on the fact that in *United States v. Wade*,[93] in which the Warren Court had declared a sixth amendment right to counsel at lineups, the lineup was held after the defendant had been indicted. In *Kirby* the Court declared that *Wade* was limited to post-indictment lineups and that there was no pre-indictment right to counsel, despite the fact that nothing in *Wade* suggested that the holding was to be so limited. These are the sorts of games conservatives felt they had to play in order to cut back on the Warren Court innovations while claiming, at the same time, to adhere strongly to the principle of stare decisis. Despite the dire predictions of liberals, no significant criminal procedure innovation of the Warren Court has actually been overruled by the Burger and Rehnquist Courts.[94] But such a posture came at a high doctrinal price because it sowed confusion as to the meaning both of the original case and of the subsequent cases that purported to, but did not really, follow it.

Recently, Justice Antonin Scalia adopted a more forthright approach to stare decisis, albeit in a narrow context. As Scalia observed, in death penalty law, as in criminal procedure, "this Court has assumed the role of rulemaking body for the States' administration of capital sentencing."[95] Also, in death penalty law, as in criminal procedure law, "the Court has gone from pillar to post, with the result that the sort of reasonable predictability upon which legislatures, trial courts and appellate courts must of necessity rely has been all but completely sacrificed."[96] In particular, Scalia pointed out that the *Furman v. Georgia*[97] line of cases, requiring "constraints on the sentencer's discretion to 'impose' the death penalty," is flatly inconsistent with the *Lockett v. Ohio*[98] line of cases, which forbids "constraints on the sentencer's discretion to 'decline to impose it.'"[99] Since, in Scalia's view, the *Furman* line of cases is closer to the text of the eighth amendment than the *Lockett* line, he concluded that he had no choice but to refuse to follow the *Lockett* line, despite stare decisis.[100]

Scalia's position in *Walton* represents a vary narrow exception to the stare decisis principle, but, to one who values clarity, he has the right idea. If the Court is going to undercut precedent, then it should overrule it, not claim to be following it. But the Court is not going to change its way of writing decisions: the fiction of stare decisis is too strongly engrained. If any sense is to be made of thirty years of revolution and counter-revolution in criminal procedure law, the entire body of law will need to be reconsidered afresh, adopting the useful innovations of the Warren Court, rejecting those that have not stood the test of time (and of more recent Supreme Court decisions), and striving for a system that, as a whole, strikes a reasonable balance between the needs of law enforcement and the protection of civil liberties.

Thus the case-or-controversy requirement limits the choice of issues; the need for flexible responses forces the Court to discard or modify clear rules; stare decisis, the tyranny of the majority opinion, the lawyer mentality, the committee problem, and the conservative's dilemma operate so the new rule and the precedent behind it will be unclear. Uncertainty is inevitable. While uncertainty is also inevitable in statutes, legislative ability to draft brief, forward-looking rules without having to account for precedents would vastly reduce the number of cases for which the rules are unclear.

Incompleteness

In addition to uncertainty, Supreme Court rulemaking suffers from incompleteness. One problem with utilizing direct interpretations of the Bill of Rights as a means of declaring rules of criminal procedure is that the Bill of Rights frequently does not have any obvious application to the regulated conduct. The Warren Court, feeling compelled to act by the failure of legislative bodies to regulate the police,[101] rubber hosed the language of the fifth amendment unmercifully in *Miranda*.* It held that a clause barring a person from being "compelled in any criminal case to be a witness against himself" required police to warn suspects of their rights to both silence and counsel before asking for voluntary, non-compelled statements prior to the beginning of the criminal "case."[102] That this exercise in judicial legislation damaged the Court is well accepted.[103]

In other cases, the Court, adhering more closely to the constitutional language, has been forced to reach unsatisfactory results. A good example of this is found in *United States v. Wade*.[104] In *Wade* the Court was obviously determined to curtail abuses in lineup procedures. Certainly, lineups as such had nothing to do with the fourth amendment[105] and, not wanting to unduly hamper police investigations, the Court was constrained to hold that the fifth amendment was not violated by requiring the defendant to appear, and even to speak, in a lineup. This left the Court the sixth amendment right to counsel as its only vehicle for lineup reform.

It held that the sixth amendment's requirement of counsel "in all criminal prosecutions" included a right to counsel at lineups. But, as anyone who has ever attended a lineup knows, this is no place for counsel. There are no witnesses to examine, no arguments to make, and no evidence to offer. Counsel may object if he or she wants, but the police are free to ignore the objections.[106]

What the Court really wanted was to ensure that lineups were fair; the best way to do this is to require that they be photographed and tape recorded (or videotaped) and that these records be produced in court. However, even the Warren Court was apparently unable to find an amendment it could squeeze hard enough to yield this result. Consequently it devised an incomplete rule based on a shaky constitutional footing. It was vulnerable to being effectively overruled by a plurality in *Kirby v. Illinois*,[107] which held that the "right to counsel" does not attach until "adversary judicial proceedings" have begun.[108] That is, the "criminal prosecution" referred to in the sixth amendment does not commence until after a formal judicial proceeding

---

*However, as Justice White pointed out, dissenting in *Miranda*, "That the Court's holding today is neither compelled nor even strongly suggested by the language of the Fifth Amendment, is at odds with American and English legal history, and involves a departure from a long line of precedent does not prove either that the Court has exceeded its powers or that the Court is wrong or unwise in its present reinterpretation of the Fifth Amendment." 384 U.S. 436, 531–32.

such as an arraignment or an indictment. Since lineups are usually held before "adversary judicial proceedings" have begun, the *Wade* Court's attempt to set rules for lineups was largely nullified.

Even in *Miranda* the Court may have felt constrained by the limits of its power. Why did *Miranda* adopt the curious requirement that criminal defendants, many of whom are in no position to comprehend the advice, must be informed of their constitutional rights in considerable detail? As in the lineup cases, a more forthright approach to the problem of the "third degree" would have been to require that confessions, and the interrogations leading up to them, be tape recorded (or, now, videotaped). But whereas the Court may have felt that its mandate extended to requiring police to inform suspects about their constitutional rights, it may not have felt empowered to require more practical solutions to the problems it addressed, simply because such solutions seemed too remote from the constitutional language.

The Court is constantly torn between memory and desire: its memory that, as it reiterated in *Moran v. Burbine,* "nothing in the Constitution vests in us the authority to mandate a code of behavior for state officials"[109] and its desire to protect the rights of criminal defendants or establish a clear rule for the police to follow. The result has been a patchwork approach that finds the Court overly involved in the details of some interests of criminal suspects—for example, the need to be warned of rights—and oblivious to other, equally important intersts.[110]

The Court's work in the confessions area well illustrates this point. Since declaring the *Miranda* rule, the Court in the ensuing twenty-odd years, has contented itself with interpreting and reinterpreting that decision. What is "custody"? What is "interrogation"? What if the defendant asserts the right to silence or counsel?[111] But in focusing on the warnings, the Court has overlooked other, equally fundamental, aspects of the interrogation process: how to guard against police fabrication of confessions; what to do if the police induce a confession by trickery;[112] what to do if, after warning the defendant, the police engage in the psychological ploys discussed in *Miranda* such as the "Mutt and Jeff" technique;[113] and how long the interrogation may last.

While the Court has endeavored to cover the entire field of fourth amendment law more zealously than it has the law of interrogation, there are also many unresolved issues in this area, such as when nighttime searches are appropriate,[114] when "no-knock" entries may be used,[115] what steps the police may take to secure premises pending the arrival of a search warrant,[116] and whether people other than the homeowner may be detained and/or frisked at a house during execution of a search warrant.[117]

In *Miranda* the Court "encourage[d] Congress and the States to continue their laudable search for increasingly effective ways of protecting the rights of the individual while promoting efficient [law] enforcement."[118] But the Court has coopted the field. One can look, almost in vain, through a criminal procedure book[119] for any reference to statutory material (or any state law, statutory or court-made) in an area that every other country, including our common law mentor, Britain, considers to be appropriately dealt with by statute.[120] As Assistant Attorney General Stephen Markman has summarized this problem, "the *Miranda* decision has effectively prevented the adoption [of better safeguards such as] electronic recording of interrogations."[121]

While this leads Markman to conclude that *Miranda* must be overruled, the *Miranda* warnings themselves are not the problem. They could easily coexist with a system that required videotaping of all confessions. The problem, rather, is that the Supreme Court, constrained by its docket, stare decisis, and the need to justify each criminal procedural innovation by a specific provision of the Bill of Rights, not to mention its frequently stated unwillingness to "mandate a code of behavior for state officials,"[122] is limited in its ability to innovate.

The problem of the Court's simply not having gotten around to deciding a case involving, for example, detention of third parties during a search can be easily solved by a rulemaking body that, unconstrained by case or controversy limitations, can anticipate, and resolve, such questions in advance. However, the problem that the Bill of Rights simply does not contain adequate constitutional language for the government to require, for example, that lineups must be videotaped would seem to apply equally to a congressionally mandated rulemaking body as to the Court. However, as will be argued in greater detail in Chapter 6, this is not necessarily a serious problem, simply because, historically, the Court has allowed Congress great leeway to determine the scope of its own constitutional authority under the fourteenth amendment. It seems highly unlikely, for example, that if a congressionally appointed rulemaking body determined that "due process" generally required lineups and/or confessions to be videotaped, the Court would overturn that determination.

Consequently, although it is probably true as a practical matter that, if enough time were allowed to pass, the Court might eventually get around to filling many of the gaps in the law of police procedures (subject to problems of uncertainty discussed above and other reasons for incompleteness discussed below), the Court itself seems to have considerable doubt about its constitutional authority to create such a comprehensive code and may in any event be unwilling to extend the reach of its "rules." It is, in my view, unlikely that the Court would express similar doubts about Congress's power to do so.

In addition to the limits of the constitutional language on which the Court's jurisdiction to declare rules is based, incompleteness also arises because the Court's rulemaking is driven by the exclusionary rule. The Court never establishes a rule that it is not prepared to back up with evidentiary exclusion. Thus, many areas, such as the post-warning interrogation issues discussed above, go unregulated because, even though a majority of the Court may feel the need for rules, they are reluctant to create new possibilities for evidentiary exclusion for defendants. Again, a more flexible approach to evidentiary exclusion would allow the creation of more complete rules for the police to follow, without necessarily increasing the number of exclusions.

Similarly, police practices that are not intended to produce evidence, such as applying strangleholds to arrestees, may never be presented for Supreme Court rulemaking. These areas could, however, be covered by statutory rules.

Legislative rulemaking thus has the advantages of being able to resolve issues immediately that have not yet been reached by the Court, for the various reasons discussed, to anticipate future problems and exceptions in advance, and to avoid some, though not all, of the problems of uncertainty that inhere in court-made rules.

Notes

1 This principle was first developed in Craig Bradley, "The Uncertainty Principle in the Supreme Court."

2. 470 U.S. 298, 320 (1985) (opinion of Brennan, J. dissenting).

3. 423 U.S. 96 (1975).

4. 384 U.S. at 473–74.

5. 423 U.S. at 106–7.

6. Compare Geoffrey Stone, "The Miranda Doctrine in the Burger Court," 134, with Yale Kamisar, "The Warren Court (Was It Really So Defense-Minded?), The Burger Court (Is It Really So Prosecution-Oriented?) and Police Investigatory Practices," 83 and n. 133 as to which of the factors cited in *Mosley* are, and which are not, "critical" to the decision of future cases.

7. Anthony Amsterdam, "Perspectives on the Fourth Amendment," 350.

8. 451 U.S. 477 (1981).

9. As I was writing this discussion, I realized that *Mosley* was decided the Term that I clerked at the Supreme Court (October Term 1975). Someone familiar with this fact might conclude that the discussion in the text is a discussion of what actually happened in *Mosley*. It is not. I have no recollection of the decisional process in that case.

10. As Yale Kamisar has observed:

> Either *Mosley* was wrongly decided or *Edwards* was. If it is inherently coercive—if it is inconsistent with *Miranda*—to renew interrogation after a suspect has invoked his right to counsel, I think it is equally wrong for the police to do so if the suspect has asserted his right to remain silent. The average person has no idea that different procedural safeguards are triggered by saying "I want to see a lawyer" . . . rather than "I don't want to say anything. . . ."

Jesse Choper, Yale Kamisar, and Lawrence Tribe, *The Supreme Court: Trends and Developments, 1982–83*, 157.

11. 110 S.Ct. 2638 (1990).

12. 110 S.Ct. at 2650.

13. 110 S.Ct. at 2654.

14. Id. at 2650 n. 14.

15. Id. at 2650.

16. See, e.g., *Florida v. Royer* 460 U.S. 491, 528–29 (1983) (Rehnquist, J., dissenting): "The question we must decide is what was *unreasonable* about the steps which *these officers* took with respect to *this* suspect in the Miami airport on this particular day."

17. 466 U.S. 170, 181–82 (1984).

18. William Rehnquist, *The Supreme Court: How It Was, How It Is*, 92.

19. R. Lea Brilmayer, "The Jurisprudence of Article III: Perspectives on the 'Case or Controversy' Requirement," 300. See, e.g., *Chicago & G.T. Ry. v. Wellman* 143 U.S. 339, 345 (1892), holding that courts may legitimately call the constitutionality of legislation into question "only in the last resort, and as a necessity in the determination of real, earnest and vital controversy between individuals" (quoted with approval in *Muskrat v. United States* 219 U.S. 346, 359 (1911).

20. *Rescue Army v. Municipal Court of Los Angeles* 331 U.S. 549 (1947).

21. See *Sup. Ct. Rule* 17.1 (c).

22. Robert Dahl, "Decision Making in a Democracy," 106.

23. See John Hart Ely, *Democracy and Distrust*, 22 for a discussion of how case-or-controversy limitations in the Slaughter House cases pushed the Court into a decision that stripped the privileges and immunities clause of any meaning, which, in turn, forced the Court to use the less likely due process clause of the fourteenth amendment as the vehicle for extending the Bill of Rights to the States.

24. 468 U.S. 897 (1984).

25. 468 U.S. 981 (1984).

26. 468 U.S. (Stevens, J. dissenting).

27. 462 U.S. 213 (1983).

28. 419 U.S. 522 (1975).

29. Id. at 538–43 (Rehnquist, J., dissenting) (discussing the lack of precedent for this view).

30. 416 U.S. 312 (1974). Four Justices argued that the case was not moot. Id. at 348–50 (Brennan, J., dissenting).

31. See *University of California Regents v. Bakke* 438 U.S. 265, 272–81 (1978).

32. Benjamin N. Cardozo, *The Nature of the Judicial Process*, 149.

33. Arthur J. Goldberg, *Equal Justice: The Warren Era of the Supreme Court*, 75.

34. John Paul Stevens, "The Life-Span of a Judge-Made Rule," 1 and n. 1.

35. *Miranda v. Arizona* 384 U.S. 436, 526 (1966) (White, J., dissenting). Similarly, Stephen Saltzburg has termed *Miranda* an "abrupt departure" from precedent. Saltzburg, "Foreword: The Flow and Ebb of Constitutional Criminal Procedure in the Warren and Burger Courts," 200.

36. 384 U.S. at 441–42.

37. Id. at 442.

38. Stone, supra note 6 at 99.

39. 401 U.S. 222 (1970).

40. "[S]tatements merely intended to be exculpatory by the defendant are often used to impeach his testimony at trial. . . . These statements are incriminating in any meaningful sense and may not be used without the full warnings. . . ." *Miranda* 384 U.S. at 477.

41. *Harris*, 401 U.S. at 224. See Alan M. Dershowitz and John Hart Ely, "*Harris v. New York*: Some Anxious Observations on the Candor and Logic of the Emerging Nixon Majority" (detailed analysis of the Court's "misleading" use of precedents).

42. *Harris*, 401 U.S. at 224.

43. 417 U.S. 433 (1974).

44. 347 U.S. 62 (1954).

45. 384 U.S. at 476.

46. See Stone, supra note 6 at 107: "[A] technical reading of *Miranda*, such as that employed in *Harris*, would enable the Court to label many critical aspects of the decision mere dictum. . . ."

47. Id. at 109.

48. 269 U.S. 20, 34–35 (1925).

49. See cases discussed in Yale Kamisar, Wayne LaFave, and Jerold Israel, *Modern Criminal Procedure*, 773–80 (including 1990 Supplement).

50. 417 U.S. at 447.

51. 384 U.S. 719 (1966).

52. Stone, supra note 6 at 123.

53. 422 U.S. 531, 539, 542 (1975).

54. 468 U.S. 897 (1984).

55. *Baltimore & O. R. R. v. Goodman* 275 U.S. 66, 70 (1927).

56. *Pokora v. Wabash Ry.* 292 U.S. 98, 106 (1934).

57. Id. at 105–6.

58. William Lloyd Prosser, *Handbook of the Law of Torts*, 188.

59. 466 U.S. 170 (1984).

60. Id. at 181 (citations omitted).

61. 442 U.S. 200, 213–14 (1979).

62. *Go-Bart Importing Co. v. United States* 282 U.S. 344, 357 (1931). See also *United States v. Rabinowitz* 339 U.S. 56, 66 (1950).

63. *United States v. Ross* 456 U.S. 798, 825 (1982).

64. These are enumerated in Craig Bradley, "Two Models of the Fourth Amendment," 1468, 1473–74.

65. See *Trupiano v. United States* 334 U.S. 699, 708 (1948): "A search or seizure without a warrant . . . has always been . . . strictly limited . . . ; *Carroll v. United States* 267 U.S. 132, 156 (1925): A warrant must be obtained if "reasonably practicable."

66. Saltzburg, supra note 35 at 154–55.
67. 267 U.S. 132 (1925).
68. Id. at 153.
69. Id. at 156.
70. 399 U.S. 42 (1970).
71. Id. at 48–49.
72. *Cardwell v. Lewis* 417 U.S. 583 (1974).
73. *Texas v. White* 423 U.S. 67 (1975) (per curiam).
74. *South Dakota v. Opperman* 428 U.S. 364 (1976).
75. 456 U.S. 798 (1982).
76. It may be that the admonition of *Coolidge v. New Hampshire* 403 U.S. 443, 461 (1971) (plurality opinion) that "[t]he word 'automobile' is not a talisman in whose presence the Fourth Amendment fades away and disappears" still retains vitality as to a car parked on private property. See *Cardwell v. Lewis* 417 U.S. 583, 593 (1974). However, Wayne LaFave has pointed out that "given the fact that neither the 'practical consideration' nor the historical underpinnings stressed by the *Ross* majority are limited to vehicles actually on the move immediately prior to police intervention, it is highly unlikely that *Ross* will be construed to be so limited." Wayne LaFave, *Search and Seizure: A Treatise on the Fourth Amendment*, § 7.2, p. 235 (citation omitted).
77. See *Robbins v. California* 453 U.S. 420 (1981); *Arkansas v. Sanders* 442 U.S. 753 (1979); *United States v. Chadwick* 433 U.S. 1 (1977) (distinguished in *Ross*).
78. The Court has recently addressed this question. In *California v. Carney* 105 S.Ct. 2066 (1985), the court found the automobile exception applicable to the reasonable search of a mobile motor home parked in a downtown lot. Reasoning that the motor home was readily mobile, licensed to operate on public streets, subject to extensive regulation, and "so situated that an objective observer would conclude that it was being used not as a residence, but as a vehicle" (id. at 2070), the Court held that the warrantless search did not violate the fourth amendment. It noted that "to fail to apply the exception to vehicles such as a motor home ignores the fact that a motor home lends itself easily to use as an instrument of illicit drug traffic and other illegal activity." Id.
79. The Court answered this question in the affirmative in *New York v. Belton* 453 U.S. 454 (1981).
80. See *Colorado v. Bertine* 479 U.S. 367 (1987); *Florida v. Wells* 58 L. W. 4454 (1990).
81. 433 U.S. 1, 11 (1977).
82. See *Arkansas v. Sanders* 442 U.S. 753 (1979) (later modified by *Ross*).
83. *California v. Acevedo* 59 LW 4559 (1991).
84. As James Haddad has observed, "If [a] search is unreasonable under all the facts, it should not be upheld simply because the facts fall within one of the well recognized exceptions. The United States Supreme Court, however, has not been true to this logic." James B. Haddad, "Well-Delineated Exceptions, Claims of Sham, and Fourfold Probable Cause," 203. On the other hand, Justice Rehnquist has criticized the Court for *striking down* essentially reasonable searches or seizures because they fail to conform to the strict terms of one of the fourth amendment exceptions. See *Florida v. Royer* 460 U.S. 491, 520 (1983) (Rehnquist, J., dissenting): "Analyzed simply in terms of its 'reasonableness' as that term is used in the Fourth Amendment, the con-

duct of the investigating officers toward Royer would pass muster with virtually all thoughtful, civilized persons not overly steeped in the mysteries of this Court's Fourth Amendment jurisprudence."

85. It is clear that a car parked in such a "public place" is subject to the automobile exception. See *Cardwell v. Lewis* 417 U.S. 583, 593–94 (1974).

86. After *Texas v. White* 423 U.S. 67 (1975) (per curiam), we must assume that a warrantless search of a car is permissible on probable cause even if the car is stopped just outside a building that houses both a police station and a court, even if the sole occupant of the vehicle is arrested, and even if a magistrate is (immediately) available. Haddad, supra note 84 at 203. This result would also be supported by the holding in *Zurcher v. Stanford Daily* 436 U.S. 547 (1978) that innocent third parties are not exempt from searches for evidence.

87. Consider also *Chimel v. California* 395 U.S. 752 (1969), in which the Court made the definitive statement of the scope of searches incident to arrest:

> When an arrest is made, it is reasonable for the arresting officer to search the person arrested in order to remove any weapons that the latter might seek to use in order to resist or effect his escape. Otherwise, the officer's safety might well be endangered, and the arrest itself frustrated. In addition, it is entirely reasonable for the arresting officer to search for and seize any evidence on the arrestee's person in order to prevent its concealment or destruction. And the area into which an arrestee might reach in order to grab a weapon or evidentiary items must, of course, be governed by a like rule. A gun on a table or in a drawer in front of one who is arrested can be as dangerous to the arresting officer as one concealed in the clothing of the person arrested. There is ample justification, therefore, for a search of the arrestee's person and the area *"within his immediate control"*—construing that phrase to mean the area from within which he might gain possession of a weapon or destructible evidence.
>
> There is no comparable justification, however, for routinely searching any room other than that in which an arrest occurs—or, for that matter, for searching all the desk drawers or other closed or concealed areas in that room itself.

395 U.S. at 762–63 (emphasis added).

In *New York v. Belton* 453 U.S. 454 (1981), the Court found that "Articles inside the relatively narrow compass of the passenger compartment of an automobile are in fact generally, even if not inevitably, within 'the area into which an arrestee might reach in order to grab a weapon or evidentiary ite[m]'" (453 U.S. at 460, quoting *Chimel* 395 U.S. at 763). Thus, in an effort to provide a "single familiar standard . . . to guide police officers" (453 U.S. at 458, quoting *Dunaway v. New York* 442 U.S. 200, 213–14 [1979]), the Court upheld the search of a jacket that was inaccessible to the defendant at the time of the search and generally approved the search of the passenger compartments of cars as incident to the arrest of people in those cars, regardless of whether the compartment was an "area within the immediate control" of the arrestee. 453 U.S. at 462–63. See LaFave, supra note 76, § 7.1 (Pocket Part, 1985), for a detailed critique of *Belton*.

88. Kamisar, supra note 6 at 62.

89. John A. Jenkins, "The Partisan," p. 35.

90. 401 U.S. 222 (1970).

91. 417 U.S. 433 (1974).

92. 406 U.S. 682 (1972).

93. 388 U.S. 218 (1967).

94. See, e.g., Silas Wasserstrom, "The Incredible Shrinking Fourth Amendment": "The Supreme Court then, has begun to dismember the body of fourth amendment law . . . developed by the Warren Court. So far, however, [the Burger Court has not] overrule[d] a single fourth amendment decision of the Warren Court." Kamisar, supra note 6 at 68: "[T]he fears that the Burger Court would dismantle the work of the Warren Court (or the Bill of Rights itself) and the reports that such dismantling was well under way, seem to have been considerably exaggerated."

95. *Walton v. Arizona* 58 L. W. 4992, 4996 (1990) (opinion of Scalia, J., concurring in part and concurring in the judgment).

96. Id. at 4999, quoting Rehnquist, J., dissenting in *Lockett v. Ohio* 438 U.S. 586, 629 (1978).

97. 408 U.S. 238 (1972).

99. 58 LW at 4997.

100. Id. at 5001.

101. See Francis Allen, "The Judicial Quest for Penal Justice: The Warren Court and the Criminal Cases," 525.

102. Of course, before the Court could torture the fifth amendment, it had to torture the fourteenth to make the fifth applicable to the states. This result also had no historical support. E.g., Henry Friendly, "The Bill of Rights as a Code of Criminal Procedure," 934. To recognize that *Miranda* required a distortion of the fifth amendment is not necessarily to disagree with the result. *Miranda*, being a legislative-type rule, *does* provide relatively clear guidance for police. Compare U.S. Dept. of Justice, Office of Legal Policy, "Report to the Attorney General on the Law of Pre-Trial Interrogation" (*Miranda* not constitutionally justified) with Stephen Schulhofer, "Reconsidering *Miranda*," (*Miranda* is constitutionally justified).

103. See Fred Graham, *The Self-Inflicted Wound.*

104. 388 U.S. 218 (1967).

105. Of course, a defendant who is seized off the street for the purpose of appearing in a lineup can challenge that seizure on fourth amendment grounds; but that is a different issue. Normally, if a non-arrested suspect is wanted for a lineup, a court order must be obtained.

106. See Leon Polsky, Richard Uviller, Vincent Ziccordi & Davis, "The Role of the Defense Counsel at a Lineup in Light of the *Wade, Gilbert,* and *Stovall* Decisions," 278, 285–86.

107. 406 U.S. 682 (1972).

108. Id. at 688–91.

109. *Moran v. Burbine* 475 U.S. 412, 425 (1986).

110. Francis Allen has expressed similar concerns about the "criminal procedure revolution" (supra note 101):

> These comments do not attack the Court's attempt to expand the rights of defendants in criminal cases, rather they indicate that narrowing one's focus to the Bill of Rights can lead to a failure to view criminal process issues

in the proper perspective of defining the judicial role in that process. The failure to question the judicial role in assuring fairness in the criminal process may lead to a restriction of the rights of the defendant as easily, and perhaps even more easily, than it may lead to an expansion of those rights.

John E. Nowak, "Due Process Methodology in the Postincorporation World," 401 (discussing Allen, supra note 101 at 540); accord Sanford Kadish, "Methodology and Criteria in Due Process Adjudication—A Survey and Criticism."

111. See Craig Bradley, Yale Kamisar, Joseph D. Grano, and James Brian Haddad, *Sum and Substance: Criminal Procedure* §§ 6.6200, 6.6300, 6.7000.

112. The Court ignored such trickery in *Oregon v. Mathiason* 429 U.S. 492, 493 (1977).

113. The Court condemned the "Mutt and Jeff" technique, wherein an interrogator who is hostile to the defendant is replaced by one who is sympathetic, in *Miranda v. Arizona* 384 U.S. 436, 452–53 (1966).

114. See *Gooding v. United States* 416 U.S. 430 (1974), upholding a federal statute allowing nighttime searches with no special showing in the warrant, but not resolving the constitutional issues.

115. See *Ker v. California* 374 U.S. 23 (1963), where the Court split on this issue.

116. In *Segurra v. United States* 468 U.S. 796 (1984) the lower court had suppressed evidence seized during a nineteen-hour period during which police improperly entered an apartment and "secured" it pending the arrival of a search warrant. The Supreme Court disapproved this police action, but did not decide whether the lower court's suppression of the evidence was appropriate. In *Murray v. United States* 108 S.Ct. 2529 (1988) the Court refused to suppress evidence seen but not seized when police illegally entered a warehouse on probable cause but without a warrant, and then obtained a warrant without using the knowledge obtained as a basis for the warrant application. Unresolved is whether evidence actually seized during the illegal entry is admissible, under what circumstances an entry to secure premises pending the arrival of a warrant is appropriate, and what steps short of such an entry the police are entitled to take.

117. See *Michigan v. Summers* 452 U.S. 692 (1981), holding that the homeowner may be detained. In *Ybarra v. Illinois* 444 U.S. 85 (1979) the Court held that patrons in a bar were not automatically subject to a frisk, absent a showing that they were armed, simply because the police were executing a search warrant in the bar. Unresolved is whether a passenger in a car, or a visitor in a home, may be subject to such a frisk because of his apparently closer relationship to the subject of the arrest or search.

118. Id. at 467.

119. See, e.g., Kamisar et al., supra note 49. Only in the relatively minor matter of joinder and severance of defendants is there any detailed discussion of Federal Rules of Criminal Procedure, and federal statutes play a major role only in the chapter on wiretapping. State statutes are, of course, not mentioned at all.

120. Police and Criminal Evidence Act, 1984, ch. 60 (Gr. Brit.). In Australia, "it is also generally accepted that what is needed is a comprehensive code setting out with as much particularity as possible the rights and duties of police, suspects and others concerned in the criminal investigation process."

P. Sallman and John Willis, *Criminal Justice in Australia*, 23. Of course continental countries have had such codes for decades. See, e.g., American Series of Penal Codes, *The German Code of Criminal Procedure (Strafprozessordnung)* (W. Germany). Accord Friendly, supra note 102 at 930 (citation omitted): "How complex the subject is, and how much it calls for the compromise that is the genius of legislation rather than the everlasting aye or nay of constitutional decision." See also American Law Institute, *Code of Criminal Procedure*.

121. Stephen Markman, "The Fifth Amendment and Custodial Questioning: A Response to Reconsidering *Miranda*," 949. Accord Mark Berger, "Legislating Confession Law in Great Britain: A Statutory Approach to Police Interrogations," 1, 3:

> The constitutional law focus of the American confession law debate has diverted attention from the substantive police interrogation issues that society should address. Instead of considering what police may or may not do to question criminal suspects, courts have had to evaluate what the judicial system can and cannot do to supervise practices in police stationhouses. . . .
> A constitutional law focus also deters legislative attempts to control the police interrogation process. . . . By repeating and elaborating the specific warnings that must be given, as well as detailing the characteristics of a valid waiver, the decision offered little indication that the Court would be satisfied with anything other than the *Miranda* procedure.

122. *Moran v. Burbine* 475 U.S. 412, 425 (1986).

Chapter 5
What Other Countries Are Doing

It is particularly useful to examine the laws of other countries in the area of criminal procedure. While American lawyers and lawmakers are largely unaware of the laws of foreign jurisdictions, especially of non-English speaking countries, the reverse is not true. Foreign lawyers, many of whom have attended graduate school in America, are acutely aware of American developments. Consequently, these countries, in formulating their rules of criminal procedure, have adopted those American innovations that seem sensible to them and rejected those that do not. Thus, while the Supreme Court's cooption of this field has essentially eliminated the states as "laboratories," where new ideas can be tested, foreign countries can play the same role. However, care must be taken. No other country studied has the high level of crime of the United States, nor the same level of racial, ethnic, and economic diversity. Consequently, just because something works in Italy or Australia does not necessarily mean that it will work in the United States. However, if a certain approach has been accepted or rejected by most of the other major countries of the world, it behooves American lawmakers to take heed.

In this chapter, the criminal procedure systems of six countries will be considered. These are the four largest countries in Western Europe—England, France, Germany, and Italy,—plus Canada and Australia. As noted in the Introduction, all of these countries have a legislatively enacted code of criminal procedure.* In all but one of them, Australia, this is a national code, applicable throughout the

*So, too, do the former Soviet Union and Japan. However, insufficient information is available in English to warrant a full discussion of these countries' practices.

country. In Australia, where the Constitution does not allow such an arrangement, some states have codes and others rely more heavily on the common law. (As will be discussed in the next chapter, the United States Constitution does not, contrary to popular belief, forbid congressional enactment of a single, nationally applicable code of criminal procedure for this country.) Even in Australia, however, there seems little debate that a code, preferably a federal code serving as a model for state codes, is the best way to go.

But while all the other major countries studied believe that a legislatively enacted code is the sensible way to declare criminal procedure law, not all countries have a well-developed code that covers all significant areas of police activity. France, in particular, while it has fairly well-developed codes, seems to repose more trust in the police to act appropriately than most Americans would deem fitting. Also, no other country has a mandatory exclusionary rule, applicable to all code violations, though the new Italian code appears to come close. However, the trend, particularly in Canada and Britain, as well as Italy and, recently, Germany, is to make increasing use of discretionary exclusion to deter police misconduct.

There follows a discussion of the criminal procedural rules of the six countries mentioned, with particular emphasis on England, which, in 1984, responding to deficiencies in the patchwork system that had developed over the centuries, enacted a comprehensive national code of criminal procedure that should serve as the starting point for any similar effort in this country. This discussion is offered not merely to advance the central thesis of this book—that a code is the best way to declare criminal procedure law—but also to suggest some possible directions that a U.S. code might take.

England and Wales*

According to Vaughan Bevan and Ken Lidstone, leading commentators on the Police and Criminal Evidence Act, 1984 (PACE):

> Before [the Act], the law governing police powers for the investigation of crime was unclear and antiquated. It had developed piecemeal since the establishment of professional police forces in the nineteenth century. Parliament had added fitfully to the few common law principles. This varied

*What will be referred to in this discussion as the "English" rules govern England and Wales. Scotland operates under separate rules, embodied in the Criminal Justice Act (Scotland), 1980. Northern Ireland is governed by rules similar to England's, embodied in the Police and Criminal Evidence Act (Northern Ireland), Order 1989, which came into force in Northern Ireland on January 1, 1990.

and scant law was supplemented by (a) rules of guidance as to the admissibility of confessions provided by the Lord Chief Justice in consultation with the judiciary; (b) national administrative guidance in the form of Home Office circulars . . . and (c) local administrative rules. The results were patchy legal obligations and powers for the police and local variations in powers. . . . A wide-ranging overhaul of the system had been due for many years. New and heavier pressures on the police and a more critical public opinion demanded the powers of the police be placed on a modern statutory footing.[1]

A Royal Commission (the Phillips Commission) issued a report in 1981 proposing a comprehensive statutory reform of police practices.[2] After extensive parliamentary debate, the Police and Criminal Evidence Act was passed in 1984. The Act, the most comprehensive code studied in this book,* comprises eight principal parts: I. Powers to Stop and Search; II. Powers of Entry, Search and Seizure; III. Arrest; IV. Detention; V. Questioning and Treatment of Persons by Police; VII. Documentary Evidence in Criminal Proceedings; VIII. Evidence in Criminal Proceedings; plus four sections on miscellaneous details. The Act is supplemented by Codes of Practice, promulgated by the Home Office, which cover such areas as interrogations, identification procedures, and searches and seizures of property. The Act has attracted criticism from both left and right for the substance of its provisions,[3] but there seems to be general agreement that the legislation successfully "codif[ies] and control[s] an area which lacked clarity and was becoming an increasing scandal."[4]

Because the English Code may serve as a useful starting point for an American codification, despite its excessive length and complexity, its provisions are considered in greater depth than those of the other countries studied.† Pertinent portions of the Act and Codes of Practice appear in the Appendices to this book.

Stop and Search

Section 1 provides that a constable may stop and search any person or vehicle upon reasonable grounds for suspecting‡ that stolen or

---

*Because the Italian code has not been translated into English, I could not assess it in this respect. It does appear to be very extensive.

†The general enthusiasm expressed in this book for the *structure* of the English system should not be read as endorsing the *practices* of British police, whose delicts have led to the creation of another Royal Commission to study these matters. See Marion McKeon, "Lawyers Urge Interim Criminal Procedure Reform" at 20.

‡The British distinguish between "reasonable grounds for suspecting," which is like our "reasonable suspicion" standard, and "reasonable grounds to believe," which is "a high standard approaching certainty of belief," seemingly somewhat stronger than our "probable cause" but, in practice, probably the same. See Vaughan Bevan and Ken Lidstone, *A Guide to the Police and Criminal Evidence Act, 1984*, §§ 2.03–2.06 for a discussion of the difference.

prohibited articles (i.e., weapons or instrumentalities of crime) may be found. This power is applicable in public places and places "accessible to the public," but not dwellings or private buildings.[5] "Reasonable grounds for suspicion" is the same as is required to justify an arrest.[6] The Code of Practice (Code A) specifies:

> Whether reasonable ground for suspicion exists will depend on the circumstance in each case, but there must be some objective basis for it . . . [Examples omitted]. Reasonable suspicion can never be supported on the basis of personal factors alone. For example, a person's colour, age, hairstyle or manner of dress, or the fact that he is known to have a previous conviction for possession of an unlawful article, cannot be used alone or in combination with each other as the sole basis on which to search that person. Nor may it be founded on the basis of stereotyped images of certain persons or groups as more likely to be committing offences.[7]

The Code of Practice makes it clear that a search in public must be "restricted to superficial examination of outer clothing"[8] but a more extensive search may occur in a nearby police van or stationhouse, if there are "reasonable grounds" for further searching. The time for which a person or vehicle may be detained is limited to what is reasonable to permit such a search to be carried out.[9] The search is limited by the nature of the suspicion. Thus, if a constable suspects that X has a gun in a coat pocket, only that pocket may be searched.[10] Each such search must be recorded and the suspect informed that such a recording will be made.[11] A separate section provides for the stopping of vehicles at roadblocks, but otherwise no special provision is made for auto searches.[12]

The differences from U.S. law are striking. The English do not draw any distinction between frisks and full searches of the person, though the "in public" search is essentially the same as the American "frisk." Thus it is the location of the search, rather than the quantum of evidence, that determines its intensity. Also, the right to search a person is limited to fruits and instrumentalities of crime, not mere evidence. The English "search" is thus broader than the American "frisk," which requires a suspicion that the subject be armed and dangerous, but narrower than the American "search," which requires probable cause, but may be for any evidence. Moreover, in England a search of the person does not flow automatically incident to arrest, as in the United States. Rather, it is limited, in both its inception and its

---

"probable cause" but, in practice, probably the same. See Vaughan Bevan and Ken Lidstone, *A Guide to the Police and Criminal Evidence Act, 1984*, §§ 2.03–2.06 for a discussion of the difference.

scope, by "reasonable grounds for suspicion."[13] However, once the suspect is actually taken to the police station, a full inventory search must be undertaken by the custody officer, as in the United States.[14]

In the section of PACE relating to the law of "stop and search," the English have succeeded in spelling out rules that it has taken our Supreme Court thirty years to develop. Moreover, many issues that are still unclear in U.S. law have been resolved by PACE. For example, PACE makes it clear that a person can only be searched in the curtilage of a house if it appears that he or she does not live there or is not there with the owner's consent.[15] A similar restriction applies to searches of vehicles on private property.[16]

Also, nearly twenty-five years after *Terry v. Ohio*[17] first authorized investigative stops, it remains unclear in the United States whether a frisk is justified absent evidence that "criminal activity is afoot." That is, can the police frisk someone on suspicion of carrying a weapon if carrying a weapon is not illegal and no independent evidence of criminality exists?[18] Also, can they stop or frisk someone for a nonserious, non-dangerous crime, such as possession of narcotics?[19] A related question is whether, given the requisite suspicion for a stop and frisk, the frisk may occur immediately, or whether the police must attempt to dispel the suspicion before frisking. *Terry* suggests that the latter course is appropriate, though common sense suggests a contrary conclusion. The courts are split.[20]

PACE resolves these matters easily (though not necessarily correctly) by allowing a stop and search any time a suspect is reasonably believed to possess "stolen or prohibited articles" (which includes weapons and illegal drugs). The Code of Practice makes it clear that "there is no power to stop or detain a person against his will in order to find grounds for a search,"[21] but "This Code does not affect the ability of an officer to speak to or question a person . . . (in the absence of reasonable suspicion) without detaining him or exercising any element of compulsion."[22] Thus, in England, a suspect may be stopped and frisked any time a weapon or contraband is reasonably suspected, there is no requirement of preliminary investigation before the frisk is performed, frisks may not be performed for mere evidence of crime, and forcible stops for investigatory purposes other than frisks are not allowed.*

---

*The astute reader may have noticed that the two sections of the Code of Practice quoted in this paragraph do not directly support the statement in this sentence that forcible stops are never permitted for investigatory purposes other than frisks. This illustrates a further advantage of statutes over court decisions. When the code writer has delineated a limited set of circumstances in which a certain action is allowed, it is reasonable to infer that such action is inappropriate in other than the defined circumstances. By contrast, when a court declares a course of action appropriate under the

Entry, Search, and Seizure

PACE provides that upon written application by the police:

(1) . . . [There are] reasonable grounds for believing that a serious arrestable offence has been committed *and* that there is material on premises specified in the application that is likely to be of substantial value (whether by itself or together with other material) *and* that the material is likely to be relevant evidence, *and* that it does not consist of or include items subject to legal privilege, *and* any of the conditions specified in §3 below applies, [a magistrate] may issue a warrant authorizing a constable to enter and search the premises. [The warrant must specifically identify the place to be searched and, if possible, the person or things to be seized.][23]

*   *   *   *

(3) The conditions mentioned in subsection (1) are—
(a) that it is not practicable to communicate with any person entitled to grant entry to the premises;

*   *   *   *

(c) that entry to the premises will not be granted unless a warrant is produced;
(d) that the purpose of a search may be frustrated or seriously prejudiced unless a constable arriving at the premises can secure immediate entry to them;[24]*

*   *   *   *

Entry may be made without a search warrant to arrest on an arrest warrant, or to arrest without a warrant for certain specified offenses (generally, those punishable by imprisonment of five years or longer[25]), provided the officer has reasonable grounds to believe that the suspect is within.[26] Such entry may also be made in hot pursuit or for the purpose of "saving life or limb or preventing serious damage to property," or to prevent a breach of peace.[27] Entry may also be made of "any premises controlled or occupied" by the arrestee after an arrest outside, if the police have reasonable grounds for believing that evidence of the instant, or related, offenses may be found inside.[28]

Unfortunately, for the purposes of understanding the English law of searches, these aspects of PACE are not the only sources of searching authority. Rather, in this area, PACE supplements previous laws, in particular the Theft Act, 1968 and the Misuse of Drugs Act, 1971,

---

facts of a certain case, it is never entirely clear what the rule is under different facts. This is true even if the court has attempted to extend the rule to other, hypothetical, cases, for such an extension can always be dismissed as dictum.

*I do not hold up this section as a model of effective draftsmanship.

which already authorized search warrants for certain items (generally, fruits and instrumentalities of drug and theft crimes, as opposed to "mere evidence").[29] PACE extended the searching authority to "mere evidence" in cases of "serious arrestable offense" (i.e., the most serious felonies, such as murder, rape, and kidnapping and other offenses leading to "serious bodily injury" or "serious financial loss").[30] Accordingly, searches for some things, in particular narcotics and stolen property, are not subject to the same restrictions as searches under PACE for evidence of "serious arrestable offenses." In any event, as Bevan and Lidstone report, the great majority of searches in England are warrantless, usually through consent (32%) or incident to arrest (55%). Twelve percent of searches are by magistrates' warrant.[31]

Again, the differences from American law are many. In order to obtain a search warrant under PACE, English police must essentially show, in addition to reasonable grounds, that consent has been or will be refused, or that to seek it would frustrate the purpose of the search. Furthermore, searches of premises are limited to serious arrestable offenses (and for drugs and stolen property under other statutes) and cannot be performed to look for privileged material. A warrantless entry apparently may not be made because of a belief that evidence is about to be destroyed.[32] None of these limitations is present in U.S. law.

The English allow a search of premises incident to arrest, even when the suspect is not arrested on the premises.[33] Moreover, the search incident to arrest is not limited to the "immediate vicinity" of the arrest, as in *Chimel v. California*, when the suspect is arrested inside.[34] On the other hand, searches of premises incident to arrest may only be performed on "reasonable grounds to believe" rather than automatically as in American law.

Consent searches

The Code of Practice (Code B) provides that consent to search premises must, if practicable, be obtained in writing after the occupant has been informed of the right to refuse consent and that anything seized may be used in evidence.[35] This provision offers substantially more protection than has the United States Supreme Court in *Schneckloth v. Bustamonte*,[36] where lax rules concerning consent searches provide police with a major loophole for avoiding the sometimes too stringent, and always confusing, fourth amendment requirements. Despite the more stringent requirements, consent searches, as noted above, remain quite common in England.

By contrast, consents to search the person need not be preceded by warnings, and need not be in writing. Moreover, the Code requirements for making a record of the search do not apply. The only restraint is that "an officer should always make it clear that he is seeking the co-operation of the person concerned."[37]

Arrest and Detention

Arrests need be based only on "reasonable grounds for suspicion" and need not be by warrant.[38] As discussed earlier, the arrestee's person may be searched only if "the constable has reasonable grounds for believing that the arrested person may present a danger to himself or others"[39] or possesses something "which he might use to escape" or "which might be evidence relating to an[y] offence."[40] As discussed above, the arrest also conveys the power, on reasonable grounds for belief, "to enter and search any premises in which [the suspect] was when arrested or immediately before he was arrested for evidence relating to the offence for which he was arrested."[41]

After arrest, a "custody officer" at each station of the rank of sergeant or above, who is independent of the investigation, must determine whether there is sufficient evidence to charge the suspect[42] and perform a full inventory search.[43] If there are not sufficient grounds for holding, the suspect must be released. An arrestee may not be held longer than 24 hours after arrival at the police station without being charged.[44] However, he or she may be held an additional 12 hours if the superintendent in charge of the station determines that this is necessary "to secure or preserve evidence relating to the offence or to obtain such evidence by questioning him," *and* the offence is a "serious arrestable offence," *and* "the investigation is being conducted diligently and expeditiously."[45] A magistrate's court may, after a hearing where the suspect is represented by counsel, authorize detention for another 36 hours where "necessary to secure evidence" and so on, as above.[46] This warrant may be extended by the magistrate's court for a total detention not to exceed 96 hours.[47] A suspect has a right not to be held incommunicado during this period and to consult with counsel,[48] subject to certain exceptions discussed below.

The Codes of Practice also provide detailed rules for the conditions of detention, medical treatment of suspects, special treatment of juveniles and mentally ill persons, and so on.[49] This area represents the most glaring omission in the American system. While in 1957, in *Mallory v. United States*,[50] the Supreme Court held that an extended interrogation (7 hours) violated the Federal Rules of Criminal Procedure (which prohibits "unnecessary delay" in bringing the suspect before a magistrate), this rule has never been extended to the states, and most states have not adopted a similar rule.[51] For some reason, the Court has assumed that, once the suspect has received the *Miranda* warnings, no further concern for what happens at the police station is required. In this area, the English system is better not only because it has rules but because of the kind of rules it has.

Interrogations

The obligation of the police to inform suspects of their rights is summed up by British authorities*:

> Suspects must be cautioned before an interview begins. The caution must expressly make it clear that there is no obligation to say anything or answer questions [and that anything said may be used in evidence].[52]

> Each new bout of questioning directed to a suspect should be preceded by a further caution, as where a person is questioned at his home, arrested, and then asked further questions in the police car on the way to the station.[53]

> The custody officer must tell [the suspect] the reasons for his arrest. . . . He must be told of his right to have somebody outside the police station informed of his whereabouts. . . . He must be told of his right to legal advice [including free legal advice from the "Duty Solicitor"].[54]

> He must also be told that he has a right to a copy of the custody record. The information to the suspect must be communicated not only orally . . . but *in writing*.[55]

Suspects' rights to notify someone of their whereabouts and to consult counsel may be delayed up to 36 hours in the case of a "serious arrestable offence" if an officer of the rank of superintendent or above has reasonable grounds for believing that the exercise of the rights:

*Readers familiar with the American experience with *Miranda* will not be surprised to learn that the police are frequently able to avoid the anticipated impact of these tough interrogation rules by "the ploy of exploiting detainees' disoriented state by rushing them through the drill so briskly that they clearly had little opportunity to absorb [the warnings]." Nevertheless, a requirement that the suspect write out a waiver of counsel in his or her own hand was rejected by Parliament and the current system—to check a box, either requesting or refusing counsel—was retained. David Wolchover and Anthony Heaton-Armstrong, "The Questioning Code Revamped," 236.

The Code of Practice further provides that a poster setting forth these rights, including a foreign language poster where appropriate, "must be prominently displayed in the charging area of every police station." Interrogation Code, supra note 48, para. 6.3.

(i) will lead to interference with or harm to evidence . . . or interference with or physical injury to other persons; or
(ii) will lead to the alerting of other persons suspected of having committed such an offence but not yet arrested for it; or
(iii) will hinder the recovery of property obtained as a result of such an offence.

*   *   *   *

Access to a solicitor may not be delayed on the grounds that he might advise the person not to answer any questions. . . .[56]

There is no right to cut off questioning by an assertion of the right to silence[57] (but subsequent questioning must not be "oppressive"). However, further questioning may not follow a request for a solicitor, subject to exigent circumstances and certain other exceptions.[58]

Any interview in a police station* must be contemporaneously recorded, unless it is impracticable to do so, in which case a record must be made of why it was impracticable. [The new Code of Practice now requires tape recording.][59] It will be regarded as impracticable to make a contemporaneous record where, for example, the suspect refuses to talk if the conversation is being recorded. However, police officers frequently claim that note-taking slows down the interrogation, gives the suspect more time to prepare and leads to stilted conversation. These problems will be reduced where tape recording is used, but they will continue to arise in relation to untaped interviews. The decisions so far suggest that a desire to maintain the spontaneity of an interview is not a sufficient reason for failing to make a contemporaneous record. . . .[60]

In the course of interviews, strategems designed to induce a confession by bringing psychological pressure to bear will not normally amount to oppression making a confession inadmissible, [but they may have that effect depending on the medical and psychological state of the suspect or if the police actively mislead the suspect and the solicitor who has the responsibility for advising the suspect].[61]

Remedies

An American reader may respond to this recitation of the English rules by saying, "These rules are all very well, but everyone knows that England doesn't enforce its rules with an exclusionary remedy." Traditionally, it was the policy of the British courts to ignore violations of the rules by police. Only involuntary confessions were subject to exclusion, on the ground that they were unreliable. Otherwise, if evidence was relevant, "it matters not how you get it; if you steal it

---

*The 1991 Code of Practice requires a contemporaneous record of all interviews, whether within or outside a police station, unless it is impracticable to do so. Interrogation Code, para. 11.5(a).

even, it would be admissible."[62] Indeed, this axiom, along with the outdated (by PACE) statement that the British "Rules do not require an admonition concerning a right to counsel at any point," was cited by the Justice Department's Office of Legal Policy in 1986 as part of a continuing effort by American conservatives to portray the American *Miranda* warnings and exclusionary rule as aberrational.[63] As discussed above, PACE specifically does require a warning as to right to counsel and, more importantly, actually affords the suspect the right to consult the attorney, rather than just requiring the police to stop questioning as *Miranda* does, and will actually provide one if the suspect cannot afford to pay (subject to a significant "exigent circumstances" exception, as noted above). The U.S. Supreme Court has never gone this far.

PACE has also completely changed the attitude of the British courts toward evidentiary exclusion as a means of enforcing the rules. David Feldman summarizes the new approach:

The judges in the Crown Courts and the Court of Appeal seem to have moved away from the traditional notion that it is not the judiciary's job to discipline the police. They treat the regulation of police practices as being at least as important an objective as procedural fairness in the [trial itself]. This seems to reflect a growing disillusionment with police pretensions to professionalism and self-regulatory capacity, a determination to make a go of the balance struck by PACE, a renewed judicial commitment to rule of law principles and the ideal of legal accountability for the exercise of police powers, and the failure of other forms of legal control over the police.[64]

There are four grounds for evidentiary exclusion under PACE. Section 76(2) provides for mandatory exclusion of confessions (a) obtained "by oppression" or (b) likely to have been rendered "unreliable" by anything said or done (by anyone). "Oppression includes torture, inhuman or degrading treatment, and the use or threat of violence. . . ."[65] When oppression is alleged the burden is on the prosecution to rebut the charge beyond a reasonable doubt.[66] In addition to these mandatory bases for exclusion, section 78(1) provides that "the court may refuse to allow evidence . . . if it appears . . . that the admission of the evidence would have such an adverse effect on the fairness of the proceedings that the court ought not to admit it." Finally, section 82(3) "saves pre-existing common law powers to exclude evidence whose prejudicial effect outweighed its probative value."[67]

On the face of it, these bases for exclusion do not seem greatly different from the old system, though the extension of the "unreliability" grounds to things done by people other than the police* is a significant addition.[68] But by drawing attention to the "oppressive-ness" of police conduct, irrespective of the reliability of the con-fession, PACE has clearly directed the judiciary to "police the police." Since PACE,

> the judges see themselves as having a disciplinary and regulatory role in maintaining the balance between the powers of the police and the protection of suspects. This balance was one of the fundamental elements in the delib-erations of the Phillips Commission and of parliamentarians debating the var-ious versions of the Police and Criminal Evidence Bill. . . . In view of the time lavished by Parliament on striking the right balance, it is not unreasonable or improper for the courts to take the resulting statute seriously and seek ways of ensuring that the police do so as well.[69]

For example, since the rights specified in PACE do not attach until after arrest and arrival at the police station,† the police may be tempted to delay arresting suspects in order to interrogate them with-out warnings. However, in *R. v. Ismail* the trial judge excluded state-ments made by the defendant where a decision to delay arrest was intended to evade the protective rules.[70] On the other hand, in *R. v. Rajakuruna*,[71] where the suspect was not properly cautioned that he was a suspect, but "was well aware of [that fact]" and declined a solici-tor, his statements were not excluded.

One area in which the English courts have been particularly protec-tive of suspects' rights is where the police delay access to counsel or communication with a third party. David Feldman elaborates:

> The statutory ground relied on to justify delay must be reasonably support-able by reference to the known facts. Thus the police cannot claim that an accomplice still at large might be alerted and escape in a case where the arrest is already public knowledge, as where a detainee was arrested in public amongst people known to him and his house had already been searched in the presence of his mother,[72] or where the suspect's mother had been told of the arrest by telephone hours before the decision to delay access to a solicitor was taken.[73] . . . [T]o delay access to a solicitor, the police must have reasonable grounds for believing that the particular solicitor is likely to be dishonest, or

---

*In *R. v. Harvey* (1988) Crim. L.R. 241 (Central Criminal Court) "the experience of hearing her lover confess to murder may have been enough to induce a psychopathi-cally disordered woman of low normal intelligence to make a false confession in order to protect her lover." §76(2)(b) was invoked to exclude her statement.

† The suspect does not have to be informed of his or her rights until after arrival at the police station. However, the Code forbids any questioning prior to the advice other than in "very exceptional circumstances." Wolchover and Heaton-Armstrong, supra note 58 at 240. Interrogation Code, supra note 48, para. 11.1.

is liable to be manipulated or duped into passing on information to a detainee's criminal confederates.[74]

David Wolchover and Anthony Heaton-Armstrong conclude that "The burden of authority is such that other than in certain categories of offence it is now virtually impossible for the police to justify the prevention of access [to a solicitor] at any stage."[75]

In a similar vein, exclusion has been ordered when the police fail to inform the suspect fully of his or her rights,[76] mislead the suspect into thinking that it is not normal to have legal advice,[77] mislead the suspect and/or the solicitor as to the strength of the evidence in possession of the police,[78] obtain a confession that is a result of an earlier, uncautioned, confession,[79] or fail to make a contemporaneous record of the interrogation.[80] The attitude of the courts is summed up by Lord Chief Justice Lane, in the latter case: "If, as we find hard to believe, police officers still do not appreciate the importance of [PACE] and the accompanying Code, then it is time they did."[81]

Evidentiary exclusions are not limited to violations of the detention and interrogation rules. In *Matto v. Wolverhampton Crown Court*[82] the breath specimen of a suspect was suppressed because of his earlier, unlawful, arrest.* In *R. v. Gall*[83] the Court of Appeals "quashed a conviction because the trial judge wrongly refused to exclude evidence of an identification parade [lineup] at which a police officer had looked into the room where the parade had been assembled and could have spoken to witnesses before they attempted to view the suspect."[84] Similarly, in *R. v. Conway*[85] the Court of Appeals quashed a conviction where no identification parade had been held, as required by the Code of Practice, and no reason was shown why a parade was impracticable.[86]

In *R. v. Taylor*[87] documentary evidence was suppressed by the trial judge in a case involving financial improprieties because, when applying for a subpoena, the police had misled the judge into believing that the investigation concerned drug trafficking. The evidence was suppressed because of police misconduct, irrespective of any concerns about reliability.[88] In *R. v. Fennelley*,[89] in a trial for possession of narcotics with intent to distribute, the trial judge suppressed the narcotics because the suspect was not told the reason why he was stopped and about to be searched by the police, as required by PACE §2(3).† Fi-

---

*See *Brown v. Illinois* 422 U.S. 590 (1975) for the United States Supreme Court's "taint of an illegal arrest" doctrine.

†David Feldman points out that *Fennelley* "might be decided differently under the new Code, since Fennelley might be held to have consented to the search and so waived his right to be given the reasons for it." Letter to author, December 17, 1991.

nally, in *Chapman v. D.P.P.*[90] a conviction for assaulting a police officer was quashed where the police entered the defendant's apartment in pursuit of a fleeing suspect without reasonable suspicion that the suspect had committed an arrestable offense.

Given the British courts' long history of ignoring violations by the police in the evidence-gathering process, the developments in exclusionary law since PACE are truly extraordinary. As David Feldman's analysis and Lord Lane's comments, cited above, suggest, the British courts have performed this about face on evidentiary exclusion in part because the code gives them new authority and in part for the simple reason that, now that the rules are clearly stated, the police can be expected to obey them.

It is particularly striking that this British "criminal procedure revolution" is occurring in the context of discretionary, rather than mandatory, exclusionary rules. The English experience strongly suggests that, if the U.S. rules were clearly stated in statutory form, then it would be possible to relax somewhat the mandatory exclusionary rule that has caused so much difficulty in this country. Such a relaxation would, in turn, make it possible to expand the coverage of the rules into areas such as detention and interrogation procedures where the Supreme Court has been unwilling to go because of the Court's commitment that any breach of its constitutionally mandated "rules" must necessarily lead to evidentiary exclusion.

My admiration for PACE is not entirely unqualified. For one thing, the system of accompanying a statute with separate, but frequently duplicative, Codes of Practice is much too complex. I would strike the balance somewhat more in the direction of simplicity, and would accompany the formal rule with explanatory notes, as illustrated in Chapter 6, but not with a separate body of law as prolix as the Codes of Practice. Also, as noted above, PACE is sometimes difficult to follow because it incorporates other statutory provisions by reference. Finally, I, of course, do not always agree with PACE as to the substantive content of individual rules. That said, PACE represents a vast improvement, from the point of view of police, defendants, attorneys, and judges alike, on the previous patchwork quilt of rules that existed in England and that continues to exist in the United States.

Australia

In 1989 I spent eight months in Canberra, the capital of Australia, studying the criminal procedure system. Australia, like the United States, is a vast, English-speaking former British colony, currently populated by people of diverse ethnic and racial origins. Its legal system is drawn from the British common law and it has a federal system of government much like our own. Moreover, Australians typically display an antipathy for police that is at least the equal of Americans'. Consequently, a study of Australia's criminal procedure system would seem to be an ideal source for constructive approaches to American problems.

Unfortunately, current Australian criminal procedure law does not bear out this expectation. In most respects it is where U.S. law was in the mid-1950s, though recent developments augur well for the future.[91] Until 1991, the "voluntariness" test as to confessions was the only basis for mandatory evidentiary exclusion, there had been little control by the High Court over state procedures, and police generally "exercise[d] personal power undisturbed by thoughts that there would ever be an accounting for its use."[92] Moreover, "in a sphere of activity involving issues of fundamental human liberty the governing rules are unclear, uncertain, out of date, difficult to find and understand and thus quite unsuitable for the age in which we live."[93]

As noted, prior to a 1991 statute discussed below there was a mandatory exclusionary rule only for "involuntary" confessions, and even they were not automatically excluded in all states.[94] Moreover, though this mandatory rule has often been mentioned in court opinions, it has rarely been invoked.[95] Beyond this mandatory rule, there are three possible grounds for discretionary evidentiary exclusion by the trial judge: (1) that the evidence in question will be unduly prejudicial; (2) that a statement given by the accused appears to be unreliable; and (3) that the evidence is the product of unfair or unlawful conduct by the police.[96] These discretionary bases of exclusion are sometimes used by trial judges to exclude confessions deemed unreliable or obtained by police overreaching.[97]

Most Australian states have fairly detailed statutory rules governing searches and arrests. For example, the New South Wales Search Warrant Act of 1985 provides for the issuance of search warrants to search houses for evidence upon a showing of "reasonable grounds" and requires that those warrants be specific.[98] However, these rules have not been taken seriously by the police because until 1990 evidence had *never* been excluded due to an illegal search in a reported case,[99] though there is ample evidence that illegal, and even brutal, searches had occurred.[100] This is true despite the fact that in the 1978 case of *Bunning v. Cross*[101] the High Court expressly broke from the British common law rule that evidence could never be suppressed due to an illegal search.[102]

In *Bunning* the Court held that, in exercising their discretion to exclude evidence due to police misconduct, trial judges should consider the following factors: (1) whether the "unlawful or improper conduct" on the part of the police was intentional or reckless on the one hand or merely accidental or "unconscious" on the other; (2) "the ease with which the law might have been complied with"; (3) "the nature of the offence charged"; and (4) whether there was evidence that the rule broken was one that reflected a "deliberate intent on the part of the legislature narrowly to restrict the police." In *Bunning* itself, the Court held that the evidence of a breathalyzer test would be admissible in a drunk driving case despite the fact that it had been taken without reasonable suspicion and without performing a preliminary roadside test as required by the statute.[103]

In the 1990 case of *George v. Rockett*,[104] however, the High Court finally did suppress evidence due to an unlawful search. In that case, police in Queensland obtained a search warrant based on a conclusory affidavit that simply related that the police had "reasonable grounds for suspicion" without setting forth the basis therefor. The High Court, sitting in its capacity as the highest court of the state of Queensland, held that the warrant was invalid and that the evidence must be suppressed. The Court ruled that the Queensland statute requiring "reasonable grounds" meant that such grounds must be set forth in the sworn affidavit so that the magistrate could satisfy himself that such grounds existed.[105] It seems likely that this holding, and particularly its repeated insistence that the terms of the statute must be followed, will lead trial judges to be substantially more receptive to the possibility of (discretionary) evidentiary exclusion in future cases involving illegal searches.

In the confessions area, in contrast to searches, no state has statutory rules governing interrogations and the law in this area has been extremely unclear. However, a recently enacted federal statute, the Crimes (Investigation of Commonwealth Offences) Act, 1991, will likely provide the basis for improved state procedures as well (if states choose to pass their own statutes using the federal statute as a model). The new statute provides that federal arrestees must be brought before a judicial officer within four hours of arrest, except that in felony cases a judge may extend the detention period to eight hours.[106] This codifies and makes mandatory the holding of the High Court in the 1986 case of *R. v. Williams*[107] in which the High Court upheld the trial judge's exercise of discretion in excluding the confession of a burglary suspect who had been arrested at 6:00 a.m. on one day and not taken to the magistrate until 10:00 a.m. the following day. *Williams* did not mandate exclusion in such a case, it simply approved the trial judge's discretionary exclusion. The combined effect of *Williams* and the statute will undoubtedly be more evidentiary exclusions in state courts on this ground than had previously been the case.

The statute goes on to require that the suspect must be informed of the right to communicate with a friend or relative and a lawyer and be allowed reasonable time to do so, and that the suspect's lawyer must be allowed to be present during questioning.[108] (This is in addition to the common law, "Judge's Rules," requirement that suspects be informed of their right to be silent and that anything they say may be used against them.)[109] However, unlike the case for England and Canada, it is not necessary for the police to inform suspects of the availability of a public defender, or that such a person even *be* available. This statute goes beyond the U.S. rules by requiring that a person under arrest must be informed if a friend, relative, or lawyer has sought information about him or her, and must provide that information to the other party unless the arrestee says not to.[110] Finally, all interviews by federal authorities must be tape recorded unless it is not reasonably practicable to do so, and, subject to this exception, untaped interviews are not admissible.[111]

In 1991 the High Court put heavy pressure on the states to adopt the tape recording requirement. In *McKinney v. R.*[112] the Court, by a 4–3 vote, held that where the (state) prosecutor seeks to use confessional evidence that is not tape recorded, the trial judge must warn the jury as to the ease with which the police might fabricate a statement that is not "reliably corroborated."[113] In this warning the court should "emphasise the need for careful scrutiny of the evidence and direct attention to the fact that police witnesses are often practised witnesses and it is not an easy matter to determine whether a practised witness is telling the truth."[114] Thus it seems that the Australian High Court, distressed by repeated allegations of police "verballing" (i.e., fabricating confessions), is determined to use any means at its disposal to stop the practice. Peter Waight reports that this case "has had the effect of putting the pressure on all Police Forces to tape/videotape interviews with suspects, and they seem to be doing this generally throughout Australia."[115]

In another important 1991 development the High Court held that silence, either during police interrogation or at trial, could not be used as evidence against a defendant.[116]

Recent developments suggest that Australia is joining the modern international trend of using statutory rules to govern the police, backed up by a mixed system of mandatory and discretionary evidentiary exclusion when the police break the statutory rules. Specifically, Australia now requires that the grounds for searches must be set forth, in advance, in writing, before a search warrant is issued, that arrestees must be fully informed of their rights before being questioned, and that police interrogations must be tape recorded if they are to be admissible in court.

The Australian experience is pertinent to this book for two reasons. First, it suggests that a "discretionary" exclusionary rule in a (partially) common law system, where the rules are often not precisely spelled out, is likely to be a failure. This conclusion is in stark contrast to the new British model, where, despite a long history of non-exclusion, the courts are actually using a discretionary rule to deter police misconduct. As the British courts have made clear, once the duties of the police are clearly defined by statute, the courts will no longer tolerate breaches of the rules as they had in the past. But where, as in the United States and Australia, the rules themselves are unclear, even a mandatory rule, as in the United States, will frequently result in the courts winking at police violations, as discussed in Chapter 3.

The second important point about Australia is that, there, "It is generally agreed" as the Australian Law Reform Commission has declared, "that what is needed is a *comprehensive code* setting out with as much particularity as possible the rights and duties of police, suspects and others concerned in the criminal investigation process."[117] Thus, Australia, despite its common law history and federal system, subscribes to the view, held everywhere but the United States, that rules governing police procedures should, if possible, be declared by a legislatively enacted code, rather than being developed case by case.

Finally, as noted, Australia appears to be joining in the international consensus as to the fundamental limits to be imposed on police searches and interrogations.

Canada

The basic principles of Canadian criminal procedure law are set forth in general terms in the 1982 Constitution's Charter of Rights and Freedoms, which is supplemented by a detailed Code. Pertinent to police procedures, the Charter states that:

> Everyone has the right to life, liberty and security of the person and the right not to be deprived thereof except in accordance with the principles of fundamental justice.[118]
> Everyone has the right to be secure against unreasonable search and seizure.[119]
> Everyone has the right not to be arbitrarily detained or imprisoned.[120]
> Everyone has the right on arrest or detention
> (a) to be informed promptly of the reasons therefor;

(b) to retain and instruct counsel without delay and to be informed of that right;

(c) to have the validity of the detention determined by way of *habeas corpus* and to be released if the detention is not lawful.[121]

Finally, the Charter declares an exclusionary rule:

where . . . a court finds that evidence was obtained in a manner that infringed or denied any of the rights or freedoms guaranteed by this Charter, the evidence shall be excluded if it is established that, having regard to all the circumstances, the admission of it in the proceedings would bring the administration of justice into disrepute.[122]

It is certainly interesting to note that, in adopting a new Charter of Rights, the Canadians chose not only to copy our fourth amendment virtually verbatim but also to adopt, as a constitutional requirement, the much maligned exclusionary rule, albeit in a more limited form.

The current Criminal Code (which is a code of both criminal law and procedure) was adopted in 1970, with substantial amendments in 1985.[123] It has been amended in various ways several times since then.[124] In Canada, all crimes are federal violations; so there is a single federal code governing the entire country.

As to searches, the Code provides for the issuance of a search warrant when a justice is satisfied by "information on oath" that there are reasonable grounds to believe that "there is in a building, receptacle or place," fruits, instrumentalities, or evidence of a crime.[125] Such prior authorization must be obtained "where feasible"[126] but may be done by radio or telephone.[127] The warrant must be executed by day unless the justice authorizes night execution.[128] A warrant is not required to search "a person, vehicle, or place other than a dwelling house," where the police have reasonable grounds to believe that an offense involving a weapon has been committed.[129]

Police do not need a warrant to effect an arrest for "an indictable offense" (except for certain theft and gambling offenses, for which a warrant must be used).[130] A warrant is not required to enter private premises to make an arrest,[131] nor to search a vehicle if there are "reasonable grounds for suspicion that the vehicle contains contraband."[132] The police may search the person and "immediate surroundings" of an accused incident to arrest, without any showing of cause beyond the arrest itself.[133] Immediately following a search incident, and prior to execution of a warrant or a consent search, the suspect must be informed of the rights to withhold consent and to counsel.[134]

Canadian law thus adopts a somewhat more police-oriented approach to searches than does U.S. law, allowing warrantless searches for offenses involving weapons, and warrantless entries to arrest, though the Canadian consent search rules are stricter.[135] By contrast, as to interrogations, Canadian law imposes, in some ways, stricter limitations on the police than does U.S. law.

Upon "arrest or detention," the suspect must be informed of the right to counsel. "The police must refrain from attempting to elicit evidence from the detainee until he has a reasonable opportunity to retain and instruct counsel."[136] "[D]etainees must be informed . . . of the existence and availability of the applicable systems of duty counsel and legal aid in the jurisdiction. . . ."[137] "Detention" occurs when the person "submits or acquiesces in the deprivation of liberty and reasonably believes the choice to do otherwise does not exist." Thus traffic stops constitute "detention," but the warnings are still not required if provincial legislation authorizing such stops allows them without warnings. Such legislation has been held to be a "reasonable limit prescribed by law" under §1* of the Charter.[138] "Detention" did occur, and the warnings were required, when an accused was "ushered into an interview room by customs officers who suspected he was carrying narcotics."[139] However, unlike the *Edwards* rule in the United States, the Canadian rules do not give the defendant any right to have counsel present during questioning (after consultation has been allowed). The Canadian Supreme Court has specifically invited police to attempt to "persuade" a counseled suspect to confess, "short of denying the suspect the right to choose or depriving him of an operating mind."[140]

Canadian police normally give the British Judges' Rules caution that the suspect has the right to silence and that "whatever you do say may be given in evidence," which appears on the standard form issued to police.[141] In the 1990 case of *R. v. Hebert*[142] the Supreme Court of Canada assumed that the right to silence included a warning as to that right, holding that "the most important function of legal advice upon detention is to ensure that the accused understands his rights, chief among which is the right to silence."[143] The Court went on to hold that, after a suspect had asserted his right to silence, an incriminating statement coaxed from the suspect by a police officer posing as a fellow prisoner must be excluded. (The Court further observed that statements made to passive undercover agents or to real prisoners who are not police agents, or overheard by a listening device, would still be admissible.)[144]

*Section 1 of the Charter provides that "The Canadian Charter of Rights and Freedoms guarantees the rights and freedoms set out in it subject only to such reasonable limits prescribed by law as can be demonstrably justified in a free and democratic society."

Thus Canada, like England, exceeds U.S. standards by requiring that the police inform detainees about the availability of free counsel and tries to ensure that detainees actually receive counsel when they ask for it, rather than simply mandating that questioning must cease.[145] Moreover, Canada requires the warnings at the onset of any arrest or detention (subject to the traffic stop exception mentioned above), rather than only prior to custodial interrogation.[146] However, neither Canada nor England has the equivalent of the U.S. rule forbidding questioning of a suspect after a request for counsel.

As noted above, the Charter sets forth a discretionary exclusionary rule to be exercised when admitting the evidence would bring the administration of justice into disrepute. The Supreme Court of Canada, in *Collins v. R.*,[147] held that this exclusionary authority should "rarely" be applied to real, as opposed to confessional, evidence, but did order exclusion in *Collins*, where the police had applied a chokehold on the subject of a search for narcotics. The Court emphasized that the purpose of the rule was not to discipline the police but to avoid "disrepute" as the Charter requires. In *R. v. Dyment*[148] the Supreme Court reversed a conviction, on the grounds of unreasonable search, where a doctor at the hospital where the suspect was being treated in connection with an automobile accident collected a sample of free-flowing blood from the suspect, without a warrant or consent, which was used to prove drunken driving. The Court noted that a "violation of the sanctity of a person's body is much more serious than that of his office or even of his home."[149]

The 1989 case of *Genest v. R.*[150] is of particular interest. There, acting pursuant to a warrant that was defective in that, inter alia, it did not specify the objects to be searched for, the police made an illegal no-knock entry into the suspect's house. The Court ruled the search unreasonable and the evidence suppressed. Though admission of the evidence did not render the trial unfair, the non-technical defects in the warrant and its execution were such that use of the evidence would bring the administration of justice into disrepute.[151] Despite the disclaimers of the Canadian Supreme Court that the purpose of exclusion is not to discipline the police, this case seems to have that effect. To the same effect is *Kokesch v. R.*,[152] where evidence of marijuana was suppressed, by a 4–3 vote of the Supreme Court, because a trespass onto the curtilage of the suspect's property provided grounds (inter alia, the odor of marijuana) for a search warrant.[153] Because the conduct of the police constituted a violation of clear statutory rules, the majority deemed it "egregious," despite the lack of any bad faith or physical force by the police.

The Canadian courts are stricter when it comes to breaches of the interrogation requirements. The reasoning is that "where, after a violation of the Charter, the accused is conscripted against himself through a confession or other evidence emanating from him, [t]he use of such evidence would render the trial unfair for it did not exist before the violation and strikes at one of the fundamental tenets of a fair trial, the right against self-incrimination."[154] This distinction seems a strange one unless it is really based on reliability concerns. Why should evidence obtained by an unreasonable search be admitted when evidence obtained by no more unreasonable interrogation techniques will not be?[155] Only, it would seem, if the latter evidence is suspected of being unreliable. However, the Supreme Court of Canada, has not declared this to be the reason for the distinction. Whether justified or not, this distinction is the stated basis for a tough-minded attitude by the Supreme Court toward police violations in the confessions area.

For example, in *R. v. Manninen*[156] the Supreme Court upheld a lower court's reversal of a conviction of a suspect who, after being informed of his rights to silence and counsel stated: "I ain't saying anything without my lawyer."[157] The police then questioned him further, inducing an incriminating response. The Court held that §10(b) of the Charter of Rights imposes a duty on police to afford suspects a reasonable opportunity to contact counsel and "to cease questioning or otherwise attempting to elicit evidence from the detainee until he has had a reasonable opportunity to retain and instruct counsel."[158]

In *R. v. Black*[159] the suspect asked for a lawyer when originally questioned and talked to her lawyer on the telephone. Later, when the victim of the suspect's knife attack died, the suspect was again informed of her right to counsel and said she wanted to speak to her lawyer. The police tried several times to contact her lawyer, but were unsuccessful. The suspect refused to try to contact another lawyer. The police then questioned her about the crime. She confessed and led them to the knife. The Supreme Court excluded the confession, and the circumstances of finding the knife (but not the knife itself, because it was "real" evidence), for the same reason as in *Manninen*.[160]

In *Amyot v. R*[161] the suspect was given the appropriate warnings and was asked to submit to a polygraph exam. Without consulting his lawyer he agreed to do so. After the test, he was informed that he had failed and, after further discussion, he made an incriminating declaration. The Quebec Court of Appeal reversed the conviction and ordered the statement suppressed, holding that the questioning of the suspect by the polygraphist after telling him he had failed was a "breach of trust . . . an example of intimidation, coercion, and undue pressure."[162] It was also a breach of his right to counsel because he was not rewarned after he became a suspect.

Finally, in *R. v. Ross*[163] a lineup identification was suppressed by the Supreme Court when the accused was made to participate without having been informed of his opportunity to consult with counsel (who could have told him that he had no legal obligation to appear in the lineup). The Court held that the identification was evidence "emanating from" the accused, as discussed in *Collins*.[164]

The Canadian system is, in a sense, the mirror image of the American. Whereas in the United States, the rules are muddled but the exclusionary formula is clear (i.e., if the rules have been broken the evidence is always excluded),* in Canada, the rules are relatively clear (at least in those areas of the law where there are codified rules), but the exclusionary requirement is, intentionally, unclear. The decision whether to exclude is left up to the trial court. However, unlike German and Australian practices, the discretionary exclusionary rule is regularly invoked, so, even if its purpose is not to deter police misconduct, it nevertheless surely has that effect.

The Canadian Code itself tends to be written in more technical language than the British PACE. Consequently, it is a less useful model for U.S. emulation. More troublesome yet is that it is not comprehensive. Instead, the Canadian system is a cross between ours and the British, with the Code spelling out some things, such as search warrant requirements,[165] and leaving other matters, such as searches incident to arrest, to be governed by judicial interpretation of the Charter.[166] Thus Canada is of interest, not because of its particular code, but because of its at least partial acceptance of the principle that a code is the way to go, that rules can be developed in advance rather than case by case, and that a discretionary, but frequently applied, exclusionary rule is the appropriate check on police misbehavior. Canada's adoption of *Miranda*-type warnings is also of interest.

France

French law recognizes three levels of crime: felonies, punishable by five years imprisonment or more, delicts, punishable by two months to five years imprisonment, and contraventions, punishable by no more than two months imprisonment.[167] A "flagrant" felony or delict is one that is in the process of being committed or has recently been

---

*Well, almost always. See *United States v. Leon* 468 U.S. 897 (1984) (good faith exception to the exclusionary rule in search warrant cases); *Illinois v. Krull* 480 U.S. 340 (1987) (reliance on statute later declared unconstitutional).

committed.[168] According to Richard Frase, the translator of the French Code, in such "flagrant" cases the code permits the authorities to

(1) search the scene of the offense and seize any evidence found there; (2) search the domicile of all persons who appear to have participated in the offense or be in possession of evidence and seize any evidence "useful to the manifestation of the truth"; (3) designate experts to conduct scientific or technical examinations; (4) detain persons on the scene until completion of the investigation; (5) summon (by force, if necessary) and interrogate (not under oath) any persons capable of furnishing evidence; and (6) place witnesses and suspects in investigatory detention for up to twenty-four hours (which can be extended to forty-eight hours with the approval of the prosecuting attorney).[169]

These search and detention powers are subject to a number of procedural safeguards. For example, house searches must respect professional secrets and the "rights of the defense" and must be witnessed by persons independent of the searching authorities; investigatory detention reports must include the dates and times of interrogation, rest, and release, and document that the detainee was advised of his right to a medical examination. On the other hand, there is apparently no particular legal standard (analogous to common law probable cause) governing where an officer may look for evidence of the offense.* Nor is there any right to counsel (or even right to silence warning) during the police interrogation, which normally takes place during investigatory detention (or at lineups).[170] Moreover, violation of the durational or other limitations on such detentions has not been found to require exclusion of the resulting confession,[171] (but violations of the rights of defense in other contexts may lead to exclusion.)[172]

In the absence of a "flagrant" offense, the investigation is, in theory, conducted by an independent magistrate (*juge d'instruction*)[173] with the police relegated to conducting only a preliminary, non-coercive, investigation in which searches for and seizures of evidence may only be done on written consent of the party affected and detention for interrogation is not allowed.† Thomas Weigand reports, however,

---

*But, as discussed below, searches of domiciles may not be undertaken on mere suspicion.

†However, a suspect who appears "voluntarily" at the police station, or is already there for some other reason, can be placed in investigatory detention for twenty-four or forty-eight hours as with "flagrant" offenses. Richard Frase, "Introduction" to *The French Code of Criminal Procedure*, 11. "Discreet allusion to the possibility of [such detention] appears often to induce garrulity in suspects and witnesses." Thomas Weigand, "Continental Cures for American Ailments," 381, 391.

that in one year only 14 percent of eligible cases were referred to the magistrate. In the other cases the police were able to obtain "voluntary" cooperation from the suspect because people were unaware of their rights or "hesitant to refuse to answer questions or otherwise obstruct police investigations lest they create or augment suspicion against themselves."[174] In those cases that are investigated by the magistrate, the magistrate has "broad discretion to issue arrest and detention orders and undertake 'all acts of investigation (including electronic surveillance) that he deems useful to the manifestation of the truth.'"[175] Furthermore, the magistrate may, and frequently does, delegate some of this investigatory authority back to the police,[176] (not including the power to issue arrest warrants or to interrogate suspects).[177]

At interrogations, which must be conducted by the magistrate, the accused must be informed of the rights to counsel and silence.[178] Failure to warn will generally result in exclusion of any statement, but not necessarily of its fruits.[179]

Finally, French law provides for identity checks, at which people are required to produce their identification papers, which need not be based on individualized suspicion, need not require any suspicion of danger for a weapons frisk, and can last up to four hours.[180]

Even these lenient rules are often ignored because, as Walter Pakter reports, they are not generally backed up with an exclusionary sanction:

French police frequently disregard Code provisions concerning the preconditions and duration of the *garde à vue* [detention for interrogation]. Most scholars have urged that courts use exclusion for Code violations; however, the Court of Cassation has consistently limited relief to individual criminal and civil actions against the police. This relief is illusory because penal sanctions for police violence have been restrictively interpreted by the courts. Furthermore, actions against the police are time consuming, expensive, and difficult to prosecute.

*   *   *   *

Administrative controls within the police department, such as promotion incentives, may prevent gross abuses of detainees. Nevertheless, the primary concern of the police is to solve crimes, and they are unlikely to pay more attention to civil liberties than the courts.

*   *   *   *

[D]etainees in France are generally treated far worse than suspects held by United States or German police interrogators.[181]

The Code's very limited restrictions on searches, such as that searches of attorneys' offices may only be carried out by a magistrate[182] and that searches may not generally be carried out at night,[183] are enforced by mandatory exclusion.[184] Other violations lead to exclusion "only if they violate 'substantial' provisions of the Code, especially 'the rights of the defense,'"[185] these rights being only loosely specified.*

In 1980 the Court of Cassation ordered the exclusion of a confession that had been obtained following a warrantless search based on mere suspicion, establishing the principle that such a search "may not be justified by mere pre-search suspicion or post-search evidence."[186] Since this decision, Pakter reports that "the Court of Cassation has reaffirmed exclusion for search and seizure violations and lower courts have excluded evidence even for good faith violations of the . . . Code."[187] Unauthorized wiretaps also may lead to evidentiary exclusion.[188]

France has a much more homogeneous population than the United States and a better trained, nationally organized police force.[189] Consequently it seems to get by with a loosely structured criminal procedure system. The French Code of Criminal Procedure (*Code de Procédure Criminal*) dates back to 1958, though it has been amended since. Whether French procedures are acceptable for France is difficult to say at this remove, though many French authorities think they are not.[190] The procedures are clearly not in keeping with the modern international trend of a detailed code of police procedure backed up by a discretionary, but frequently invoked, exclusionary rule to ensure that the police follow the rules. Thomas Weigand reports that "reform of criminal procedure is very much on the agenda in France" and a "semi-official" commission has recommended major reforms in a 1991 report.[191]

Germany

The German Code of Criminal Procedure (*Strafprozessordnung*) was introduced in 1877 and most recently repromulgated in 1975.[192] It is more detailed, and places more restrictions on the police, than

---

*Frase describes the "rights of the defense" as "a vaguely defined group of procedural guarantees, often not based on any particular Code provision, which are deemed to be implicit in principles of justice and equity. Violations . . . do not necessarily lead to exclusion of evidentiary "fruits" and . . . usually require a strong showing of prejudice to the defendant's interests." Frase, "Comparative Criminal Justice as a Guide to American Law Reform," 586 n. 254.

does the French code, but is relatively undemanding by modern standards.[193]

For example, the dwelling and person of anyone "suspected" of a crime may be searched by the police "for the purpose of apprehending such person or if it may be presumed that such search will lead to the discovery of evidence."[194] Although Article 13 of the Constitution (*Grundgesetz*) provides that searches may be ordered only by a judge, that article and the Code permit searches to be ordered "by the prosecution and its auxiliary officials" (the police) if there is "danger in delay."[195] Under the Code, search warrants need not be in any particular form, need not be grounded on probable cause or any particular evidentiary showing (merely "suspicion"), and may be given orally, or simply dispensed with, if there is danger in delay.

However, in a dramatic (by German standards) new development, the Constitutional (highest) Court has "interpreted" the Code to require more. To search the home of a suspect, the Code, as noted, requires only mere suspicion ("*verdächtig*").[196] This is in contrast to searches of the homes of third persons, in which case a higher standard (which sounds like our probable cause), "facts upon which it may be concluded that evidence may be found," must be set forth.[197] However, in the Decision* of September 3, 1991,[198] the Constitutional (Highest) Court rejected a warrant that simply declared that the police wanted to search the suspect's home "on suspicion of murder,"[199] without setting forth the grounds for the suspicion, and ordered the evidence to be excluded. (This wording was typical on warrant applications prior to this time.[200]) The Court declared that the warrant violated the constitutional protection of the "free development of the personality"[201] as well as Article 13, discussed above. Specifically, the warrant was defective in that it did not set forth details of the offense suspected and did not specify the nature of the evidence to be sought or define the areas to be searched narrowly enough.[202] Such specificity is necessary so that the magistrate can make an independent judgment as to whether the intrusion into the suspect's "private sphere" occasioned by the search and seizure is proportional to the crime suspected.[203]

While the decision stops short of requiring more than mere suspicion to justify a search, its implication is that something more akin to the factual showing required to search non-suspects is now required. Anything less would, in the usual case, make it difficult for

---

*German cases are cited by date and have no other name, though sometimes they develop an informal name in subsequent discussion (e.g., the "Diary Case"). A Judgment has a stronger precedential effect than a "Decision."

the magistrate to make an "independent" judgment declaring the search consistent with the constitutional principle of proportionality. Moreover, since the Constitutional Court excluded the evidence in this case, it demonstrated its willingness to back up its pronouncements with meaningful remedies. This is in contrast to the frequent past practice of declaring a search illegal but then admitting the evidence anyway.[204]

In addition to this recent development, the German Constitution imposes other restrictions on the criminal justice system. It

> affords a fair trial before a legally appointed and independent judge in which constitutional guarantees are observed; specifically the dignity of the person, the right to free development of the personality, the freedom of the person, the equality before the law . . . as well as the prohibition against inhumane treatment.[205]

In addition, the *Rechtsstaatsprinzip* (principle of a just state—similar to our due process requirement) forbids police brutality and deceit both in the seizure of evidence[206] and in interrogations.[207]

Although evidence must be excluded if the seizure itself was in violation of the *Rechtsstaatsprinzip*,[208] regardless of its probative value or the seriousness of the crime under investigation,[209] the practical effect of this broad exclusion is limited by the fact that the German courts have analyzed searches and seizures separately. Thus, in a case in which a search order violated the *Rechtsstaatsprinzip* because it failed to specify the crime being investigated and the evidence sought, this constitutional defect alone did not lead to suppression of the evidence seized pursuant to the order.[210] Instead, the seizure was evaluated independently of the illegal search to determine whether it had been accomplished through brutality or deceit.[211] The court reasoned that the question of the validity of the search itself was not properly presented,[212] because the seizure was the actual source of the evidence.[213] As a result, unconstitutional seizures (i.e., seizures achieved through brutality or deceit) will lead directly to suppression,[214] whereas unconstitutional searches and merely illegal seizures (those that violate the rules of criminal procedure) will not necessarily have that effect.[215]

However, as noted above, the Decision of September 3, 1991, which involved not a seizure accomplished by brutality or deceit but rather a defective search warrant, seems to be changing the German approach and mandating exclusion as a remedy for police misconduct for *either* search or seizure violations.

The second relevant constitutional principle is that of *Verhältnismäs-*

sigkeit (principle of proportionality).[216] Under this doctrine, the methods used in fighting crime must be proportional to the "seriousness of the offense and the strength of the suspicion"[217] as well as to the constitutional interests at stake; thus, what would be appropriate in some cases may not be justifiable in others. The courts also employ a form of "least drastic means" analysis when assessing police actions under the principle of proportionality: if less intrusive measures will suffice, a greater intrusion will not be permitted.[218] This approach is illustrated by the federal constitutional court's Judgment of June 10, 1963,[219] in which taking spinal fluid from a suspect to determine his possible insanity, though generally authorized by the code of Criminal Procedure,[220] was held to be out of proportion to the misdemeanor charge against him.[221] The warrant application in the 1991 case was also held to violate the principle of proportionality because it did not give the magistrate sufficient information to determine whether the search was a proportional measure.[222]

German courts therefore engage in a two-step analysis when addressing constitutionally based challenges to the use of evidence. First, the court determines whether the evidence at issue was seized or obtained in violation of the *Rechtsstaatsprinzip*. In cases in which there is a violation, the judiciary must exclude the evidence to preserve the purity of the judicial process (*Reinheit des Verfahrens*).[223] If the evidence is not excluded in the first step, the court then considers the principle of proportionality. Weighing the appropriate factors, the court decides whether to use the evidence in question. If the court determines that the individual privacy rights of the accused outweigh society's interest in having all relevant evidence presented,[224] the evidence will be excluded. The legality of the seizure is not necessarily dispositive on this issue.

The mechanics of the German system are demonstrated by three cases in which the courts excluded a diary,[225] a tape recording of a private conversation,[226] and the files of a drug rehabilitation clinic[227] on the ground that use of the evidence in court would violate the privacy rights of the defendant. The courts reached these results even though the legality of the seizures was conceded in the first two cases. In the Diary Case [228] the federal court of appeals considered whether the defendant's diary was properly admissible in a perjury trial. The police had been given the diary by the wife of the defendant's lover, in whose home it had been concealed. Applying the balancing test required by the principle of proportionality, the court reversed the defendant's conviction on the ground that using the defendant's private diary against her in court violated her privacy rights under articles 1 and 2 of the Constitution.[229] The court emphasized, however, that the mere fact that the defendant's privacy rights were implicated did not automatically require exclusion, and stressed that exclusion was appropriate in this instance because the gravity of the intrusion outweighed the minor nature of the criminal charge. The court suggested that criminals' diary entries concerning their felonies, or foreign agents' entries concerning their spying activities, would not be protected,* because the interests of the state in prosecuting the offense would outweigh the privacy interests of the defendant.[230] Similarly, business papers that did not expose the personality of the author would not be excluded, because there would not be a privacy interest to weigh against the state's interest in securing the admissibility of all relevant evidence.[231]

This case illustrates some of the differences in the operation of exclusionary rules between Germany and the United States. In the United States the diary would have been admissible because it was obtained without police misconduct,[232] whereas a gun obtained pursuant to a defective search warrant would have been excluded.[233] In contrast, the diary was excluded in Germany, whereas an illegally seized gun would be admissible because its use would not interfere with the free development of the defendant's personality. Only a brutal or deceitful seizure that violated the defendant's most fundamental constitutional rights under the *Rechsstaatsprinzip* would result in excluding a gun. A diary is subject to different treatment, however, because its use in court constitutes a harsh incursion into an individual's personal privacy, whether or not the evidence is legally obtained.†

By excluding a legally seized diary but holding that diaries or other private personal papers may be used as evidence in prosecutions of more serious crimes, the court in the Diary Case gave the police little guidance in deciding when such documents should be seized. As the case indicates, the admissibility of all evidence—unless seized in violation of the *Rechtsstaatsprinzip* or a statute requiring exclusion—is open to consideration by the court, which decides on an ad hoc basis

---

*Indeed, in 1989, the Constitutional Court affirmed, by an equally divided court, the conviction of a murderer whose legally obtained, diary-like notes were used against him. Judgment of Sept. 14, 1989, BVerfG, 2 BvR 1062.

†A recent reaffirmation of the Diary Case may be found in the Judgment of January 4, 1988 by the supreme court of Saarbrucken, 5 Qs 149. In that case, the police, acting pursuant to a search warrant, seized the diaries of the defendant's "girlfriend," who, unbeknownst to the police, had become his wife, at the apartment where they both lived. The court held that the diary would not be admissible against either of them because the seizure violated the constitutional principle of "free development of the personality."

whether to admit or exclude. Thus the purpose of the German exclusionary rule is not to deter police misconduct.[234] Instead, through balancing, the rule operates to maximize privacy interests consistently
with society's interest in prosecuting serious crimes.[235]

To similar effect is the Judgment of January 31, 1973,[236] in which
the federal constitutional court (the highest German court) excluded
a tape recording of the planning of a fraud that had been made by
one of the parties to the transaction and turned over voluntarily to
the police. The court held that use of taped conversations in court
intruded upon the "private sphere" of the individual and such recordings would only be admissible in the event of an overriding public
interest, which was not present here. While the court held that the
tape recording was not admissible in this fraud prosecution, it noted
that the result might have been different had the tape been evidence
of a crime of violence.[237]

Finally, in the Judgment of May 24, 1977,[238] the constitutional court
held that the records of a narcotics treatment center could not be
used when they were obtained during an unwarranted "fishing expedition" by the police. However, the court again cautioned that in an
investigation of a serious crime, or a properly limited search for specific narcotics violations, seizure and use of such records might be
appropriate.[239]

In a 1985 article reviewing German exclusionary law, especially the
Judgment of March 17, 1983,[240] in which the federal appeals court
excluded evidence when an unlawful wiretap was used in combination with deception, Walter Pakter concluded that "Recent decisions indicate that the BGH (federal appeals court) now recognizes
that illegal searches by the police occur, and the current trend is to
expand the use of exclusion to deter misconduct by police or other
state officials."[241] But while this may be the "trend" in Germany, such
exclusionary decisions are still too rare to have a consistent impact on
police behavior, and the disciplining of police is explicitly not the basis
for evidentiary exclusion.[242] This is especially true because a decision
by the trial court "excluding" evidence does not mean that the fact
finders (a mixed panel of judges and private citizens) do not find out
about the excluded evidence. Rather, knowing of it, they are enjoined
to disregard it, and the evidence cannot be used to support the statement of reasons that must accompany each judgment to the appellate
court. This arrangement obviously tends to dilute the impact of any
exclusionary rules.[243] Nevertheless, the Decision of September 3, 1991,
does seem to reinforce Pakter's view.

In the confessions area, §136 of the Code of Criminal Procedure
provides that, prior to any questioning in court,

the accused shall be informed of the act with which he is charged and of the applicable penal provisions. It shall be pointed out to him that the law grants him the right to respond to the accusation, or not to answer regarding the charge, and at all times, even before his examination, to consult with defense counsel of his choice.

Although this section does not apply, on its face, to police interrogations, the federal appeals court has held that the police are required to give these warnings.[244] However, until 1992, exclusion by the trial judge of a confession obtained after a failure to give the warnings was not required.[245] In the important Decision of February 27, 1992[246] the Fifth Senate of the Federal Court of Appeals (BGH), in an opinion subscribed to by other Senates[247] (and thus, apparently, the final word on the subject), changed this. Citing *Miranda v. Arizona* and noting that Britain, France,* Denmark, Italy, and the Netherlands also have a mandatory exclusionary rule for such violations, the Court declared that if the interrogation of an accused by the police has not been preceded by the section 136 warnings "the admissions may not be used."[248] Only minor exceptions, such as where the accused already was aware of his or her rights, were discussed, so the exclusionary rule appears to be mandatory. Also, the warning requirement applies "before [the subject] is questioned as an accused."[249] Thus going further than *Miranda* it applies to all interrogations, without regard to whether the suspect is "in custody" or not. Finally, also going further than the United States Supreme Court, the German Code requires that the suspect must be accurately informed of the crime with which he or she is being charged.[250]

In addition to the warning requirement, §136a of the Code provides that

The freedom of the accused to determine and to exercise his will shall not be impaired by ill-treatment, by fatigue, by physical interference, by dispensing medicines, by torture, by deception or by hypnosis. . . . Statements which were obtained in violation of these prohibitions may not be used even if the accused agrees to such use.

Thus, in the Judgment of May 31, 1990,[251] the BGH excluded a confession from an accused who had been informed that the police were investigating a "missing person" report when, in fact, they had already found the body and were investigating a murder. However, subsequent statements, made after the accused had been informed of the true nature of the investigation, were admissible. Similarly, earlier

---

*The German Court correctly noted, as discussed above, that the warning requirement in France applies only to judicial, not police, interrogations.

cases had excluded confessions where an accused confessed after being arrested at 5:00 a.m. and deprived of sleep for thirty hours,[252] and where the accused had been confronted with the corpse of his three-year-old son, whom he was accused of murdering.[253] By the same token, according to Walter Pakter, "arbitrary prolongations of arrest and mistreatment of suspects are no longer considered a problem. . . . [A]ny statement obtained [after the permitted 24 hour time limit on detentions][254] would be excluded under §136(a)."[255]

In conclusion, Germany, in common with the growing international trend, has a fairly detailed code of procedure that generally requires search warrants and *Miranda*-type warnings prior to interrogation. Moreover, the Germans are increasingly using evidentiary exclusion as a means of enforcing the mandates of the Code.

Italy

In 1989 Italy adopted a new code of criminal procedure to replace the Fascist-inspired *Codice Rocco* that, with many alterations and amendments, had been in effect for fifty years.[256] The new code contains 746 articles that cover the entire criminal process from investigation to appeals.[257] In general, the thrust of the Code has been to transform Italy's criminal justice system from the inquisitorial to the accusatorial model and to codify "many aspects of the American Supreme Court's 'criminal procedure revolution' of the 1960's."[258] Because the Code has apparently not yet been translated into English, I have had to rely on the commentators, particularly Lawrence Fassler's 1991 article in the *Columbia Journal of Transnational Law*.[259]

Concerning police procedures, under the new Code, frisks may be made only of persons caught in flagrante delicto, or pursuant to an arrest warrant.[260] Warrantless searches of specific places may only be performed under three circumstances: of the crime scene when a person is caught *in flagrante delicto* or when an arrest warrant has been issued, or of other places when delay would prejudice the case.[261] There is a major exception, however, that has the effect of swallowing up much of the rule: police may also perform warrantless searches of places where weapons are thought to be hidden. "In practice, this distinction allows police to search domiciles for contraband or evidence of other non-weapons-related crimes as long as the search is ostensibly undertaken to look for weapons. . . ."[262] (Presumably it also allows frisks for weapons even when the suspect is not caught red-handed.) However, this power is limited to "cases of necessity and urgency,"[263] so the Italian courts may, in theory at least, exclude evidence found when the police cannot make such a showing.

The interrogation rules, in contrast to the search restrictions, are extremely stringent:

Statements taken from an interrogation of a suspect without a defense attorney present cannot be recorded or used during the judicial proceeding itself though the police may act on such statements for the immediate continuation of the investigation.[264]

Persons who begin to make incriminating statements before being officially put under investigation must be interrupted, cautioned that such declarations might cause investigations to turn against [them] and invited to nominate an attorney.[265]

Statements made without an attorney present may not even be used to impeach.[266] The only circumstance under which a suspect's confession may be used in the prosecution's case-in-chief is when it is made to the prosecutor, with the attorney present.[267] Thus not only has Italy, in essence, adopted the *Miranda* warnings, it has completely barred confessions from the trial unless the confession is given in the attorney's presence.* This situation seems extreme, and raises concerns that the courts will find ways to get around strict enforcement of the rules. If Italy is concerned about the police falsifying or forcing confessions, a tape recording requirement similar to Australia's would largely eliminate the first concern and help to alleviate the second.

In addition to a right to counsel at any interrogation, the suspect has a right to counsel during the suspect's "confrontation with witnesses or codefendants, scientific tests . . . [and] finally, when physical examinations, searches or seizures are required."[268] This right can be avoided by the police only if "justified urgency" requires them to proceed without counsel being present.[269]

Finally, and most significantly, the code expressly provides that "Evidence acquired in violation of prohibitions established by law cannot be utilized [in court]."[270] Unfortunately, because of the newness of the code, the Italian experience with this, the first far-reaching mandatory exclusionary rule outside the United States,[271] has not yet been reported in English. Because of the broad "weapons" exception to the warrant requirement discussed above, Fassler concludes that the code's exclusionary rule "is best considered as a prohibition against illegally coerced testimonial evidence."[272] However, this may prove to be an underestimation of the exclusionary rule's impact, since requiring counsel at the various stages of the investigation listed above, absent "justified urgency," also seems ripe for police violation and hence exclusionary sanction.

---

*Statements made to the police, with the defense attorney present, may be used only to impeach, not in the prosecution's case-in-chief.

There is some tradition of evidentiary exclusion under the old code. The inadmissibility of uncounseled confessions, for example, was established in 1974.[273] In 1985, Pakter declared that "exclusion plays a central role in Italian law in controlling police interrogations."[274] The police are permitted to seek, and may use, statements made before counsel arrives for investigatory purposes, but the statements themselves are inadmissible in court and excluded from the dossier.[275] Statements made without warnings as to silence and counsel are "unusable in any way."[276] That is, even evidence derived from unwarned, as opposed to uncounseled, statements is inadmissible.[277] As to searches, in contrast to the German courts, which distinguish the illegal search from the seizure and only exclude automatically if the latter is performed inappropriately, the Italian Court of Cassation has held:

Once the nullity of a search has been ascertained on the basis of [the Code] the consequences cannot be avoided. That is, if the act of the search was void, the efficacy of the seizure is no longer discussable, and thus the evidence gained from the seizure cannot be used.[278]

Thus Italy, with the most recent recodification of the countries studied, stands as an important example of the fact not only that other countries consider a code to be the way to declare rules, and use an exclusionary rule to deter police violations, but that limitations on the police as strong, and in some cases stronger, than those imposed by the Warren Court are sometimes deemed appropriate.

Conclusion

Four trends stand out from the comparative analysis in this chapter. First, these six countries, unlike the United States, agree that declaring criminal procedure rules is, at least primarily, the province of the legislative not the judicial branch. Second, in most of them *Miranda*-type warnings are required prior to interrogation; if the U.S. requirement of such warnings was once aberrational, that is no longer the case. Third, exclusionary remedies are finding increasing favor as a means of deterring police breaches of the rules. Fourth, these exclusionary remedies tend, except in the case of coerced confessions, to be discretionary, rather than mandatory, as in the United States, but to be enforced often enough, at least in Canada and England, and increasingly in Germany and, perhaps Italy and Australia, to have an impact on the police.

The United States has developed criminal procedure rules that, as even the Supreme Court's fondest admirers must admit, are unclear.

Then those rules are backed up with a mandatory exclusion policy whenever a violation is found. It is hardly surprising that this system causes great consternation among both liberals and conservatives. Liberals criticize the courts, with ample justification, for ignoring the rules (or, in the case of the Supreme Court, watering them down) in order to avoid suppressing evidence. Conservatives criticize the courts, again with ample justification, for excluding evidence in cases of technical and unimportant violations by the police, or, even worse, in cases where "if the Chief Justice were riding in the back of the police car" he could not have definitively told the police what to do.

It seems that the other countries may have it right. Develop, either directly through the legislature or by a legislatively appointed body, a comprehensive set of rules, all of which may be enforced with the exclusionary remedy so that the police are encouraged to obey them. Then, use that remedy often, but only when, on balance, the use of the evidence would be unfair, or bring the administration of justice into disrepute. The clearer the rules that the police are supposed to follow, the more likely it is that their failure to follow them will bring the administration of justice into disrepute. Thus, on the admittedly frequent occasions when the statutory rules do not give the police clear guidance, evidentiary exclusion would ordinarily be inappropriate, but when the rules are clear, evidentiary exclusion would be the norm, at least for violations of non-technical rules.

Because excluding evidence interferes with the truth-seeking process, the goal of any exclusionary remedy should be to achieve maximum deterrence with minimum actual evidentiary exclusion. It is far better to do this openly, by only excluding evidence when the breach by the police is serious, than to do it surreptitiously, by ignoring police violations, or by claiming that what appeared to be a violation actually was not, and in the process watering down the rules for future cases.

My experiences in Germany in 1982 and Australia in 1989 had led me to believe that a "discretionary" exclusionary rule was no exclusionary rule—a remedy that was paid lip service by the courts but was not seriously enforced, and hence had no substantial impact on police behavior. However, my study of the British and Canadian systems, as well as recent developments in Italy, and in Germany and Australia themselves, has convinced me that a discretionary system can work as long as it is based on clear, codified rules and taken seriously by the courts, particularly the nation's highest court. I see no reason to believe that U.S. courts, with a thirty-year tradition of evidentiary exclusion to deter police misconduct, could not be trusted to apply a discretionary rule rigorously, just as British and Canadian courts, with no such tradition, seem to have done.

It should also be noted that this proposal is not based on unqualified admiration of the systems studied. On the contrary, only England (and possibly Italy) has a code that is comprehensive enough to serve as a meaningful model for a U.S. code, and the English Code is much too complicated.* Moreover, it is obvious that most of the countries studied have been heavily influenced by the innovations of the United States Supreme Court. The widespread requirement of pre-interrogation warnings and the increasing use of an exclusionary remedy to deter police misconduct have clearly been influenced by American developments. But just as these countries were willing to learn from us, so should we be willing to learn from them.

I realize that the suggestion of a discretionary or limited exclusionary rule is contrary to the thrust, and indeed the plea, in other parts of this book that any changes in a newly adopted code of procedure should be aimed at clarifying and simplifying the rules, not at changing their ideological content. This suggestion seems to be a major shift in a conservative direction from the current system. As indicated in the preceding paragraphs, it is not so clear that such a shift would actually occur if a discretionary rule were adopted. As I found in a study of fourth amendment cases in state courts,[279] police violations of procedural rules are frequently swept under the rug by U.S. courts, in part, presumably, because the courts know that condemning the police will necessarily lead to exclusion. If the two questions "Was there a violation?" and "Must the evidence be suppressed?" were separate, the law as to what constitutes a violation could be clarified and expanded since police misconduct could be criticized without the "criminal [necessarily] going free." Moreover, as the British experience in particular suggests, a discretionary exclusionary rule, or a mandatory rule limited to violations of clear code provisions, does not necessarily lead to the courts' winking at police rulebreaking.

Thus a switch to a non-mandatory exclusionary rule would in most cases lead to the same result (non-exclusion) as the current "mandatory" but not consistently enforced rule does.† Still, such a proposal is, in theory, a major departure from current law. Consequently, if I were actually drafting legislation to be approved by Congress, I might not include this suggestion. As a matter of public interest, by contrast, as well as a predictor of possible developments in the Supreme Court,

---

*As noted earlier, I have not read the Italian code and thus cannot comment on its quality.

†Such a switch only makes sense if it accompanies a comprehensive code that more clearly spells out the rights and duties of both police and citizenry. Our current confusing rules too easily lend themselves to legitimate police confusion, and hence, to discretionary non-exclusion.

the uniform practice of other countries in this regard cannot be ignored.

Notes

1. Vaughan Bevan and Ken Lidstone, *The Investigation of Crime: A Guide to Police Powers*, 1.
2. *Report of the Royal Commission on Criminal Procedure*.
3. Cf. Leslie Curtis, "Policing the Streets," 95 (too restrictive of law enforcement) with David Ashby, "Safeguarding the Suspect," 183.
4. Ashby, supra note 3 at 188.
5. PACE, §1 (see Appendix A); Richard Stone, "Police Powers After the Act," 54.
6. Code of Practice for the Exercise by Police Officers of Statutory Powers of Stop and Search, para 1.5 (see Appendix B) (hereafter Stop and Search Code).
7. Id., paras. 1.6–1.7.
8. Id., para. 3.5.
9. PACE, §§2(8), 2(9). Stone, supra note 5 at 57.
10. Stop and Search Code, at para. 3.3. Stone, supra at 57.
11. PACE §2(3). Stone, supra at 57.
12. PACE §4.
13. Id. §1(3).
14. Id. §54.
15. Id. §1(4).
16. Id. §1(5).
17. 392 U.S. 1 (1968).
18. See Wayne LaFave, *Search and Seizure: A Treatise on the Fourth Amendment* §9.4(a), discussing this issue.
19. See id., at §9.2(c), discussing disagreement on this point.
20. Id.
21. Stop and Search Code, para. 2.1.
22. Id., para. 1, Notes for Guidance 1B.
23. PACE, §17.
24. Id. §8.
25. Id. §24.
26. Id. §17.
27. Id. §§17(1)(d), (e); §17(6).
28. Id. §18.
29. E.g., the Theft Act, 1968, §26(1) provides that, on reasonable cause shown, a justice of the peace may issue a search warrant to search for and seize stolen goods. If the suspect has been convicted of a theft offense within the last five years, a police superintendent may issue such a warrant. §26(2).
30. PACE §116.
31. See Bevan and Lidstone, supra note 1 at §4.06.
32. The reference to "preventing serious damage to property" quite clearly refers to the protective, rather than the evidence-gathering, function of the police. See id. at 74–75 for examples of cases in which the police may enter under this section.
33. U.S. law is to the contrary. *Vale v. Louisiana* 399 U.S. 30 (1970).

34. Bevan and Lidstone, supra note 1 at §4.16.

35. Code of Practice for the Searching of Premises by Police Officers, para. 4 (see Appendix B).

36. 412 U.S. 218 (1973).

37. Stop and Search Code, Notes for Guidance 1D.

38. PACE §24(4).

39. Id. §32(1).

40. Id. §32(2) and (5).

41. Id. §32(2)(b).

42. Id. §37(2).

43. Id. §54.

44. Id. §41(2)(a).

45. Id. §42(1).

46. Id. §43(1).

47. Id. §44(3)(b).

48. Code of Practice for the Detention, Treatment, and Questioning of Persons by the Police, para. 5 (see Appendix B) (hereafter Interrogation Code).

49. Id., paras. 8, 9, 13.

50. 354 U.S. 449 (1957).

51. Yale Kamisar, Wayne LaFave, and Jerold Israel, *Modern Criminal Procedure*, 429.

52. Interrogation Code, para. 10.4. However, contrary to U.S. practice, see *Doyle v. Ohio* 426 U.S. 610 (1976): though the prosecution may not "suggest that an accused's silence was suspicious, they could inform the jury that the accused was silent. Nothing could prevent the jury from drawing adverse inferences from the fact of silence if they chose to do so." M. Zander, *The Police and Criminal Evidence Act, 1984*, 144.

53. David Feldman, "Regulating Treatment of Suspects in Police Stations: Judicial Interpretation of Detention Provision in the Police and Criminal Act 1984," 463, citing Interrogation Code, paras. 10.4, 11.2.

54. Interrogation Code, para. 6: "[Arrestees] shall be informed in writing of these options and of the fact that option (b) [the duty solicitor] will always be free of charge."

55. Michael Zander, "The Act in the Station," 126.

56. Interrogation Code, Annex B.

57. See Mark Berger, Legislating Confession Law in Great Britain: A Statutory Approach to Police Interrogations," 39.

58. Interrogation Code, para. 6.6. See David Wolchover and Anthony Heaton-Armstrong, "The Questioning Code Revamped," 238, discussing this issue in greater detail.

59. Code of Practice on Tape Recording (see Appendix B). For a full discussion of British interrogation law under PACE, including the tape-recording requirements, see Berger, supra note 57 at 56–57.

60. Feldman, supra note 53 at 463.

61. Id. at 464 and cases cited therein.

62. *R. v. Leathan* 121 E.R. 589 (1861).

63. U.S. Department of Justice, Office of Legal Policy, "Report to the Attorney General on The Law of Pretrial Investigation" and "The Search and Seizure Exclusionary Rule."

64. Feldman, supra note 53 at 452 and 468.

65. PACE §76(8).

66. Zander, supra note 55 at 189.

67. Feldman, supra note 53 at 453.

68. Birch, "The PACE Hots Up: Confessions and Confusions Under the 1984 Act"': "Subsection 2(b) represents a break with the past. . . . [A] court's duty to exclude [now] comes into play wherever anything may have been said or done to cause the potentially unreliable confession; it does not matter by whom."

69. Feldman, supra note 53 at 469.

70. Id. at 454, discussing *R. v. Ismail* (1990) Crim. L.R. 109. Similarly, in *R. v. Sparks* (1991) Crim. L.R. 128, the Court of Appeal held that a "friendly conversation" about the crime between the suspect and a constable of his acquaintance prior to any arrest was an "interview" at which the suspect was entitled to be cautioned and the police were required to make a record. This, despite the fact that the constable was not purposely trying to evade the requirements of PACE.

71. (1991) Crim. L.R. 458. Accord *R. v. Dunford* (1991) Crim. L.R. 370 and cases cited in Commentary.

72. Feldman, supra note 53 at 458, citing *R. V. Alladice* (1988) 87 Cr. App. R. 380, (C.A.).

73. Id., citing *R. V. Samuel* (1988) Q.B. 615 (C.A.).

74. Id., citing, inter alia, *R. v. Davison* (1988) Crim. L.R. 442 (Central Criminal Court).

75. Wolchover and Heaton-Armstrong, supra note 58 at 232, 234.

76. Id. at 455 and cases cited therein.

77. Id.

78. *R. v. Beales* (1991) Crim. L.R. 118 (suspect alone misled by police); Accord, *R. v. Blake* (1991) Crim. L.R. 119; *R. v. Mason* (1987) 3 All E.R. 481 (suspect and solicitor misled by police).

79. *R. v. McGovern* (1991) Crim. L.R. 124. Compare *Oregon v. Elstad* 470 U.S. 298 (1985) where, on somewhat similar facts, the United States Supreme Court reached the opposite result. In *McGovern* the first confession was made, in the absence of a solicitor, by an emotionally upset woman with an IQ of 73. The court of appeal held that the absence of the solicitor was likely to render the first confession unreliable. Since the second confession, though made with full warnings and in the presence of the solicitor, was the result of the first, it too must be excluded. The court did not seem to rely on this defendant's peculiar vulnerability, however, noting that "the very fact" that the first interview was "in breach of the rules" is "likely to have an effect on the person in the course of the second interview." (1991) Crim. L.R. at 125.

80. *R. v. Canale* (1990) Crim. L.R. 329. See also *R. v. Scott* (1991) Crim. L.R. 56 where an incriminating statement was suppressed by the Court of Appeal because the police failed to have the defendant read and sign the record of the interview as required under para. 12(12).

81. Id.

82. (1987) R.T.R. 337 (D.C.)

83. Cited in Feldman, supra note 53 at 468.

84. Id.

85. (1990) Crim. L.R. 402.

86. Accord *R. v. Britton and Richards* (1989) Crim. L.R. 144 and cases cited therein.

87. Cited in Feldman, supra note 53 at 468–69, citing *The Independent*, January 19, 1990, p. 1.

88. Id.

89. (1989) Crim. L.R. 142.

90. (1988) Crim. L.R. 843.

91. The discussion of Australian law found in this section is drawn from Craig Bradley, "Criminal Procedure from the Land of Oz: Lessons for America."

92. *Report of the Board of Inquiry into the Enforcement of Criminal Law in Queensland*, 91 (hereafter Lucas Report).

93. Peter Sallman and John Willis, *Criminal Justice in Australia*, chap. 20.

94. In New South Wales exclusion is also automatic for confessions secured by deliberately untrue statements. Crimes Act, 1990, §410. Victoria and the Australian Capital Territory do not automatically reject all involuntary confessions. Crimes Act, 1958 (Vic), §149; Evidence Act, 1971 (A.C.T.), §68.

95. Bradley, supra note 91 at 107.

96. Id. at 107–110.

97. "[T]his 'police misconduct' discretion is actually *used* from time to time, at least in confession cases, though not with any regularity or consistent logic." Id. at 112 and cases discussed therein.

98. Search Warrant Act of 1985, N.S.W. Stat. §§5, 6.

99. Id. at 116.

100. Bradley, supra note 91 at 119–20.

101. 141 CLR 54 (Australia 1978).

102. Id. at 569 (Stephan and Aickin, JJ.).

103. Bradley, supra note 91 at 100–11 and citations therein.

104. 64 A.L.J.R. 384 (1990).

105. Id. at 386–87.

106. Parliamentary Research Service, Digest of Crimes (Investigation of Commonwealth Offenses) Amendment Bill 1990 (now "Act 1991").

107. 161 CLR 278 (Australia 1986).

108. Digest, supra note 106 at 3.

109. Bradley, supra note 91 at 103. Prior to the statute, this "requirement" seems to have been honored more in the breach than in the observance. See, e.g., *Van der Meer v. R.* 62 A.L.J.R. 656 (1988), where the accused were questioned for eleven hours prior to receiving the caution and the High Court nevertheless held that an earlier caution was not required.

110. Digest, supra note 106 at 4. Cf. *Moran v. Burbine* 475 U.S. 412 (1986).

111. Digest, supra note 106 at 4.

112. 65 A.L.J.R. 241 (1991).

113. Id. at 243.

114. Id.

115. Peter Waight, letter to author, June 25, 1992.

116. *Petty v. R.* 65 A.L.J.R. 625 (1991).

117. (Australian) Law Reform Commission, Report No. 2 at 23.

118. Constitution Act, 1982, §7.

119. Id. §8.

120. Id. §9.

121. Id. §10.

122. Id. §24(2). I consider this to be a "discretionary" exclusionary rule in the sense that exclusion does not follow automatically from the finding of a

constitutional violation, as in America. The Canadian Supreme Court, however, insists that §24(2) "does not confer a discretion on the trial judge but a duty to admit or exclude as a result of this finding [of disrepute]" *R. v. Collins* 56 C.R. (3rd) 193, 204 (1987). The burden of establishing "disrepute," even after a finding of a Charter violation, is on the defendant. Id. at 208. See Y.-M. Morissette, "The Exclusion of Evidence Under the Canadian Charter of Rights and Freedoms: What to Do and What Not to Do," 538, cited with approval in *Collins* at 209.

The decision whether to exclude depends on "all the circumstances," including the nature of the evidence, what Charter right was violated, whether the violation was serious or technical, willful or inadvertent, whether it occurred in circumstances of urgency, whether the evidence would have been obtained in any event, whether the offence was serious, and whether the evidence was essential to substantiate the charge. *Collins* at 210–11.

In *Collins* the Supreme Court chose the "lower threshold" French version of the constitutional text "*could* bring the administration of justice into disrepute" rather than the English "*would* bring. . . ." Id. at 213.

123. Revised Statutes of Canada R.S.C. 1970, c. C-34; R.S.C. 1985, ch. C-46.

124. R.S.C. 1985, ch. 11 (1st Supp.). See *Martin's Annual Criminal Code* 1991, p. CC-1.

125. *Martin's Annual Criminal Code* §487.

126. Id., Annotation p. CC-540.

127. Id. §487.1(1).

128. Id. §488.

129. Id. §101(1).

130. Id. §495.

131. Id., Annotation to §495, p. CC-568.

132. Id., Annotation, pp. CH-15–16 and cases cited therein. This limitation of vehicle searches to "contraband" rather than all evidence of a crime appears only in the Annotation, not in the Code itself, and apparently simply reflects the holding of a particular case. There is no reason to suppose that, if confronted with such a case, the Canadian courts would not extend vehicle searches to other evidence as well.

133. Id.

134. Id. Failure to inform the accused of the right to counsel prior to a consent search is likely to render the search unreasonable under §8 of the Charter. Id. at CH-16. Violation of the right to counsel in other search contexts is not. Id. Accord Scott Hutchinson and James Morton, *Search and Seizure Law in Canada*, 7-2.

135. Although the United States Supreme Court has recognized over twenty exceptions to the warrant requirement, searches in cases involving weapons are not among them. See Craig Bradley, 1474. In *Payton v. New York* 445 U.S. 573 (1980), the Court held that an arrest warrant was required to arrest someone in his or her home.

136. Id. at CH-21 and cases cited therein.

137. Id.

138. Id. at CH-20.

139. Id. at CH-20 and cases cited therein.

140. *R. v. Hebert* 77 C.R. (3rd) 145, 147; 57 C.C.C. (3rd) 1 (1990).

141. See, e.g., *R. v. Manninen* 58 C.R. (3rd) 97, 100 (1987).

142. 77 C.R. (3rd) 145.

143. Id. at 146.
144. Id. at 147.
145. See *Miranda v. Arizona* 384 U.S. 436 (1966).
146. Cf. *United States v. Gouveia* 467 U.S. 180 (1984), where the Court held that prisoners held in administrative detention for up to 19 months during the investigation of the murder of fellow inmates were not entitled to counsel.
147. 33 C.C.C. (3rd) 1 (1987).
148. 66 C.R. (3rd) 348 (1988).
149. Id. at 367, quoting *Pohoretsky v. R.* 58 C.R. (3rd) 113, 116 (1987), a case where the same result was reached on similar facts. Compare *Schmerber v. Cal* 384 U.S. 757 (1966), allowing the warrantless extraction of blood from a drunk driving suspect under an "exigent circumstance" rationale.
150. 67 C.R. (3rd) 224 (1989).
151. Id. at 225 (English digest of case reported in French).
152. 1 C.R. (4th) 62 (1990).
153. But see *R. v. DeBot* 73 C.R. (3rd) 129 (1989) for a recent case in which evidence found during a frisk was not suppressed by the Supreme Court, despite the police's failure to advise the accused of his right to counsel prior to the frisk. As Justice Sopinka pointed out, concurring in the result, it would be an empty gesture to inform the accused of his right to counsel, since the majority concluded that it was not necessary for the police to suspend the search if the accused invoked that right. Id. at 158.
154. *R. v. Collins* 56 C.R. (3rd) 193 (1987). See also Roger Salhany, *Canadian Criminal Procedure*, 69–70.
155. Accord *R. v. Meddoui* 2 C.R. (4th) 316 (1990), where the Alberta Court of Appeal excluded evidence found as a result of an illegal search. "[A]ny attempt to draw a line around Charter protection based upon personal involvement of the accused is bound to produce curious, even absurd, results." Id. at 336.
156. *R. v. Manninen*, 58 C.R. (3rd) 97 (1987).
157. Id. at 100.
158. Id. at 104. Cf. *Edwards v. Arizona* 451 U.S. 477 (1981) to the same effect. See also *R. v. Duguay* 67 C.R. (3rd) 252 (1987), where the Supreme Court suppressed physical evidence that was the fruit of a statement given when the accused had been interrogated without having been informed of his right to counsel.
159. 70 C.R. 97 (1989).
160. Id. at 117. The Court also observed that "the knife would undoubtedly have been uncovered by the police in the absence of the Charter breach. . . ." Id. The fact that the Court felt it necessary to invoke this "inevitable discovery" rationale casts further doubt on the firmness of the Court's resolve to admit real evidence absent unusual circumstances. Compare *Oregon v. Elstad* 470 U.S. 298 (1985), similarly refusing to apply the "fruit of the poisonous tree" doctrine to *Miranda* violations.
161. 78 C.R. (3rd) 129 (1990).
162. Id. at 129–30 (English digest of opinion in French).
163. (1989) 67 CR (ed) 209. Cf. *Kirby v. Illinois* 406 U.S. 682, 692 (1972), finding no right to counsel at preindictment lineups. For an excellent comparative analysis of Canadian and American criminal procedure, see Robert Harvie and Hamar Foster, "Ties That Bind? The Supreme Court of Canada,

American Jurisprudence and the Revision of the Canadian Criminal Law Under the Charter."

164. Id.
165. §487
166. See *Martin's Annual Criminal Code* §495, p. CC-568, "Search Incident to Arrest."
167. Richard S. Frase, "Introduction" to *The French Code of Criminal Procedure*, 1 (hereafter "Introduction").
168. Id. at 9.
169. Id. at 10.
170. Richard S. Frase, "Comparative Criminal Justice as a Guide to American Law Reform: How Do the French Do It, How Can We Find Out and Why Should We Care?" (hereafter "Comparative Justice"), 585.
171. Frase, "Introduction" at 10.
172. Id. at 16, n. 105. In particular, "violations of the provisions of Articles 63 and 64, governing investigatory detention, might lead to exclusion if it were shown that 'the search for truth was fundamentally tainted.'"
173. Id.
174. Thomas Weigand, "Continental Cures for American Ailments: European Criminal Procedure as a Model for Law Reform," 391.
175. Frase, "Introduction" at 13, quoting the French Code of Criminal Procedure (Code de Procédure Criminal, CPP) Arts. 91, para. 1 and 82, para. 1. Frase reports that electronic surveillance is now regulated more closely by Law No. 91-646 (July 10, 1991), which limits the duration of and places other restrictions on electronic surveillance. Letter to author, May 14, 1992.
176. Frase, "Introduction" at 15.
177. Id.
178. Id. at 14.
179. Id. at 16. See also Frase letter, supra note 175.
180. Frase, "Comparative Justice" at 580.
181. Walter Pakter, "Exclusionary Rules in France, Germany, and Italy," 13–15. Accord Frase, "Comparative Justice" at 586:

[A]lthough some American observers have suggested that French rights are effectively enforced by means of administrative discipline, the French themselves are skeptical of such remedies: "experience proves that the sole ordinary sanction is exclusion." (citations omitted)

182. CPP Art. 56-1.
183. Id. Art. 59(1).
184. Id. Art. 59(3) provides that "The formalities mentioned in Articles 56, 57, and the present articles are imposed upon pain of nullity." See also Art. 78-3(11), providing for mandatory exclusion as to the limitations on detention for the purpose of identity checks.
185. Frase, "Introduction" at 16.
186. Pakter, supra note 181 at 36.
187. Id. at 36.
188. Id. at 38.
189. Frase, "Comparative Justice" at 554–57.

190. Frase reports that scholarly opinion in France favors evidentiary exclusion as the remedy for police misconduct. Id. at 586.
191. Thomas Weigand, letter to author, Jan. 8, 1992.
192. Id.
193. See, generally, Craig Bradley, "The Exclusionary Rule in Germany," from which much of the discussion in this section is drawn. See also American Series of Penal Codes, *The German Code of Criminal Procedure* (*Strafprozessordnung*) (StPO) §102.
194. Id. at 1038 quoting StPO §102.
195. StPO §105. Constitution (Grundgesetz GG) Art 13(2).
196. StPO §102.
197. StPO §103.
198. *Bundesverfassungsgericht* (BVerfG) (2d Senate), Wistra 1992, Heft 2, p. 60.
199. Id.
200. Conversation with Heinz Wagner, University of Kiel, June 16, 1992.
201. Grundgesetz Art 2:

(1) Everyone shall have the right to the free development of his personality. . . .
(2) Everyone shall have the right to life and to inviolability of his person. . . .

202. Id. at 61.
203. Id.
204. See Bradley, supra note 193 at 1040–41, 1046. The contrast with American search and seizure law is striking. Searches may be performed on mere "suspicion," rather than probable cause, and a written search warrant is frequently not used at all in Germany. Most significantly for the purposes of this book, violation of a search order requirement or failure to provide the required information does not lead to the exclusion of evidence derived from the search.
205. Theodor Kleinknecht, *Strafprozessordnung*, Einleitung 19 (citations omitted).
206. Judgment of Mar. 17, 1971, Bundesgerichtshof (BGH), W. Ger., 24 Entscheidungen des Bundesgerichtshof in Strafsachen (BGHSt) (decisions of the federal appeals court panel for criminal cases) 125, 131.
207. The rules forbidding brutality and deceit in interrogation are statutory (see StPO §136a), but the statute in turn rests on constitutional principles. Bradley, supra note 193 at 1049–50.
208. Kleinknecht, supra note 205, Einleitung para. 54.
209. Id.; cf. *Rochin v. California* 342 U.S. 165 (1952) (excluding brutally seized evidence on due process grounds in a decision preceding extension of the exclusionary rule to the states).
210. See Judgment of May 24, 1977, BVerfG, 44 BVerfG 353.
211. Id. at 371–72; see Bradley, supra note 193 at 1406. In this case, the seizure was held unconstitutional for essentially the same reason for which the search was held unconstitutional: the police were not investigating a specific crime, and a "fishing expedition" could not justify an action as intrusive as the seizure of the private medical records of a drug rehabilitation clinic. If, however, the police had found illegal narcotics rather than merely medical

records, it is likely that the evidence would not have been suppressed, despite the defects in the search; in deciding in favor of exclusion, the court placed great emphasis on the private nature of the evidence seized.

212. Accord Judgment of May 24, 1977, BVerfG, 42 BVerfG 212, 218. In this earlier case, the court did not conclude that it would never exclude evidence on the basis of an illegal search, but found that the issue was not ripe.

213. See Judgment of May 24, 1977, BVerfG, 44 BVerfG at 383–84. In view of the fact that the German Constitution guarantees the inviolability of the home (GG Art. 13; see Judgment of May 26, 1976, BVerfG, BVerfG at 219) this distinction makes little sense. Breaking down the door of a house to find evidence is certainly as serious an intrusion as snatching the evidence from the defendant's hand. Because the German system provides alternate grounds to exclude evidence, however, this distinction does not create as much mischief in Germany as it might in the United States. This point is illustrated by the Supreme Court's decision in *Irvine v. California* 347 U.S. 128 (1954). When police broke into the defendant's home and installed a microphone, the Court condemned the police behavior as a flagrant violation of the fourth amendment (id. at 132), but declined to exclude the evidence (the conversations of the occupants), because the Court had not yet held the exclusionary rule applicable to the states. Id. at 132–34; see *Wolf v. Colorado* 228 U.S. 25 (1949), overruled by *Mapp v. Ohio*, 367 U.S. 643, 665 (1961). In Germany the courts would not have difficulty excluding such evidence, not because of illegal police behavior but because private conversations in the home generally are not admissible, however obtained. See, generally, Bradley, supra note 193 at 1044–46 (discussing the tape recording case).

214. Judgment of May 24, 1977, BVerfG, 44 BVerfG at 383–84.

215. Thus a night search that is prohibited by StPO §104, for example, can nevertheless yield admissible evidence unless use of that evidence would violate the principle of proportionality; see Bradley, supra note 193 at 1041.

216. As though the principle of proportionality is also considered to be a component of the *Rechtsstaatsprinzip* (see K. Hesse, *Grundzuge des Verfassungrechts der Bundesrepublik Deutschland*, 77) in the German decisions it is usually discussed as a separate principle.

217. Kleinknecht, supra note 205, Einleitung para. 20.

218. Judgment of Aug. 5, 1966, BVerfG, 44 BVerfG 162, 187; see also James Carr, "Wiretapping in West Germany" discussing application of this doctrine in wiretapping cases.

219. Judgment of June 10, 1963, BVerfG, 16 BVerfG 194.

220. A physical examination of the accused may be ordered for the ascertainment of facts that are important for the proceeding. For this purpose the taking of blood samples and other penetrations of the body, made by a physician pursuant to the rules of medical science . . . are permissible without the consent of the accused, provided no resulting detriment to his health is to be feared. StPO, §81a.

221. Judgment of June 10, 1963, BVerfG, 16 BVerfG at 202. Because this case arose on appeal from the order authorizing examination, the evidence was never obtained, and the question of suppression was not directly addressed. See also Judgment of Aug. 5, 1966, BVerfG, 20 BVerfG 162, 187, holding that search of a press room requires a higher standard of cause than do other searches; such a search "must promise success in producing appropriate evidence" rather than being grounded on mere suspicion.

222. Decision of 3 Sept. 1991, supra note 198 at 61.

223. But see Klaus Rogall, "Gegenwärtiger Stand und Entwicklungsten-denzen der Lehre von den Strafprozessualen Beweisverboten," 1, 12, discussing and criticizing the focus on the purity-of-the-process doctrine.

224. See generally Ewald Löwe and Werner Rosenberg, *Die Strafprozessordnung und das Gerichtsverfassungsgesetz mit Nebengensetzemi: Grosskommentar,* chap. 14, para. 1, observing that the search for truth in criminal investigations is limited by the commands of justice, which forbid investigatory means that "are unreasonable, violate the proportionality principle, offend human dignity, or are not related to the development of the truth," and claiming that "The exclusionary rules serve the purpose of enforcing these interests."

225. Judgment of Feb. 21, 1964, BGH, 19 BGHSt 325.

226. Judgment of Jan. 31, 1973, BVerfG, 34 BVerfG 238.

227. Judgment of May 24, 1977, BVerfG, 44 BVerfG 353.

228. Judgment of Feb. 21, 1964, BGH, 19 BGHSt 325.

229. Id. at 326–27; GG Art. 2, para. 2. The Diary Case was the first to hold explicitly that exclusion could be based on a violation of constitutional rights. The court reached this result even though the exclusionary provisions of the Code of Criminal Procedure—for example, StPO §136a, which excludes coerced confessions—were not applicable, and thereby prepared the way for the subsequent expansion of the exclusionary rule based on the broad constitutional principles discussed above. The basic concept of exclusion, however, is not a new one in Germany; it was first set forth in 1903. Ernst Beling, *Die Beweisverbote als Grenzen der Wahrheitserforschung im Strafprozess in Strafrechtlichen Abhandlungen,* Heft 46 at 37.

230. Judgment of Feb. 21, 1964, BGH, 19 BGHSt at 331.

231. Id.

232. The diary would be admissible in the United States even if it were turned over to the police by a thief who had ransacked the defendant's home. See *Burdeau v. McDowell* 256 U.S. 465, 476 (1921). The focus in the United States is on police misconduct, without regard to whether a substantial invasion of the defendant's privacy has occurred. But see Craig Bradley, "Constitutional Protection for Private Papers," arguing that past Supreme Court decisions and constitutional theory provide support for the proposition that private papers should receive greater constitutional protection than do guns and narcotics.

233. See, e.g., *Whiteley v. Warden* 401 U.S. 560, 568–69 (1971) (excluding tools and old coins).

234. See, e.g., Karl-Heinz Gössel, "Kritische Bemerkungen zum gegenwartigen Stand der Lehre von den Beweisverboten im Strafverfahren," 651. But see F. Dencker, *Verwertungsverbote im Strafprozess,* 52 and n. 169. Dencker notes that some scholars contend that the rule should have a deterrent purpose (id. at 52, n. 169), but concludes that it "is not possible to assume that the legislature created the 'evidence use prohibitions' that are in existence for disciplinary reasons. . . ." Id. at 53, 55.

235. The efficient administration of justice is itself a constitutionally guaranteed interest. Judgment of May 24, 1977, BVerfG, 44 BVerfG 353, 374.

236. Judgment of Jan. 31, 1973, BVerfG, 34 BVerfG 238.

237. Id. at 248. In a recent case the BGH did admit an illicit tape-recording to prove arson. 1989 *Neue Juristiche Wochenschrift* 2760.

238. Judgment of May 24, 1977, BVerfG, 44 BVerfG 353.

239. Id. at 379. Similarly, in the Judgment of May 8, 1972, the federal constitutional court held that information from a doctor's files concerning his treatment of the defendant, though seized pursuant to a valid warrant, must be excluded from the defendant's extortion trial. 32 BVerfG 373, 379.

240. Judgment of March 17, 1983, BGH, 31 BGHSt 214, 304 (1983).

241. Pakter, supra note 181 at 48.

242. Bradley, supra note 193 at 1044 and authorities cited therein.

243. This problem is discussed in more detail in id. at 1063–64.

244. Judgment of June 7, 1983, BGH, 31 BGHSt 395.

245. Id. at 400.

246. Decision of Feb. 27, 1992, 1992 *Neue Juristische Wochenschrift* 2760.

247. Id. at 1467.

248. Id. at 1463.

249. Id. at 1464.

250. Cf. *Colorado v. Spring* 479 U.S. 564 (1987), where the Supreme Court held that it was not necessary that the suspect be accurately informed of the subject matter of the investigation.

251. Judgment of May 31, 1990, BGH, 4 StR 112.

252. Judgment of March 24, 1959, BGH, 13 BGHSt 60.

253. Judgment of Oct. 7, 1960, BGH, 15 BGHSt 187.

254. StPO, §128.

255. Supra note 181 at 20.

256. Codice di Procedura Penale, enacted by Presidential Decree-Law No. 477 of September 22, 1988, No. 250 Gazz. Uff. (Oct. 24, 1988) (effective Oct. 24, 1989). For a discussion of the background of the code reform in Italy, see Note, "Plea Bargaining and Its Analogues Under the New Italian Criminal Procedure Code and in the United States: Toward a New Understanding of Comparative Criminal Procedure," 221–22.

257. Id. at 223.

258. Lawrence Fassler, "The Italian Penal Procedure Code: An Adversarial System of Criminal Procedure in Continental Europe," 246. According to Note, supra note 256, there are three major aspects to the Italian reform: (1) creating a "more partisan relationship between the public prosecutor and the defense counsel, while the judge retains a more impartial position in the process" (id. at 224); (2) making the trial more than a "brief public formality at the end of the investigation" as it was under the old system (id. at 225); and (3) introducing "special procedures to eliminate the majority of cases before the trial stage" such as plea bargaining and summary trials (id. at 226). In particular, at trial the accused now has a right to counsel, a right to silence, and a right to confront, and have counsel cross-examine, witnesses against him. Fassler at 267 et seq.

259. Id.

260. Lawrence Fassler, letter to author, Dec. 3, 1991.

261. Id. at 253.

262. Id. at 256. Compare Canada's "weapons exception" to the search warrant requirement, discussed supra at note 134, which does not apply to domicile searches.

263. Id. at 255.

264. Id. at 254. Accord Ennio Amodio and Eugenio Selvaggi, "An Accusatorial System in a Civil Law Country: The 1988 Italian Code of Criminal Procedure," 1222–23.

265. Fassler, supra note 258 at 256. "When 'specific and exceptional reasons' exist the code permits the preliminary investigation judge to delay the accused's right to confer with an attorney for up to seven days. (But uncounseled statements still may not be used at the trial.) Additionally, where the suspect has been arrested, the prosecutor can delay the right up until the suspect's first appearance [in court] which might not occur until five days after the arrest." Id. at 256–57, n. 70.

266. Fassler to author, supra note 260. Fassler cites a judgment of Italy's Constitutional Court of May 23, 1991, plus discussions with an Italian trial judge in support of this surprising restriction.

267. Id. Statements made to the *police* with the defense attorney present may only be used to impeach.

268. Amodio and Selvaggi, supra note 264 at 1222.

269. Fassler, supra note 258 at 253, n. 50.

270. Id. at 255, quoting Code of Penal Procedure, art. 191, para. 1.

271. Fassler, supra note 258 at 255.

272. Id. at p. 256.

273. Pakter, supra note 181 at 24, and sources cited therein.

274. Id.

275. Id. at 24. Cf. the German method, discussed above, where "excluded" evidence is not referred to in court but remains in the dossier.

276. Id. at 33, quoting Judgment of Feb. 20, 1974, Corte cassazione 127 Giur. It. II 432, 436 (1975).

277. Pakter, supra note 181 at 33.

278. Id. at 51, quoting Judgment of Sept. 26, 1980, Corte cassazione 133 Giur. It. II 113 (1981) (evidence nevertheless admitted because issue first raised on appeal).

279. Craig Bradley, "Are the State Courts Enforcing the Fourth Amendment? A Preliminary Study."

Chapter 6
What Is To Be Done?

The position taken in this book is that the attempt by the United States Supreme Court to declare "rules" of criminal procedure has led to a body of criminal procedure law that is largely incomprehensible. The reasons for this lie mostly in the nature of the Supreme Court as an institution rather than in the political direction of its opinions or the quality of individual decisions.

There is, however, a very good reason why criminal procedure rules have had to originate with the Supreme Court, despite that institution's fundamental incapacity to perform the function adequately—namely, because it is widely believed that the Supreme Court is the only institution capable of enacting rules applicable nationwide. It was reasonable for the Warren Court to conclude, particularly in light of the consistent refusal of the southern states to recognize civil rights of blacks, that matters concerning such fundamental constitutional rights as the right to a fair trial and the right not to be subjected to coercive police interrogation must not be left to the mercies of the individual states. But no national institution had clear power to act. The Supreme Court simply assumed that power by concluding that the due process clause of the fourteenth amendment "incorporated" the Bill of Rights and made it applicable to the states. Once the Court did this, both Congress and state legislatures largely abandoned the field, leaving a legal system that has come to assume that the Supreme Court is the only body capable of declaring nationally applicable rules of criminal procedure to protect the nationally applicable Bill of Rights. It is the principal point of this book that the Court is neither the only nor the best source of such rules. Rather, what is needed, as other countries recognize, is a comprehensive, nationally applicable, statutory scheme.

The problem with statutes is two-fold. The first is simply getting them passed. Many years and three statutory schemes after criminal procedure reform was first attempted in Australia, nothing has yet been done.[1] On the other hand, comprehensive reforms have been achieved in Britain and Italy and, to some extent, in Canada, and Germany has long had a fairly detailed code. Such an effort in the United States might succeed if devoted largely to codifying and clarifying current Supreme Court law, and to making the rules more comprehensive, rather than substantially changing the law's ideological content.

As will be discussed, the job must not be performed by Congress itself, which is too political and too lacking in expertise to perform such a complex and continuing task. Rather, Congress should appoint a special commission, or expand the mandate of the committee that currently drafts the Federal Rules of Criminal Procedure. Congress should limit itself to voting either for or against the product of this committee, or otherwise avoid detailed reconsideration of the rules. The committee should maintain a continuing existence to deal with unforeseen problems and reversals in the courts. In short, the American rules of criminal procedure should be dealt with in essentially the same way that such rules are dealt with in the other countries I have discussed—as a uniform, nationwide system of codified rules, which are promulgated and amended by a body created specifically for that purpose, but which remain subject to constitutionality review in the courts.

The second "problem," common to the United States and Australia, but not other countries, is federalism.* The criminal investigation bills proposed in Australia would only apply to the federal authorities because the federal government has very limited powers vis-à-vis the states. It is generally assumed that Congressional power is similarly constrained in the United States. This is a serious problem because such fundamental rights must be enforced uniformly nationwide, not subjected to the differing whims of state legislatures or state courts. This would seem to be the major reason why the Supreme Court has undertaken the job of declaring nationally applicable "rules" of criminal procedure.

In my view, this problem is a chimera in the United States. Congress has the power to prescribe a national code of criminal procedure. If Congress can provide a tort remedy for violation of constitutional rights by state officers, which the Supreme Court has said it can,[2] then

---

*Germany and Canada are also federal republics for many purposes, but the authority of the national government to promulgate nationally applicable codes of both criminal law and procedure is beyond question in those countries.

Congress can also legislate the precise obligations that those rights place on the police, as well as an exclusionary remedy.

The fourth, fifth, and sixth amendments have all been applied to the states by the Supreme Court through the fourteenth amendment.[3] It was this "incorporation" of the Bill of Rights into the fourteenth amendment that enabled the Court to declare rules applicable to the states. But that amendment also provides, in section 5, that "Congress shall have power to enforce, by appropriate legislation, the provisions of this article."[4] Because the criminal procedure amendments have been incorporated into the due process clause of the fourteenth amendment, it is clear that Congress is now empowered to enforce them "by appropriate legislation"[5]—that is, by a national code of criminal procedure. Such a code would provide the uniformity necessary for enforcing federal constitutional rights,* combined with a relative certainty as to the scope of those rights. This is currently unattainable by reference to case- and precedent-bound Supreme Court decisions.[6]

That such an arrangement would pose no federalism problems is quite clear. The Supreme Court has repeatedly declared that the power of Congress to enact nationally applicable remedies under section 5 of the fourteenth amendment is at least as great as, and probably greater than, the Court's own power. Thus in *Katzenbach v. Morgan* the Court recognized that the purpose of section 5 of the fourteenth amendment was "to grant Congress the same broad powers expressed in the Necessary and Proper Clause, Art. I§8, cl. 18."[7] In short, "§5 is a positive grant of legislative power authorizing Congress to exercise its discretion in determining whether and what legislation is needed to secure the guarantees of the Fourteenth Amendment."[8] In the 1991 case of *Gregory v. Ashcroft* the Court, while generally offering a paean to strong state governments within the federal system, specifically noted that "the principles of federalism that constrain Congress' exercise of its Commerce Clause powers are attenuated when Congress acts pursuant to its powers to enforce the Civil War Amendments."[9]

As discussed in Chapter 5, it is the opinion of many other countries that, as the Australian Law Reform Commission put it, "what is needed is a comprehensive code setting out with as much particularity as possible, the rights and duties of police, suspects and others concerned in the criminal investigation process."[10] In the early days of

---

*Such a code would not, of course, prevent individual states from holding their own police to higher standards, as they are currently free to do. *Oregon v. Haas* 420 U.S. 714, 719 (1975). But it would provide uniformity as to the bottom line, the most fundamental rights.

the criminal procedure revolution, many prominent people in this country also recognized that courts were not the appropriate bodies for declaring rules of criminal procedure—that these should come from legislative, or legislatively appointed, bodies. Thus in 1966 Herbert Packer of Stanford Law School, recognizing that the Supreme Court's actions were due to a "law-making vacuum," deemed the Court's establishment of criminal procedural rules "moves of desperation." He concluded that "the rules of the criminal process, which ought to be the subject of flexible inquiry and adjustment by law-making bodies having the institutional capacity to deal with them, are evolved through a process that its warmest defenders recognize as to some extent awkward and inept."[11] Judge Friendly declared that the subject called for "the compromise that is the genius of legislation rather than the everlasting aye or nay of constitutional decision."[12] Finally, Paul Bator and James Vorenberg of Harvard Law School, the reporters of the Model Code of Pre-Arraignment Procedure, recognized the "peculiar appropriateness of legislation to the solution of the major issues of criminal procedure."[13]

However, none of these commentators recognized the possibility that such rules could be declared nationally, as a result of federal legislation. Rather their efforts were confined to trying to encourage the states to adopt rules, preferably in conformance with a national standard such as the Model Code of Pre-Arraignment Procedure promulgated by the American Law Institute. Not surprisingly, these efforts failed. Even if the states had been inclined to develop comprehensive rules, the steady stream of new mandates emanating from the Supreme Court, which constantly changed the ground rules, would have doomed such an effort at its inception. (Nevertheless, that code, along with the English Police and Criminal Evidence Act in Appendix A, would be the obvious starting points for the national code proposed in this book).

Only one commentator at that time recognized the possibility of Congress' legislating nationally applicable rules of criminal procedure. In an article in the *Journal of Criminal Law, Criminology and Police Science* Donald Dowling, a private practitioner in Chicago who was serving as the Illinois reporter to the American Bar Foundation's Indigent Accused Persons Project, made the following observations:

If the states are to operate the state-federal criminal system, they ought to be allowed to participate in the full panoply of governmental processes which control that system. . . .

*　*　*　*

If the Congress is intelligently advised, perhaps through a Committee on state-federal criminal law . . . legislation meeting the demands of decency and efficiency as to the citizens prosecuted and the state as law enforcer could be passed and included in a title to the United States Code.

*   *   *   *

There is nothing inherent in our system, other than Congressional lethargy, some lack of imagination, the force of legislative inertia at rest, and the willingness to pass the buck to judicial interpolation, that restricts Congress from legislating fourteenth amendment requirements for state criminal process.[14]

Any doubt about the authority or ability of Congress to legislate a comprehensive code of criminal procedure should be allayed by reference to the federal wiretapping statutes, Title III of the Omnibus Crime Control and Safe Streets Act of 1968.[15] Title III provides for comprehensive federal control, binding on the states,[16] of all electronic eavesdropping activity, which, since *Katz v. United States*[17] in 1967, has been recognized by the Supreme Court as trenching on vital fourth amendment concerns. Despite criticism,[18] Title III seems to have provided relatively clear rules and, in the view of a leading commentator on the subject, Michael Goldsmith, "virtually every level of protection afforded by the statute transcends constitutional demands."[19] This is true despite the fact that Title III was drafted as ordinary legislation rather than by an independent commission, as recommended here.

Congress could base a code on its general authority to enforce the fourth, fifth, and sixth amendments without necessarily tying each rule to a specific constitutional violation. It could thereby avoid the "patchwork" problem that has plagued the Court's work in this area. Thus Congress could declare that fair conduct of lineups implicates defendants' due process rights and that lineups must therefore be photographed and tape recorded (or videotaped) in order for the results to be admissible at trial, without specifying precisely which constitutional phrase required this rule.[20] This approach is reminiscent of that used in the loan-sharking statutes,[21] where Congress simply declared that loan-sharking affected interstate commerce without requiring proof of the effect in a given case. The Supreme Court approved this approach in *Perez v. United States*.[22] A grateful Court, relieved at last of its burden of declaring, case by case, rules for the police to follow, while retaining its authority to pass on the constitutionality and the application of the rules that had been devised, would likely support such legislation.

In the past the states, through members of Congress, might have resisted such legislation as trenching on matters that were exclusively of state concern. However, in the thirty years since *Mapp* everyone has become so accustomed to criminal procedure as a federal matter that it seems unlikely that serious states' rights arguments would be raised. Moreover, as Dowling has observed, such a legislative system would give the states more input, through their representatives in Congress as well as through their police officials' testimony before the drafting authority, than they have now.

Such a constitutionally based code would continue to be a "bottom line," as in the current system. States would be free to provide more expansive protection for the rights of their citizens if they so desired. Also, such a code, while it could deal broadly with such fundamental concerns as fair lineups and interrogation procedures, would not extend to non-constitutional details such as the form of search warrant returns and when preliminary motions must be filed before trial. Such matters, which do not entrench upon federally protected constitutional rights, would continue to be dealt with by separate state and federal codes of procedure. This is not to suggest that the drafters must assume that only matters that have already been addressed by the Court fall within the ambit of constitutional protection. On the contrary, matters such as the rights of police to lie to a suspect and the outer time limits for interrogations, while they have not been resolved by the Court, should be covered by the rules to the extent that they raise "constitutional issues," interpreting that term broadly. Following the British example, it would be best to err on the side of making the code too comprehensive, and running the risk that the Supreme Court might (but probably would not) strike portions of it down as wholly beyond constitutional concern, than not to make it comprehensive enough, and continue to leave the police without guidance in significant areas.

To the extent that local conditions required different rules in different states, the drafting commission should simply refrain from acting, even in the constitutional sphere, if they feel that the local concerns outweigh the federal rights. However, it is generally the case that conditions vary far more within states, between rural and urban areas, than they do between states. Consequently, it is difficult to imagine significant areas of constitutional law that can be better resolved state by state than at the federal level, although the drafters might feel that such areas exist. It would not seem inappropriate for the drafters to consider reasoned distinctions between high-crime urban and low-crime rural areas, which seem much more meaningful than state-to-state distinctions.

As noted, it would seem that there are two reasonable ways to accomplish this task. The first would be to create a Criminal Procedure Rules Commission. While the Sentencing Commission was created to serve quite a different function, it may serve as at least a partial model.[23] The Sentencing Commission comprises seven voting members appointed by the President with the advice and consent of the Senate. A representative of the Attorney General is an *ex officio* non-voting member. The Commission is charged with promulgating sentencing guidelines, periodically reviewing and revising those guidelines, and "consult[ing] with authorities on, and individual and institutional representatives of, various aspects of the Federal criminal justice system."[24] A similar makeup and charge of a criminal procedure commission would seem appropriate. However, given the fundamental rights protected by a criminal procedure code, it would make sense for Congress to appoint a bipartisan commission itself and to retain the authority to approve or disapprove (but not to tinker with) the final product.

Given the Supreme Court's approval of the delegation of congressional power to the Sentencing Commission in *Mistretta v. United States*, such a delegation to a criminal procedure commission would seem to pose no separation of powers problems.[25] Moreover, since such a set of rules would always be subject to the Supreme Court's authority as the final arbiter of the scope of the fourth, fifth, and sixth amendments, there could be no claim that Congress was usurping the Court's powers. As for federalism concerns, as previously noted, the states get little input into the current "rulemaking" procedures, other than briefs in Supreme Court cases, so such objections have already been rendered nugatory.

The Sentencing Commission has come in for a good deal of criticism. However, that criticism seems aimed at the fact that the Commission has undertaken a peculiarly difficult task: to determine the *exact* sentence applicable to *each* criminal defendant convicted in federal court *in advance*. Obviously the job of determining a particular defendant's sentence, in the abstract, without reference to the characteristics or representations of the defendant, flies in the face of many strongly felt notions about how the punishment should fit both the defendant and the crime. Moreover, it intrudes substantially into the traditional authority of federal judges. It is hardly surprising, then, that the *New York Times* reports that a "Chorus of Judicial Critics Assail Sentencing Guides."[26] By contrast, police are used to having to abide by criminal procedure rules, and such rules would not, and could not, attempt to decide whether or not a given factual setting produced, for example, a valid search. Determining "probable cause" or "reasonable suspicion" must necessarily be left to the trial judge, though clearer direction as to the meaning of those terms than the Supreme Court's Delphic musings is surely possible.

The other possible route that Congress could take to form a rule-making body would be to expand the mandate of the Federal Rules Advisory Committee, which promulgates the Federal Rules of Criminal Procedure, which are currently applicable only in federal courts and do not govern police activities such as warrantless searches. Under current law (18 U.S.C. §§3771, 3772), the Supreme Court is empowered to prescribe rules of "pleading, practice and procedure with respect to any and all proceedings" both prior to and after verdict or guilty plea, "in the United States district courts. . . ." In practice, the process is somewhat more complicated. The Supreme Court has delegated all federal rulemaking responsibility to the Judicial Conference of the United States, which is chaired by the Chief Justice and comprises twenty-four other federal judges, including the Chief Judges of all the circuits.[27] The Judicial Conference only meets twice a year and apparently does not spend a great deal of time reviewing proposed rule changes.[28] Rather it appoints a Standing Committee on (all) Rules of Practice and Procedure to oversee the work of a series of advisory committees, which actually draft the rules in the various areas—criminal procedure, civil procedure, evidence, and so on. The Advisory Committee on Criminal Rules comprises federal judges, the federal Public Defender, Justice Department officials, practitioners, and academics. They are appointed by the Chief Justice in his capacity as chairman of the Judicial Conference.[29] After the proposed rules are drafted, they are circulated for public comment and published in Federal Rules Decisions.[30] Following any revision based on the comments, the draft is passed on to the Standing Committee, the Judicial Conference, and the Supreme Court, none of whom are likely to make any substantial changes.[31] The Chief Justice then submits the draft to Congress.

While the statute seems to give Congress no power to disapprove or modify them,[32] in practice Congress has assumed that it has retained such power.[33] In recent years, Congress has changed rules it has received from the Court, or modified the Federal Rules of Criminal Procedure on its own, in particular in the Comprehensive Crime Control Act of 1984.[34]

The current structure seems unduly complicated. It would seem that the Judicial Conference and the Standing Committee levels could be eliminated, with the Advisory Committee reporting directly to the Supreme Court, which would then submit the proposed rules to Congress. Whatever the precise structure might turn out to be, the current federal rulemaking process provides a useful basis on which to construct a rulemaking body to promulgate a national code of criminal procedure. Given that the Supreme Court, without benefit of expert opinion or public comment, has undertaken to promulgate such rules informally for the last thirty years, formalistic objections that such advisory committees are not suited to draft rules for police, as opposed to court, procedures can reasonably be brushed aside.

The latter proposal has the advantage of using a preexisting structure and of getting the Supreme Court involved during the rulemaking stage, thus avoiding the prospect of evidence being suppressed because the Supreme Court did not agree with the rule upon which the police had relied (as opposed to the issues of whether the police correctly followed a rule or whether the rules adequately covered a particular police activity). On the other hand, the process would benefit greatly from having the selection of the drafting committee done in the open by Congress, on a bipartisan basis, rather than by the Chief Justice acting alone. Furthermore, such a committee should have the opportunity and obligation to hold hearings concerning proposed rules, in order to maximize public and expert input before the final product is submitted to the Court and Congress for approval, rather than simply seeking written comments. Consequently, a bipartisan drafting committee that partakes of some aspects of the Sentencing Commission, and some of the Federal Rules Advisory Committee, would seem to be the best approach.

The presence of the Supreme Court in such a rulemaking process may pose constitutional problems. The participation by the Court in the current federal rulemaking process is less problematic because these are rules governing the behavior of federal courts, over which the Supreme Court has supervisory authority. As argued, Congress has the authority to legislate rules governing the conduct of state and local police and courts insofar as their conduct interferes with rights incorporated in the fourteenth amendment. However, it is not clear whether the Supreme Court is empowered to involve itself in the preliminary stages of a process over which it lacks supervisory authority. *Garcia v. SAMTA*, which granted Congress essentially unlimited power to override state authority under the Commerce Clause, stressed that this power would be checked by the fact that the states are represented in Congress.[35] Since this scheme grants Congress only limited authority to vote the proposed rules up or down, but would allow the Supreme Court to tinker with them, this could be viewed as a violation of separation of powers. On the other hand, it could be argued that Congress's broad power to legislate to enforce the fourteenth amendment and the Supreme Court's historic participation in the (federal) rulemaking process combine to legitimate this process.

In any case, Supreme Court participation in the drafting process, while desirable to avoid future problems, is not essential. The Advisory Committee could report directly to Congress.

In my view, it would be a mistake for Congress to retain the authority to make changes in nationally applicable rules of criminal procedure. As described in Chapter 2, this is a subject that can raise considerable political passion. If Congress were to involve itself in a line-by-line review of the rules, the chances are that a code would be produced that overemphasized crime control at the expense of civil rights. The Supreme Court would then have to strike down the offensive aspects of such a code, leaving the state of the law no better off than it was before. If, by contrast, the role of Congress were limited to voting for or against such rules, its members could disclaim individual responsibility and thus insulate themselves from individual political consequences of painful decisions, much as they did in the military base closing process.

Judge Jack Weinstein has reflected on the desirability of limited congressional involvement in the drafting of the Federal Rules of Criminal Procedure:

It would be a mistake . . . for Congress to insist on reviewing proposed rules in minute detail. Rulemaking is delegated so the Congress may profit from the expertise of courts and specialists in areas of litigation procedure with which they are far more conversant than Congress. Unless Congress confines itself to the basic policy issues submitted to it, the ends sought to be achieved by the delegation [of drafting authority to the Advisory Committee] will be undercut.[36]

When the first Federal Rules of Criminal Procedure were promulgated in 1944, Justice Frankfurter refused to vote to approve them on the ground that the Supreme Court was too far removed from the trial arena to be promulgating rules governing trials. Obviously the Court is even farther removed from the police investigatory process, but that has not stopped it from attempting to produce "rules" governing the conduct of police investigations. As Justice Frankfurter noted, "experience proves that justice profits if the responsibility for such rulemaking be vested in a small, standing, rule-making body rather than be left to legislation generated by particular controversies."[37] Justice Frankfurter would surely have expanded his admonition to "judicial decisions generated by particular controversies" had he foreseen, in 1944, the direction in which the law of criminal procedure was headed. A similar sentiment was expressed to Frank Remington of the Advisory Committee on the Criminal Rules by Chief Justice Burger, who urged that "rulemaking was the way to make significant improvement in criminal procedure rather than waiting, as had too often been done in the past, for the litigated case to come along in which the Court could deal with the issue, usually as an issue of constitutional law."[38]

Even if the Supreme Court participated in the rulemaking process, its function would not be limited to approving rules of criminal procedure in advance. It would still retain its constitutional authority to decide, in individual cases, whether a given police search, interrogation, or identification procedure squared with the Constitution, either because the police failed to follow the applicable rule, because there was no applicable rule, or, in rare cases, because the applicable rule was, for some reason unforeseen at its drafting, unconstitutional.* It would then be up to the Standing Committee to amend the rules to reflect this decision. Thus, the *Committee* would be charged with distilling the essence from a Supreme Court holding and putting it into rule form, rather than requiring thousands of individual police departments and officers to try to do this on their own, as the current system demands. A standing committee could also respond to unforeseen difficulties, omissions, and so on that came to light as the rules were applied in practice.

Of course, it must be admitted that a system of written rules will still leave many unanswered questions that will have to be resolved by the courts. Certain issues, such as whether there was probable cause in a particular case, can *only* be resolved by the courts. Will the process of resolving these questions cause the new rules to become as "murky and difficult" as the Court rightly admits the old rules have become? It is possible. If the Court, in a new political age, considers the old rules totally wrong, then it may begin to chip away at them as it has at *Miranda*. But *Miranda* would never have been promulgated by a bipartisan committee in the first place. If the rules, or at least the process of declaring the rules, is perceived as even-handed at inception, the desire to change or limit the rules will not be as strong. One need only consider the makeup of the Court in the October Term 1965 to realize that the Court that decided *Miranda* was dominated by very liberal people: Warren, Fortas, Brennan, Black, and Douglas (the *Miranda* majority) as well Harlan, Stewart, Clark, and White (the *Miranda* dissenters). It is thus imperative that, whatever the makeup of the drafting committee, the rules attempt to codify, clarify, and fill in the gaps of current Supreme Court law (which has been made moderate—

---

*However, in such a case the evidence would likely not be excluded. *Illinois v. Krull* 480 U.S. 340 (1987) (police reliance on unconstitutional statute subject to good-faith exception to exclusionary rule).

though incomprehensible—by a conservative Court's attempt to cut back on liberal doctrine without overruling it), without significantly changing the overall ideological direction of current law.

Although in the 1960s there seems to have been considerable sentiment among commentators that the rules of criminal procedure ought to be codified, there is reason now to doubt whether a change in the system is desirable. This view is ably exemplified in a letter to the author by William Stuntz of the University of Virginia Law School commenting on an earlier draft of this book. Stuntz suggested that the problems that Chapters 3 and 4 identified in the criminal procedure system were a temporary phenomenon:

> It is not surprising that in the first two decades after *Mapp* and *Miranda* there has been a lot of ebb and flow, and consequently a good deal of misprediction, by lawyers as well as police officers. But much of that is over now. *Miranda* doctrine, *Massiah* doctrine, and large chunks (I would argue a large majority) of search and seizure law are fairly clear and fairly stable. . . . [M]ost of your examples, in Chapter 4, . . . are examples of the problem of fleshing out general principles. They do not, I think, undermine the point that *now* there is a lot more certainty to the law than there was 20 or even 10 years ago.[39]

Stuntz then goes on to cite the *Ross* automobile search decision—which held that cars could be searched on probable cause alone, without a warrant—as a good example of a "rule that the police have an easy time understanding and applying."

If one views the current state of the law of criminal procedure as fondly as Stuntz does, then it may be correct to apply the maxim, "If it ain't broke, don't fix it." Obviously, I do not take such a sanguine view of the state of criminal procedure law. Nor, it would seem, does the Supreme Court itself, since the majority recently recognized "the extent to which our Fourth Amendment jurisprudence has confused the courts"[40] and terms its interrogation law "murky and difficult."

I do agree with Stuntz that, since the Supreme Court undoubtedly has the authority to act in every significant area of criminal procedure, eventually it may get around to declaring law in areas, such as what happens at an interrogation after the *Miranda* warnings are given, that it has heretofore left to the states.[41] However, given the strict constructionist outlook of the current Court, it seems unlikely that it will expand its mandate into many new areas in the foreseeable future, despite the fact that these areas may greatly need clarification. In any event, Stuntz's comments address themselves only to the "incompleteness" problem with the current law, not to the "uncertainty" problem. If, as argued in Chapter 4, judicial opinions inherently tend to create more uncertainty than they resolve (and more uncertainty than statutes do), then Supreme Court action in a given area of the law will make matters worse, not better.

I also agree with Stuntz that, unlike many areas such as airport stops and searches, the clear, legislative-like pronouncement of the *Ross* automobile search case has probably resolved more questions than it has raised. However, it has not resolved as many questions as a statute would have. Left open by *Ross* were such questions as whether a container placed in the car was also subject to a warrantless search when the police had probable cause only that the container held contraband, whether an RV could be searched without a warrant, and the scope of "less than probable cause" searches, such as inventory searches. It took the Court ten years after *Ross* to answer these questions.[42] Still unanswered are questions that Yale Kamisar posed at the time *Ross* was decided:[43] whether the *Ross* emphasis on the mobility of automobiles is meant, as the dissent suggests, to render the decision inapplicable to parked cars and whether the *Ross* limitation of its holding to cases in which there is "probable cause to believe the vehicle *contained contraband*" is meant to preclude seizure of non-contraband evidentiary items. In general the *Ross* reliance on *two* aspects of automobiles to justify its result—mobility and reduced expectation of privacy—will lead to confusion whenever one of those aspects is not present.* (See the discussion of "The Lawyer Mentality" in Chapter 4.)

Finding all these questions unanswered after *Ross* is only half the battle. It remains for me to construct a statute that would have solved all, or at least most, of the problems posed by *Ross* and the other automobile search cases, in advance. Again, it must be stressed that *Ross* is an unusually straightforward holding where the Court explicitly sought to establish a clear rule that the police could easily follow. Consequently, it will be harder to construct a statute that improves on *Ross* than it would be to improve on the law of stop and frisk or searches incident to arrest, for example. Nevertheless, *Ross* can easily be bettered:

Vehicle Searches

Definition: A vehicle is any car, truck, van, bus, motorcycle, bicycle, trailer, boat, plane, or similar conveyance, whether motorized or not, which appears immediately capable of leaving the scene.

1. *Searches for Evidence*: The police may seize and fully search any vehicle

---

*For example, if a disabled car is parked in a driveway, may it be searched without a warrant? What if it is parked on a highway? Does it matter whether the police can tell that it is disabled? What if it is a disabled RV? For a discussion of some of these issues, see Wayne LaFave, *Search and Seizure: A Treatise on the Fourth Amendment* §7.2 (pocket part).

which they have probable cause to believe contains evidence of any felony or misdemeanor.

2. *Searches Incident to Arrest*: During or after the custodial arrest of any person in a vehicle, the police may search the passenger compartment of that vehicle and any containers, including the glove compartment, found therein. The trunk, and other areas separate from the passenger compartment, may only be searched pursuant to §§1 or 3.

3. *Inventory Searches*: If the police, acting pursuant to written departmental guidelines, impound any vehicle, they may fully search that vehicle, and seize, search, and inventory items found therein, to the extent authorized by the guidelines.

Drafter's Notes: This statute is essentially a codification of Supreme Court cases. In the interest of simplification, it goes further than the Court in allowing a full search of a car when probable cause is limited to the contents of a container found in the car. *California v. Acevedo* 111 S.Ct. 1982 (1991) only allowed a search of the car for the container and a search of the container. Given what an *Acevedo* search would normally entail, this is an insignificant expansion and one which the Supreme Court would likely adopt if presented with such a case, even though it expressly declined to decide the issue in *Acevedo*.[44]

Section 1 stresses apparent mobility, thus allowing a search of a car that appears to be, but is not, mobile. Because mobility rather than the elusive "expectation of privacy" aspect is stressed, it follows that any conveyance that appears to have an immediate potential for mobility is included within the definition of "vehicle." On the other hand, cars missing wheels, trailers up on blocks, and so on are not "vehicles." (But see Searches of Abandoned Property §____). Section 1 allows a "full search" of the car, which means a search as extensive as the probable cause indicates, including, if appropriate, searches under the hood, removal of seats, and so on. This is consistent with current law.

Section 2 of the statute codifies *New York v. Belton* 453 U.S. 454 (1981). However, it answers several questions left unresolved by *Belton*, such as whether a locked glove compartment, a locked suitcase in the passenger compartment, or the back of a station wagon may be searched incident to arrest (yes as to all three). Given the privacy intrusion already occasioned by the arrest and search incident thereto, the clarity achieved by extending *Belton* to every aspect of the "passenger compartment" outweighs any further intrusion on privacy. Section 2 also resolves an issue raised in Justice Brennan's dissent in *Belton* by providing that areas inaccessible to passengers, such as the trunk, the area under the hood, the area under the floorboards, and the area behind door panels may not be searched incident to arrest. This section follows *Michigan v. Thomas* 458 U.S. 259 (1982) in not requiring that the search incident be contemporaneous with the arrest,* but does limit searches of vehicles incident to arrest to cases where the suspect is arrested "in a vehicle." Section 2 purposely does not mention passengers. They, consistently with current Supreme Court law in *Ybarra v. Illinois* 444 U.S. 85 (1979), can only be frisked

---

*But see the British Police and Criminal Evidence Act §32 (Appendix A), which limits searches incident to arrest to cases where police have "reasonable grounds" for believing that the arrestee is dangerous or that evidence will be found.

upon reasonable suspicion that they are armed and searched upon probable cause. They may, of course, be ordered out of a vehicle during a search. Section 3 codifies *Colorado v. Bertine* 479 U.S. 367 (1987) and *Florida v. Wells* 110 S.Ct. 1632 (1990). It explicitly requires written standards, which *Bertine* and *Wells* do not. Furthermore, it reposes no discretion in the individual officer except to the extent that such discretion is allowed in the guidelines, consistently with *Wells*. The statute does not spell out, but assumes, the limitation stated in *Wells*, that "The policy . . . governing inventory searches should be designed to produce an inventory. The individual police officer must not be allowed so much latitude that inventory searches are turned into 'a purposeful and general means of discovering evidence of crime.'"[45] Accordingly, an inventory search will not be as intrusive as a full-scale search for concealed evidence. It is not deemed necessary to spell out the requisites of a proper inventory policy because counsel for police can consult *Wells* and *Bertine* in drafting such a policy. The statute contains the only admonition that the individual police officer needs to know: follow the written guidelines.

Considering the amount of time and effort and the number of pages in the U.S. Reports that the Supreme Court has devoted to vehicle searches, only to produce doctrine that the Court itself consistently denigrates, this statute, including the drafter's comments, is a model of brevity and, hopefully, clarity. It attempts to reflect Supreme Court holdings in this area, deviating from those holdings only to the extent necessary to achieve consistency or clarity. In one sense, it illustrates the opposite of Stuntz's point that a statute might have been a good idea thirty years ago, but is no longer needed. On the contrary, thirty years ago, a statute writer would have had no guidance as to where the Supreme Court might go in a given area, and little guidance as to what problems lay hidden in each area of the law. Today, after thirty years of Court decisions since *Mapp* extended the Court's reach to the states, and academic commentary as to the shortcomings of those decisions, the problems and possibilities are much more apparent. It is much easier to draft a statute that encapsulates Supreme Court law than one that anticipates it.*

Consider the advantages of a code in dealing with the problems that have faced the Court in promulgating criminal procedure rules, as discussed in Chapter 4. First, the incompleteness problem can be instantly solved, rather than waiting another decade or two for the right cases to come before the Court. The "gray area" problem will, unavoidably, arise in a statutory scheme, but will be far smaller than in the current arrangement because the drafters of the rules will be able to anticipate, and deal with, many problems in advance.

---

*Even the doubtful Stuntz concedes that this statute "provides more predictability than the current scheme." Letter of Aug. 2, 1991. However, he goes on to doubt whether a real-life legislative body could produce such a rule.

For similar reasons, the "case or controversy," stare decisis, and "tyranny of the majority opinion" limitations are absent from legislative rulemaking.

Of course, the very clarity and simplicity of such rules may tend to lead to unjust results in some cases where disobeying the rule seems, under the circumstances, the most reasonable course of action, though the fact that some contingencies can be anticipated when the rule is drafted gives legislative rulemaking an inherent advantage over the case method. The clear rules/flexible response problem is frequently avoided under the current system by courts adjusting the rules on an ad hoc basis and claiming that the police did not violate them. It makes more sense, as discussed in the previous chapter, to repose discretion in trial courts to acknowledge the violation forthrightly, but decline to exclude the tainted evidence, on the ground that the use of the evidence would not bring the administration of justice into disrepute, that the rule was not sufficiently clear, or some other flexible standard. The use of a discretionary exclusionary rule would also free the hands of drafters, allowing them to propose a tough and comprehensive code without fear that including detailed standards in certain areas would lead to wholesale evidentiary exclusion.

As discussed in the previous chapter, there is a risk that trial judges, invited to exercise their discretion, will always exercise it in favor of the police, thus rendering the exclusionary rule nugatory. However, this risk inheres in the current system as well, especially since many constitutional claims are now shielded from federal habeas review. Only the determination of state appellate courts, and of the United States Supreme Court, to deter police misconduct through use of the exclusionary sanction causes the current "mandatory" rule to have any deterrent impact. Otherwise, trial judges can ignore the "mandatory" rule with impunity. There is no reason to believe that this determination would weaken if courts were allowed to recognize a violation without being forced to exclude evidence, rather than being forced, as in the current system, to alter the rules in order to avoid exclusion when police behavior seemed reasonable.

The Canadian and British experiences suggest that when trial courts are faced with police violations of clear, codified rules, evidentiary exclusion will frequently be used to punish violations of those rules. However, any attempt to alter the exclusionary rule, even if it does not diminish its overall deterrent efficacy, might meet with such fervent opposition that, as discussed in Chapter 5, it might be politically unwise to attempt it in the context of a code revision.

Do legislative rules suffer from problems that do not bedevil judge-made rules? None that inhere in the process. However, political concerns are obviously much more likely to afflict a legislative body than a group of judges appointed for life. These may take the form of not producing a rule at all, or of allowing political expediency to overwhelm common sense or decency. I have tried to guard against this by suggesting a rulemaking body that is reasonably shielded from, but not immune to, political concerns.

It must be reemphasized that, unless such a statutory scheme is "revenue neutral" (i.e., like the tax code revision, but using the term "revenue" to refer to political capital), it will fail. The overall effort must be aimed at clarification, simplification, and completeness, not at a change in the ideological direction of the law. But this is not to say that, in a given area, the drafters should take adherence to current Supreme Court doctrine as their overriding goal. An effort to define the "best," most efficient, or most easily followed rule should naturally be undertaken. But current Supreme Court law should nevertheless be the guiding star of the codification effort as a whole.

The experience of the Justice Department in trying, but failing, to achieve a much needed reform of the federal criminal law (a bill labeled "S1") because the bill also tried to achieve a conservative political agenda should be ample evidence of the unwisdom of a politically motivated reform of criminal procedure law.[46]

Will Congress ever adopt the approach suggested in this book? Who knows? It might be that conservatives will like it because they will reason, despite the above admonition, that since Congress is generally conservative when it comes to crime, the result will move the law to the right of where even the Rehnquist Court, hindered by stare decisis, has been willing to go. On the other hand, conservatives will not like the idea of legitimating federal control over criminal procedure law, which they still consider to be a matter for the states. Conservatives may also fear being squeezed by the fact that any codification cannot be much more conservative than current Supreme Court law because the Court may strike it down,[47] whereas the Court can have no objection if Congress chooses to grant more rights to criminal suspects than the Court might have done. On the other side of the aisle, liberals may be for it because they fear the direction that the current Supreme Court is going or against it because they expect the second coming of Earl Warren in a future "Clinton Court" and do not trust Congress. Police and other criminal justice professionals should be for it because it will give police clearer, more comprehensive guidelines and therefore result in the exclusion of less evidence than is currently the case. But there is one group that should welcome this proposal like the return of a prodigal son—the Supreme Court. After thirty years of sinking ever deeper into the tarpit of their own creation that is criminal procedure law, the members of the Court should not let Congress rest until it adopts this reform.

Notes

1. The Criminal Investigations Bills of 1976 and 1981 were rejected by Parliament. A more recent proposal by the Law Reform Commission is currently being studied by governmental agencies and seems to have better prospects for passage. Telephone conversation with Stephen Mason, Secretary and Director of Research, Law Reform Commission, March 2, 1989.

The police lobby has been highly influential in opposing and defeating previous efforts at reform. "The Victoria Police responded to the findings . . . of the Beach Inquiry with remarkable vigour and hostility, and fought a largely successful campaign . . . to prevent the implementation of its procedural recommendations." Peter Sallman and John Willis, *Criminal Justice in Australia*, 18.

In response to the Criminal Investigation Bill of 1981, the President of the Police Federation of Australia and New Zealand threatened a police strike if the procedural protections of the bill were enacted. 26 *Reform* 63 (April 1982). Senator Evans, then Attorney General, "suggested that the police response to the Bill . . . demonstrated 'a profound indifference to the constraints of existing law.'" Id.

2. 42 U.S.C. §1983 (1982); see *Monroe v. Pape* 365 U.S. 167 (1961).

3. *Malloy v. Hogan* 378 U.S. 1 (1964) (fifth amendment); *Gideon v. Wainwright* 372 U.S. 335 (1963) (sixth amendment); *Mapp v. Ohio* 367 U.S. 643 (1961) (fourth amendment).

4. U.S. Constitution, amend. XIV, §4.

5. The holding of *The Civil Rights Cases* 109 U.S. 3 (1883) that the fourteenth amendment gives Congress no authority to regulate the behavior of private individuals would have no bearing here since Congress would be limiting the conduct of a quintessential state/local governmental agency—the police. See *Katzenbach v. Morgan* 384 U.S. 641, 650–51 (1966) (holding that Congress has independent authority to interpret the provisions of the fourteenth amendment). See, generally, Irving Gordon, "The Nature and Uses of Congressional Power Under Section Five of the Fourteenth Amendment to Overcome Decisions of the Supreme Court"; Robert Burt, "*Miranda* and Title II: A Morganatic Marriage."

6. It might be argued that the power to "enforce" includes only the power to provide remedies, not to declare rules. This seems an unduly crabbed reading of the fourteenth amendment, especially in view of the statutes already enacted to "enforce" it, such as 42 U.S.C. §1983, and 18 U.S.C. §§241, 242 (1988). A power to "enforce" without the power to flesh out the vague terms of the amendment with statutory rules would be largely meaningless.

7. 384 U.S. 641, 650 (1966).

8. Id. at 651. See also *Regents of the Univ. of Cal. v. Bakke* 438 U.S. 265, 302 n. 41 (1978): "We have previously recognized the special competence of Congress to make findings with respect to the effects of identified past discrimination and its discretionary authority to take appropriate remedial measures."

9. 10.59 LW 4714, 4718–19 (1991).

10. Australian Law Reform Commission, Report No. 2, p. 23.

11. Herbert Packer, "The Courts, the Police, and the Rest of Us," 240.

12. Henry Friendly, "The Bill of Rights as a Code of Criminal Procedure," 930.

13. Paul Bator and James Vorenberg, "Arrest, Detention, Interrogation, and the Right to Counsel: Basic Problems and Possible Legislative Solutions," 63–64. Accord Francis Allen, "The Judicial Quest for Penal Justice: The Warren Court and the Criminal Procedure Revolution," 542:

A new allocation of responsibilities is required. The role of the Court will remain critical. It has shown its capacity to identify and dramatize problems in criminal justice administration; this role is an essential catalyst for reform. The Court will have to make the ultimate decisions on the constitutional validity of the solutions devised. Nevertheless, its role is better adapted to review than to initiation. If categorical rules for the system are needed, it is better that other institutions formulate most rules.

14. Donald Dowling, "Escobedo and Beyond: The Need for a Fourteenth Amendment Code of Criminal Procedure," 143, 153, 154, 156. Dowling cited *Ex Parte Virginia* 100 U.S. 339, 345–46 (1879) to support the proposition that Congress had the power, under §5 of the fourteenth amendment, to enact such a code of criminal procedure. In *Ex Parte Virginia* the Court held that "Whatever legislation is . . . adapted to carry out the objects the amendments have in view . . . is brought within the domain of congressional power." Id. Accord *Monroe v. Pape* 365 U.S. 167, 171–72 (1961).

15. 18 U.S.C. §§2510–20.

16. Id. §2516(2).

17. 389 U.S. 347 (1967).

18. See sources cited in Wayne LaFave and Jerold Israel, *Criminal Procedure*, §4.2.

19. Michael Goldsmith, "The Supreme Court and Title III: Rewriting the Law of Electronic Surveillance," 170.

20. See *Katzenbach v. Morgan* 384 U.S. 641, 650–51 (1966), holding that Congress has independent authority to interpret the provisions of the fourteenth amendment. Cf. Burt, supra note 5 at 81.

21. 18 U.S.C. §§891–896 (1988).

22. 402 U.S. 146 (1971).

23. The Sentencing Commission was created under the Sentencing Reform Act of 1984, as amended, 18 U.S.C. §3551 et seq. (1982 ed., Supp. IV) and 28 U.S.C. §§991–998 (1982 ed., Supp. IV).

24. 18 U.S.C. §994.

25. *Mistretta v. United States* 109 S.Ct. 647 (1989).

26. Sunday, April 12, 1992, p. 1.

27. Winifred Brown, *Federal Rulemaking: Problems and Possibilities* (Washington, D.C.: Federal Judicial Center, 1981), p. 29.

28. Id. at 29.

29. Id., n. at 9.

30. Id. at 16.

31. See Gene Shreve and Peter Raven-Hansen, *Understanding Civil Procedure*, 7–8.

32. See text and annotations following 18 U.S.C.A. 3771.

33. Frank Remington, "A Quarter of a Century of Rulemaking with Particular Attention to the Federal Rules of Criminal Procedure," 236.

34. Charles Wright, *Federal Practice and Procedure*, §4.

35. 469 U.S. 528, 556.

36. Jack B. Weinstein, "Reform of Federal Court Rulemaking Procedures," 929–30.

37. Id. at 4.

38. Remington reports this conversation in supra note 35 at 225.

39. William Stuntz, letter to the author, Nov. 13, 1990, on file at Indiana University (Bloomington) Law Library.

40. *California v. Acevedo* 111 S.Ct. 1982, 1990 (1991).

41. Actually, in *McNabb v. United States* 318 U.S. 332 (1943) and *Mallory v. United States* 354 U.S. 449 (1957) the Court, acting under its supervisory power, did hold that a seven-hour delay in presenting the suspect to the magistrate violated F.R. Crim. P. 5(a). Also, in *Riverside Co. v. McLaughlin* 111 S.Ct. 1661 (1991) the Court held that a suspect arrested without a warrant must have a judicial probable cause hearing within 48 hours.

42. In *California v. Acevedo* 111 S.Ct. 1982 (1991) the Court held that if there is probable cause to search a container in a car, then the container may be searched without a warrant, even though it could not have been searched had it not been placed in the car.

In *California v. Carney* 105 S.Ct. 2066 (1985) the Court held that an RV may be searched without a warrant unless it is rendered immobile, such as being up on blocks in a trailer park.

In *New York v. Belton* 453 U.S. 454 (1981) the Court held that a search incident to arrest extends to the entire passenger compartment of an automobile (but not the trunk) even if the defendant has been removed from the car prior to the search.

43. Yale Kamisar, *The Supreme Court, Trends and Developments, 1981–82*, 86ff.

44. "[A] search of the entire car would have been . . . unreasonable under the Fourth Amendment." 111 S.Ct. at 1991.

45. *Florida v. Wells* 110 S.Ct. 1632, 1635 (1990).

46. For a relatively recent report on the status of, and need for, federal criminal code revision, see Ronald Gainer, "Report to the Attorney General on Federal Criminal Code Reform."

47. But see Gordon, supra note 6 at 656, arguing that Congress can both enhance and diminish rights granted by the Supreme Court.

Chapter 7
Alternative Models of Criminal Procedure

The statutory model of criminal procedure proposed in the last chapter runs counter to the training and experience of American lawyers, who are steeped in the notion that case law is the way to develop constitutionally based rules. This fact, combined with the possible political objections that this proposal may face, discussed in the previous chapter, means that it may never be enacted. This book is not intended merely as an academic exercise, but is, rather, designed to provide practical solutions to the practical problems facing the criminal justice system. Consequently, this chapter proposes three alternative approaches that do not require a total revamping of the current system of Supreme Court-created criminal procedure law. The first two, which I originally proposed in a 1985 article in the *Michigan Law Review* entitled "Two Models of the Fourth Amendment," suggest new approaches that the Supreme Court itself could take to the vexing problems of fourth amendment, and all criminal procedure, law. The third proposal simply suggests that the Advisory Committee for the (federal) Criminal Rules expand the coverage of those rules to include police procedures, and thus serve as a model for the states.

Two Models of Criminal Procedure

As I argued at length in the *Michigan Law Review*, there are two ways in which the Supreme Court could avoid some of the problems that inhere in its attempts to declare rules of criminal procedure discussed in Chapter 4. They could either declare a clear rule and stick to it, even if it led to unsatisfactory results in a particular case (Model I), or declare a standard that was so obviously *not* a clear rule that it would not have to be compromised case by case (Model II). It was, essentially, this latter standard that was in effect prior to the criminal procedure revolution, when the fourteenth amendment's requirement that no one be deprived of liberty but by "due process of law" was the only constitutional limitation on state police procedures. Under this regime, to be admissible confessions had to be "voluntary,"[1] identification procedures not "so unreasonably suggestive [as to be] conducive to irreparable mistaken identification,"[2] and searches must not have shocked the conscience.[3] In general, as Justice Frankfurter writing for the Court in *Rochin v. California* put it, "Due process of law . . . precludes defining, and thereby confining, these standards more precisely than to say that convictions cannot be brought about by methods that offend 'a sense of justice.'"[4]

As discussed in Chapter 2, the Warren Court concluded that such vague pronouncements were inadequate if the Court was regularly going to exclude evidence as a result of defective state procedures, and thereby cause the release of convicted criminals. Consequently, the Court set out to develop clear rules for the states to follow. As to the fourth amendment, the principal new rule was that "search warrants are always required" (except under "exigent circumstances"). As to confessions, the Court held in *Miranda* that admissions obtained via "custodial interrogation" could never be admitted unless warnings as to the rights to silence and counsel were given to the defendant before questioning.[5] Finally, as to lineups, the Court required that counsel be present at a lineup if that procedure were to be admissible at trial.[6]

Despite police objections, the latter two rules were not only clear but workable, and the police were able to adapt to them. Had the warrant requirement really been enforced, subject only to the "emergency" exception, which was the only exception that the Court, at least in theory, originally recognized,[7] it too would have been a workable rule that the police would have disliked at first but learned to follow. This would have been especially true if telephonic warrants, as currently allowed by the federal rules,[8] had been held to satisfy the warrant requirement, thus reducing the number of cases in which an "emergency" required that a warrant not be sought.

But, as discussed in Chapter 3, the Warren Court, perhaps sensitive to criticisms that it was "soft on crime," tried to help the police out by recognizing several exceptions to the strict warrant requirement— such as searches incident to arrest, stop and frisk, and automobile searches—as well as by attempting to refine its definition of just what was a proper search under various circumstances. The Burger Court accelerated this trend until, by 1985, there were over twenty exceptions to the warrant requirement.[9] While the Court still claims, in the face of myriad holdings to the contrary, that there is a warrant requirement, recent cases show that this is nothing but window dressing.[10] Meanwhile the cases defining what is or is not a proper search have proliferated, creating a lengthy, and confusing, body of law on the subject.

In the interrogations area the *Miranda* requirements, while limited to custodial interrogation, did not originally admit of any exceptions once custodial interrogation was found, reflecting the Model I "clear rule" approach. Moreover, *Miranda* imposed a second clear requirement: if, after warnings, the suspect asserts the right to silence or counsel, "interrogation must cease."[11] Unfortunately both for doctrinal consistency and for the police and citizenry alike, the Court has diluted these clear rules, creating a doctrine that the Court itself now deems "murky and difficult." First it has created two exceptions to the basic *Miranda* holding: the "public safety"[12] and "booking question"[13] exceptions. Second it has held that the suspect's assertion of the right to silence does not necessarily mean that questioning must cease altogether,[14] but that the assertion of the right to counsel still does.[15] Even this latter clear rule is qualified by a holding that if the suspect "initiates" further conversation, questioning may resume, even if the "initiation" is nothing more than asking, "What is going to happen to me now?"[16] In short, the more the Court has "clarified" the *Miranda* doctrine over the years, the more uncertainty it has created as to the scope of that doctrine.

In addition to the uncertainty about what *Miranda* now requires, that case never did resolve all the problems in the interrogation area because it did not address itself to the question of what the police could do after the warnings were given (Was deception appropriate? How long could the interrogation last? . . .). Still, it had the virtue of presenting the police with two clear rules that they could learn to follow and that, contrary to predictions, did not have the effect of cutting off confessions. The current direction of the Court, chipping away at *Miranda* without overruling it, is leading toward a body of law that is as hopelessly confused as that of the fourth amendment.

In the area of identification procedures, the law has developed in a third way. In *Wade*, the Warren Court adopted a clear rule that counsel must be present at all lineups. It was not a very good rule, since photographs and tape recordings would be a better way to ensure fairness than counsel's presence, but at least it was clear, reasonably helpful to suspects, and not harmful to the investigation process. However, in *Kirby v. Illinois*[17] the Burger Court reverted to the old "no rules" due process approach by holding that *Wade* only applied to post-indictment lineups (i.e., after the right to counsel attaches anyway). Most lineups are held before the indictment (to determine whether there is anyone to indict). Thus *Wade* has largely been wiped out, and for most lineups the applicable rule is the old due process approach that they must not be "unnecessarily suggestive and conducive to irreparable mistaken identification." This "no rules" standard seems to work out fairly well, especially since police and prosecutors have recognized that being able to reproduce the lineup through tape recordings and photographs, or videotapes, makes it more valuable evidence in court.[18]

Thus, the Court itself has adopted each of the two models, "no rules" or "clear rules," in different contexts. The *Miranda* rule was clear in its instruction to the police and reasonably clear in its applicability (i.e., in all cases of "custodial interrogation"). The identification rule, starting out as a Model I "clear rule" and reverting to the old due process Model II, is admittedly unclear, but has proved workable. The development of the law of the fourth amendment would have benefited had the Court adopted either of these approaches: that warrants are always required prior to any search, subject only to a narrowly defined emergency exception (Model I)*, or that searches must simply be "reasonable," taking into account all relevant factors such as the seriousness of the crime, the level of suspicion, whether a warrant was obtained, and so on (Model II).

Justice Scalia advocated abandoning the fictitious warrant requirement in his concurring opinion in *California v. Acevedo*, decided in 1991.[19] He noted that the fourth amendment, by its terms, imposes no warrant requirement, and that, in any case, a "requirement" that had over twenty exceptions was meaningless. Accordingly, he proposed returning to the sort of "no lines" approach that had governed the Court prior to the Warren era—a requirement that searches only need be "reasonable." However, he qualified this statement, by allowing that "changes in the surrounding legal rules . . . may make a warrant indispensable to reasonableness where [at common law] it was not."[20] It is not clear how this proposal differs from the current warrant non-requirement imposed by the majority, but at least Scalia has recognized the anomalies created by the current law.

In short, any system of criminal procedure law that requires the Supreme Court constantly to "fine tune" it will produce hopeless confusion because of the Court's tendency to create more questions than it resolves, as detailed in Chapter 4. Consequently, a system that the Court can put in place, and then largely leave alone, would work best,

---

*Searches or seizures (e.g., *Terry* frisks), which have never been subject to the probable cause requirement, would not be subject to such a warrant requirement.

in part because it might encourage more states to develop comprehensive codes.* Had the Court confined itself in the interrogation area to answering such post-*Miranda* questions as "what is custody?" and "what is interrogation?" and "what are the limits on the police after the warnings are given?" and then stopped, we might have a body of law that is more comprehensible today (though the "uncertainty principle" would have assured that it was far less comprehensible than a code). As it is, the law of both interrogations and searches has become such a tangled web that it is unlikely that the Court alone can ever extricate itself from the mess.

But if the Court were to revert to a "no lines" standard, such as that confession be reliable and not obtained by police oppression or that searches must be "reasonable," would it not get itself into the same sort of mess it was in prior to *Miranda*? This is possible, and is one reason I favor statutory rather than court-created rules. If a "no lines" approach is to work, in either the interrogation or the search area, the Court must restrict itself to recognizing that each case is fact-specific, not a vehicle for "clarifying" or "modifying" the standard. It may be that the states have become so attuned to the constitutional limits on police conduct that they may effectively enforce such a "no lines" standard without the necessity of Supreme Court intervention to curb outrageous police practices. Or, even if the Supreme Court did intervene, if it did so in a brief opinion that simply set forth the facts and declared the particular police behavior unacceptable, it would avoid most of the uncertainty problems that it is prone to. However, unless each state drafts a comprehensive code itself, and one that sticks closely to Supreme Court guidelines, this will simply move the problem of uncertainty from the federal to the state level, leading to pressure on the Court to intervene once again to protect the rights of citizens in states that are not prepared to protect those rights themselves.[21]

The Models at Work

The test of any proposal is whether it can resolve real cases better than they are currently being resolved. An acid test is provided by *New York v. Belton*,[22] where the Court found itself confronted with the

---

*Currently about a third of the states have comprehensive codes adopted since the Warren Court began its intense scrutiny of the criminal procedure area. Wayne LaFave and Jerold Israel, *Criminal Procedure*, vol. 1, §1.5(c). These state rules differ greatly in terms of both their coverage and their substantive requirements. See Barry Latzer, *State Constitutions and Criminal Justice*.

task of integrating two of its confusing doctrines, the automobile exception (to the warrant but not the probable cause requirement) and the search incident to arrest exception (to both) into a single decision. In *Belton* a highway patrolman stopped a speeding car, smelled marijuana, and saw an envelope on the floor marked "Supergold," which he associated with marijuana. He then ordered the four occupants out of the car, informed them that they were under arrest, and searched the passenger compartment of the car, finding marijuana in the envelope and cocaine in the zippered pocket of a black leather jacket.

The Court upheld the search, citing the need for "a set of rules which, in most instances, makes it possible [for the police] to reach a correct determination beforehand as to whether an invasion of privacy is justified." [23] Accordingly, the 5–4 majority held that the passenger compartment of an automobile may always be searched "incident to arrest" of the occupants (i.e., without a warrant or probable cause to search) because that compartment is "generally, even if not inevitably," an "area into which an arrestee might reach in order to grab a weapon or evidentiary ite[m]." [24]

Thus *Belton* like *Ross* [25] tried to make things easier for the police by establishing a "bright line" that was applicable in a limited class of cases—arrests from automobiles. Such an effort is doomed to failure because the class of cases in which the "bright line" is to apply does not itself have clear boundaries. As Justice Brennan argued in dissent, the new rule

leaves open too many questions and, more important, it provides the police and the courts with too few tools with which to find the answers.*

Thus, although the Court concludes that a warrantless search of a car may take place even though the suspect was arrested outside the car, it does not indicate how long after the suspect's arrest that search may validly be conducted. Would a warrantless search incident to arrest be valid if conducted five minutes after the suspect left his car? Thirty minutes? Three hours? Does it matter whether the suspect is standing in close proximity to the car when the search is conducted? . . . [W]hat is meant by "interior"? Does it include locked glove compartments, the interior of door panels, or the area under the floorboards? Are special rules necessary for station wagons and hatchbacks, where the luggage compartment may be reached through the interior, or taxicabs, where a glass panel might separate the driver's compartment from the rest of the car? Are the only containers that may be searched those that are large enough to be "capable of holding another object"? Or does the new rule apply to any container, even if it "could hold neither a weapon nor evidence of the criminal conduct for which the suspect was arrested"?

*Note that the questions raised by Justice Brennan would be answered by the model statute on vehicle searches proposed in Chapter 6.

The Court does not give the police any "bright-line" answers to these questions. More important, because the Court's new rule abandons the justification underlying *Chimel, it offers no guidance to the police officer seeking to work out these answers for himself.*[26]

Beyond leaving unanswered questions, the result in *Belton* as in *Ross*[27] will lead to inconsistent results in many cases. While the Court continues to assert that one has a constitutional right not to have one's automobile searched without at least probable cause unless there is some good reason for doing so, *Belton* converts the fact that there may be a good reason to permit such warrantless, non-probable-cause searches in some cases into a rule permitting such searches in all cases.[28] The "clear rule" of *Belton* is neither clear nor just.

A statutory approach to the problems of vehicle searches has already been suggested in Chapter 6. Either of the two models suggested in this chapter can also resolve the *Belton* issues without creating a precedent that will cause mischief in the future. Under Model I the resolution is simple. There is nothing to indicate that the patrolman had any sense of emergency in the case. He could have radioed his evidence (which clearly constituted probable cause) to the magistrate at his convenience (presumably after help had arrived), obtained an authorization, and searched the car. (Of course, the original, non-probable-cause traffic stop would not require a Model I warrant, nor would the non-probable-cause plain view of the "Supergold" envelope.) If Model I were in effect, it could readily have been complied with in this case, and the extensive litigation that *Belton* engendered would have been avoided. If Model I were not complied with, the evidence would have to be suppressed. In a case in which there is probable cause to arrest the occupant of a car but not to search the car (e.g., a suspect is arrested on a fugitive warrant), under Model I police would not, and should not, be able to search the car just because they could not get a warrant (*Belton* allowed such a search).[29] It is difficult to imagine an automobile case where an emergency would justify dispensing with a Model I warrant, since the police should be able to control the car and its occupants while awaiting search approval.

The application of Model II to this case is less clear cut but still not difficult. Here the patrolman had evidence amounting to a virtual certainty that marijuana was present in the car. Moreover, he was dealing with a car and not a house. On the other hand, the suspected offense was a minor one and there was no emergency. One could resolve this case either way, and, since the resolution would have little precedential value, it is not terribly important what that resolution might be. In my view the stronger argument is that the intrusion on protected interests was sufficiently slight and the probable cause so strong that the policeman acted reasonably. Had he opened a locked container in the passenger compartment, judges undoubtedly would split as to whether this was "reasonable."[30] If he had proceeded to demand the keys to the trunk and to go through suitcases found there, I would conclude that he should have obtained a warrant before doing so.[31]

When the goal of providing definitive answers in advance is demonstrably unachievable, tolerance for uncertainty is the only alternative. A system that tolerates uncertainty only in relatively close cases is far preferable to a system in which, as in *Belton*, clear rules dictate unjust results. At least if the evidence is suppressed under Model I, it will be suppressed on the basis of the bottom line of the fourth amendment—that the search was unreasonable—and not because a court determines that a locked container is not part of the passenger compartment of the car. This latter question, which *Belton* forces the courts to ask, is an irrelevant abstraction that completely loses track of the fundamental fourth amendment requirement of "reasonableness."

Still, the experience of other countries with codes suggests that relatively clear and detailed rules are achievable. Consequently, if the political will can be mustered, it would be better to proceed with a code system, which is comprehensive and can decide many future cases in advance, than for the Supreme Court to attempt to revise its way of dealing with criminal procedure issues.

Expanding the Federal Rules

If none of the approaches suggested so far comes to pass, there is a fourth, even less ambitious, reform that could be adopted. That is simply to expand the mandate of the current Federal Criminal Rules Advisory Committee to drafting rules that cover (federal) police procedures. Since the FBI, DEA, ATF, Postal and Secret Service agents engage in a range of searches, interrogations, and identification procedures that are similar to those in the states, rules promulgated to govern them could be used as a model for the states. Indeed, in *Miranda* the Court relied on the fact that the FBI required its agents to give suspects warnings as to their rights to silence and counsel as the basis for the *Miranda* requirements.[32]

Currently, the Federal Rules are based upon the old view of "criminal procedure" discussed at the beginning of this book—that it is limited to court procedures. Thus there are standards for search warrants issued by magistrates (Rule 41) but no standards for warrantless searches. Interrogations are indirectly limited by the requirement that suspects must be taken before a magistrate "without unnecessary delay" (Rule 5), but no warnings requirement is delineated. Of course, *Miranda* applies to the federal authorities as much as it does to the states; so it is not surprising that development of the federal rules has been somewhat coopted by what has occurred in the Supreme Court. However, by the same token, federal authorities receive no clearer guidance from confusing Supreme Court rules than do state authorities, and they could benefit greatly from codification and simplification of those Supreme Court dictates.

While Sara Beale has argued that the Supreme Court's supervisory authority does not extend to making non-constitutional rules for the governance of federal courts (as it did in *McNabb v. United States*[33] and *Mallory v. United States*[34]), she agrees that "amendments to the Federal Rules of Criminal Procedure may properly regulate some matters that have been the subject of highly questionable supervisory power rulings. . . ."[35]

As discussed earlier, I believe that rules concerning such subjects as the length of interrogation and whether deceit may be used can properly be considered to be matters of due process, and hence made applicable to the states through federal statute or Supreme Court pronouncement. Failing that, however, if the Federal Rules were expanded to govern police procedures, they, and the litigation (or lack of it) that they would engender in the federal courts, could serve as a very useful model for improving and codifying state procedures.

Finally, it must be noted that neither this model of advisory federal rules nor the main proposal in this book for mandatory federal rules is inconsistent with the Supreme Court's adopting the Model II (no rules) approach, which is exactly the direction that the Court is currently headed in the fourth amendment area. If the Court walks out of the game by refusing to try to spell out rules and just striking down an occasional unreasonable search (or interrogation), then it may eventually occur to legislative rulemakers at either the state or the federal level that they must move to fill this vacuum in order that the police and citizens receive more guidance as to appropriate police procedures. In other words, the very course of action that the Court urged upon legislatures nearly thirty years ago in *Miranda*, and then proceeded to undermine by coopting the field itself, may once more become viable if the Court gives up its failed attempt to declare the rules of criminal procedure. If the Federal Rules Advisory Committee expanded its role, the Court could encourage the process by citing the federal rules as guidelines for what searches are reasonable and what interrogations are appropriately conducted, thus encouraging the states to follow the federal government's lead—as in Australia.

Why is this not the best approach? Certainly, many conservatives who would agree that the Supreme Court has not produced comprehensible doctrine would argue that returning the rule-creation authority to the states would be ideal. Even assuming that the states would make and enforce rules with some regard for the constitutional rights involved, I cannot endorse this approach as anything more than a pale substitute for a national code of criminal procedure. The first problem is getting the Supreme Court to cooperate. While the Court would probably be willing to cede its role of declaring the rules of procedure to a coordinate branch of the federal government, it seems unlikely that it would be willing to turn the clock back to pre-incorporation days and return this power to the states. The temptation, on the part of the Court, to tinker with, and make more uniform, state rules of procedure, or to continue to declare rules for those states that have failed to act (which decisions would necessarily also apply to those states that *had* followed the model rules) would be too great and, given the likely rules some states would produce, would be entirely justified. The "reform" would end up looking just like the current system. Second, it makes no sense to say that Bill of Rights guarantees that the Court has required to be applied uniformly to all citizens for thirty years may now vary from state to state. Of course, the Court could avoid these problems by consistently holding up the federal rules as the only acceptable model for the states to follow, thus bringing in through the back door what I have proposed to bring in through the front.

But while I do not advocate model federal rules as the best approach to the problems of criminal procedure, expanding those rules to cover police procedures would certainly be a good start, as it would give both the states and the Supreme Court a compass by which to steer their course in creating later rules.

Notes

1. *Brown v. Mississippi* 297 U.S. 278 (1936).
2. *Stovall v. Denno* 388 U.S. 293, 302 (1967). In *Stovall* the Court speaks of this as a "recognized ground of attack upon a conviction," though it had not been recognized by the Supreme Court prior to *Stovall* itself.
3. *Rochin v. California* 342 U.S. 165, 172 (1952).
4. Id. at 173.
5. *Miranda v. Arizona* 384 U.S. 436 (1966).
6. *United States v. Wade* 388 U.S. 218 (1967).

7. E.g., in *McDonald v. United States* 335 U.S. 451, 455 (1948) the Court held that:

Absent some grave emergency, the Fourth Amendment has interposed a magistrate between the citizen and the police. . . . We cannot be true to [the Constitution] and excuse the absence of a search warrant without a showing by those who seek exemption from the constitutional mandate that the exigencies of the situation made that course imperative.

However, in *Chimel v. California* 395 U.S. 752 (1969), which quoted the above passage with approval, the Court approved warrantless, non-emergency searches incident to arrest, and reiterated its approval the prior Term, in *Terry v. Ohio* 392 U.S. 1 (1968), of warrantless stops and frisks.

8. F.R. Crim. P. 41(c), (2).

9. Craig Bradley, "Two Models of the Fourth Amendment," 1473.

10. The 1988 case of *Murray v. United States* 108 S.Ct. 2529 (1988), is a particularly striking example of this trend. In *Murray*, the DEA had probable cause that a certain warehouse contained marijuana. While one officer went for a warrant, the others entered the warehouse and found marijuana. No exigent circumstances were claimed. Without seizing anything, the agents awaited the arrival of the search warrant. When it came, they entered and seized 270 bales of marijuana. The Court allowed the admission into evidence of all the seized marijuana. The majority reasoned that the actual seizure of the marijuana was accomplished through an "independent source," namely the search warrant, which was not tainted by the prior illegal entry. However, the key point in *Murray* is that an unjustified warrantless search went unpunished by the exclusionary remedy. The Court went even further in dictum, declaring that even if the officers had seized the marijuana during the illegal search it would have been admissible. Justice Marshall was correct in averring, in dissent, that this holding "emasculates" the warrant requirement. Obviously, the Court did not really care about the warrant requirement or it would have made its violation more costly in *Murray*.

11. 384 U.S. 436, 473–74 (1966).

12. *New York v. Quarles* 467 U.S. 649 (1984).

13. *Pennsylvania v. Muniz* 110 S.Ct. 2638 (1990).

14. *Michigan v. Mosley* 423 U.S. 96 (1975).

15. *Edwards v. Arizona* 451 U.S. 477 (1981).

16. *Oregon v. Bradshaw* 462 U.S. 1039 (1983).

17. 406 U.S. 682 (1972).

18. Jerold Israel, "Criminal Procedure in the Burger Court, and the Legacy of the Warren Court," 1368–71.

19. 111 S.Ct. 1982, 1992 (1991).

20. Id. at 1993.

21. Readers interested in a full explication of the advantages and disadvantages of these two models should consult Bradley, supra note 9.

22. 453 U.S. 454 (1981).

23. Id. at 458 (quoting Wayne LaFave, *Search and Seizure: A Treatise on the Fourth Amendment*, 142).

24. *New York v. Belton*, 453 U.S. at 460, quoting *Chimel v. California* 395 U.S. 752, 763 (1969).

25. *United States v. Ross* 456 U.S. 798 (1982).

26. 453 U.S. at 469–70 (Brennan, J., dissenting) (emphasis in original).

27. *United States v. Ross* 456 U.S. 798 (1982).

28. For a detailed criticism of *Belton* see LaFave, supra note 23, §7.1 at 208–14 (Supp. 1985).

29. Of course a mistake by the magistrate in assessing probable cause would be subject to the good faith exception to the exclusionary rule announced in *United States v. Leon* 468 U.S. 897 (1984).

30. This assumes they would ignore the *Belton* holding itself, which allowed a search of "any containers found within the passenger compartment." *New York v. Belton* 453 U.S. at 460.

31. Of course, adopting Model I would not preclude the use of Model II (radioed, tape-recorded) warrants. *Ross* currently seems to allow such a warrantless search.

32. 384 U.S. 436, 483–85 (1966).

33. 318 U.S. 332 (1943).

34. 354 U.S. 449 (1957). In *Mallory* the Court held that a delay of seven hours between arrest and presentment before a magistrate violated F.R. Crim. P., which required presentment "without unnecessary delay."

35. Sara Sun Beale, "Reconsidering Supervisory Power in Criminal Cases: Constitutional and Statutory Limits on the Authority of the Federal Courts," 1521–22.

Appendix A
Excerpts from the Police and Criminal Evidence Act 1984 [as amended] (Great Britain)*

*Reprinted under license from Her Majesty's Stationer's Office. Citations and some technical sections (identified in the Contents list by a †) are not reprinted; they may be found in the appendix to Michael Zander, *The Police and Crminial Evidence Act, 1984*. As noted in Chapter 5, I consider PACE and the accompanying Codes of Practice prolix and complex. They are reproduced here not as models for an American statutory scheme but as a starting point for those who draft such statutes.
† Not reprinted.

79. Time for taking accused's evidence. †
80. Competence and compellability of accused's spouse. †
81. Advance notice of expert evidence in Crown Court. †

* * * *

PART I
POWERS TO STOP AND SEARCH

Power of constable to stop and search persons, vehicles etc.

1 (1) A constable may exercise any power conferred by this section—
   (*a*) in any place to which at the time when he proposes to exercise the power the public or any section of the public has access, on payment or otherwise, as of right or by virtue of express or implied permission; or
   (*b*) in any other place to which people have ready access at the time when he proposes to exercise the power but which is not a dwelling.

(2) Subject to subsection (3) to (5) below, a constable—
   (*a*) may search—
      (i) any person or vehicle;
      (ii) anything which is in or on a vehicle,
         for stolen or prohibited articles or any article to which subsection (8A) below applies; and
   (*b*) may detain a person or vehicle for the purpose of such a search.

(3) This section does not give a constable power to search a person or vehicle or anything in or on a vehicle unless he has reasonable grounds for suspecting that he will find stolen or prohibited articles or any article to which subsection (8A) below applies.

(4) If a person is in a garden or yard occupied with and used for the purposes of a dwelling or on other land so occupied and used, a constable may not search him in the exercise of the power conferred by this section unless the constable has reasonable grounds for believing—
   (*a*) that he does not reside in the dwelling; and
   (*b*) that he is not in the place in question with the express or implied permission of a person who resides in the dwelling.

(5) If a vehicle is in a garden or yard or other place occupied with and used for the purposes of a dwelling or on other land so occupied and used a constable may not search the vehicle or anything in or on it in the exercise of the power conferred by this section unless he has reasonable grounds for believing—
   (*a*) that the person in charge of the vehicle does not reside in the dwelling; and
   (*b*) that the vehicle is not in the place in question with the express or implied permission of a person who resides in the dwelling.

(6) If in the course of such a search a constable discovers an article which he has reasonable grounds for suspecting to be a stolen or prohibited article (or an article to which subsection (8A) below applies), he may seize it.

(7) An article is prohibited for the purposes of this Part of this Act if it is—

(*a*) an offensive weapon; or

(*b*) an article—

    (i) made or adapted for use in the course of or in connection with an offence to which this sub-paragraph applies; or

    (ii) intended by the person having it with him for such use by him or by some other person.

(8) The offences to which subsection (7)(b)(i) above applies are—

(*a*) burglary;

(*b*) theft;

(*c*) offences under section 12 of the Theft Act 1968 (taking motor vehicle or other conveyance without authority); and

(*d*) offences under section 15 of that Act (obtaining property by deception).

(8A) This subsection applies to any article in relation to which a person has committed, or is committing or is going to commit an offence under section 139 of the Criminal Justice Act 1988.

(9) In this Part of this Act—

"offensive weapon" means any article—

(*a*) made or adapted for use for causing injury to persons; or

(*b*) intended by the person having it with him for such use by him or by some other person.

Provisions relating to search under section 1 and other powers

2   (1) A constable who detains a person or vehicle in the exercise—

(*a*) of the power conferred by section 1 above; or

(*b*) of any other power—

    (i) to search a person without first arresting him; or

    (ii) to search a vehicle without making an arrest,

need not conduct a search if it appears to him subsequently—

    (i) that no search is required; or

    (ii) that a search is impracticable.

(2) If a constable contemplates a search, other than a search of an unattended vehicle, in the exercise—

(*a*) of the power conferred by section 1 above; or

(*b*) of any other power, except the power conferred by section 6 below and the power conferred by section 27(2) of the Aviation Security Act 1982—

    (i) to search a person without first arresting him; or

    (ii) to search a vehicle without making an arrest,

it shall be his duty, subject to subsection (4) below, to take reasonable steps before he commences the search to bring to the attention of the appropriate person—

    (i) if the constable is not in uniform, documentary evidence that he is a constable; and

    (ii) whether he is in uniform or not, the matters specified in subsection (3) below,

and the constable shall not commence the search until he has performed that duty.

(3) The matters referred to in subsection (2)(ii) above are—
(a) the constable's name and the name of the police station to which he is attached;
(b) the object of the proposed search;
(c) the constable's grounds for proposing to make it; and
(d) the effect of section 3(7) or (8) below, as may be appropriate.

(4) A constable need not bring the effect of section 3(7) or (8) below to the attention of the appropriate person if it appears to the constable that it will not be practicable to make the record in section 3(1) below.

(5) In this section "the appropriate person" means—
(a) if the constable proposes to search a person, that person; and
(b) if he proposes to search a vehicle, or anything in or on a vehicle, the person in charge of the vehicle.

(6) On completing a search of an unattended vehicle or anything in or on such a vehicle in the exercise of any such power as is mentioned in subsection (2) above a constable shall leave a notice—
(a) stating that he has searched it;
(b) giving the name of the police station to which he is attached;
(c) stating that an application for compensation for any damage caused by the search may be made to that police station; and
(d) stating the effect of section 3(8) below.

(7) The constable shall leave the notice inside the vehicle unless it is not reasonably practicable to do so without damaging the vehicle.

(8) The time for which a person or vehicle may be detained for the purposes of such a search is such time as is reasonably required to permit a search to be carried out either at the place where the person or vehicle was first detained or nearby.

(9) Neither the power conferred by section 1 above nor any other power to detain and search a person without first arresting him or to detain and search a vehicle without making an arrest is to be construed—
(a) as authorising a constable to require a person to remove any of his clothing in public other than an outer coat, jacket or gloves; or
(b) as authorising a constable not in uniform to stop a vehicle.

(10) This section and section 1 above apply to vessels, aircraft and hovercraft as they apply to vehicles.

Duty to make records concerning searches

3   (1) Where a constable has carried out a search in the exercise of any such power as is mentioned in section 2(1) above, other than a search—
(a) under section 6 below; or
(b) under section 27(2) of the Aviation Security Act 1982,
    he shall make a record of it in writing unless it is not practicable to do so.
(2) If—
(a) a constable is required by subsection (1) above to make a record of a search; but
(b) it is not practicable to make the record on the spot,
    he shall make it as soon as practicable after the completion of the search.

(3) The record of a search of a person shall include a note of his name, if the constable knows it, but a constable may not detain a person to find out his name.

(4) If a constable does not know the name of a person whom he has searched, the record of the search shall include a note otherwise describing that person.

(5) The record of a search of a vehicle shall include a note describing the vehicle.

(6) The record of a search—

(a) shall state—

(i) the object of the search;

(ii) the grounds for making it;

(iii) the date and time when it was made;

(iv) the place where it was made;

(v) whether anything, and if so what, was found;

(vi) whether any, and if so what, injury to a person or damage to property appears to the constable to have resulted from the search; and

(b) shall identify the constable making it.

(7) If a constable who conducted a search of a person made a record of it, the person who was searched shall be entitled to a copy of the record if he asks for one before the end of the period specified in subsection (9) below.

(8) If—

(a) the owner of a vehicle which has been searched or the person who was in charge of the vehicle at the time when it was searched asks for a copy of the record of the search before the end of the period specified in subsection (9) below; and

(b) the constable who conducted the search made a record of it, the person who made the request shall be entitled to a copy.

(9) The period mentioned in subsections (7) and (8) above is the period of 12 months beginning with the date on which the search was made.

(10) The requirements imposed by this section with regard to records of searches of vehicles shall apply also to records of searches of vessels, aircraft and hovercraft.

Road checks

4   (1) This section shall have effect in relation to the conduct of road checks by police officers for the purpose of ascertaining whether a vehicle is carrying—

(a) a person who has committed an offence other than a road traffic offence or a vehicles excise offence;

(b) a person who is a witness to such an offence;

(c) a person intending to commit such an offence; or

(d) a person who is unlawfully at large.

(2) For the purposes of this section a road check consists of the exercise in a locality of the power conferred by section 163 of the Road Traffic Act 1988 in such a way as to stop during the period for which its exercise in that way in that locality continues all vehicles or vehicles selected by any criterion.

(3) Subject to subsection (5) below, there may only be such a road

check if a police officer of the rank of superintendent or above authorises it in writing.

    (4) An officer may only authorise a road check under subsection (3) above—

    (*a*) for the purpose specified in subsection (1)(a) above, if he has reasonable grounds—

       (i) for believing that the offence is a serious arrestable offence; and

      (ii) for suspecting that the person is, or is about to be, in the locality in which vehicles would be stopped if the road check were authorised;

    (*b*) for the purpose specified in subsection (1)(b) above, if he has reasonable grounds for believing that the offence is a serious arrestable offence;

    (*c*) for the purpose specified in subsection (1)(c) above, if he has reasonable grounds—

       (i) for believing that the offence would be a serious arrestable offence; and

      (ii) for suspecting that the person is, or is about to be in the locality in which vehicles would be stopped if the road check were authorised;

    (*d*) for the purpose specified in subsection (1)(d) above, if he has reasonable grounds for suspecting that the person is, or is about to be, in that locality.

    (5) An officer below the rank of superintendent may authorise such a road check if it appears to him that it is required as a matter of urgency for one of the purposes specified in subsection (1) above.

    (6) If an authorisation is given under subsection (5) above, it shall be the duty of the officer who gives it—

    (*a*) to make a written record of the time at which he gives it; and

    (*b*) to cause an officer of the rank of superintendent or above to be informed that it has been given.

    (7) The duties imposed by subsection (6) above shall be performed as soon as it is practicable to do so.

    (8) An officer to whom a report is made under subsection (6) above may, in writing, authorise the road check to continue.

    (9) If such an officer considers that the road check should not continue, he shall record in writing—

    (*a*) the fact that it took place; and

    (*b*) the purpose for which it took place.

    (10) An officer giving an authorisation under this section shall specify the locality in which vehicles are to be stopped.

    (11) An officer giving an authorisation under this section, other than an authorisation under subsection (5) above—

    (*a*) shall specify a period, not exceeding seven days, during which the road check may continue; and

    (*b*) may direct that the road check—

       (i) shall be continuous; or

      (ii) shall be conducted at specified times, during that period.

    (12) If it appears to an officer of the rank of superintendent or above

that a road check ought to continue beyond the period for which it has been authorised he may, from time to time, in writing specify a further period, not exceeding seven days, during which it may continue.

(13) Every written authorisation shall specify—

(a) the name of the officer giving it;

(b) the purpose of the road check; and

(c) the locality in which vehicles are to be stopped.

(14) The duties to specify the purposes of a road check imposed by subsections (9) and (13) above include duties to specify any relevant serious arrestable offense.

(15) Where a vehicle is stopped in a road check, the person in charge of the vehicle at the time when it is stopped shall be entitled to obtain a written statement of the purpose of the road check, if he applies for such a statement not later than the end of the period of twelve months from the day on which the vehicle was stopped.

(16) Nothing in this section affects the exercise by police officers of any power to stop vehicles for purposes other than those specified in subsection (1) above.

* * * *

PART II
POWERS OF ENTRY, SEARCH AND SEIZURE

SEARCH WARRANTS

Power of the justice of peace to authorise entry and search of premises

8   (1) If on an application made by a constable a justice of the peace is satisfied that there are reasonable grounds for believing—

(a) that a serious arrestable offence has been committed; and

(b) that there is material on premises specified in the application which is likely to be of substantial value (whether by itself or together with other material) to the investigation of the offence; and

(c) that the material is likely to be relevant evidence; and

(d) that it does not consist of or include items subject to legal privilege, excluded material or special procedure material; and

(e) that any of the conditions specified in subsection (3) below applies,

he may issue a warrant authorising a constable to enter and search the premises.

(2) A constable may seize and retain anything for which a search has been authorised under subsection (1) above.

(3) The conditions mentioned in subsection (1)(e) above are—

(a) that it is not practicable to communicate with any person entitled to grant entry to the premises;

(*b*) that it is practicable to communicate with a person entitled to grant entry to the premises but it is not practicable to communicate with any person entitled to grant access to the evidence;

(*c*) that entry to the premises will not be granted unless a warrant is produced;

(*d*) that the purpose of a search may be frustrated or seriously prejudiced unless a constable arriving at the premises can secure immediate entry to them.

(4) In this Act "relevant evidence", in relation to an offence, means anything that would be admissible in evidence at a trial for the offence.

(5) The power to issue a warrant conferred by this section is in addition to any such power otherwise conferred.

Special provisions as to access

9   (1) A constable may obtain access to excluded material or special procedure material for the purposes of a criminal investigation by making an application under Schedule 1 below and in accordance with that Schedule.

(2) Any Act (including a local Act) passed before this Act under which a search of premises for the purposes of a criminal investigation could be authorised by the issue of a warrant to a constable shall cease to have effect so far as it relates to the authorisation of searches—

(*a*) for items subject to legal privilege; or

(*b*) for excluded material; or

(*c*) for special procedure material consisting of documents or records other than documents.

Meaning of "items subject to legal privilege"

10   (1) Subject to subsection (2) below in this Act "items subject to legal privilege" means—

(*a*) communications between a professional legal adviser and his client or any person representing his client made in connection with the giving of legal advice to the client;

(*b*) communications between a professional legal adviser and his client or any person representing his client or between such an adviser or his client or any such representative and any other person made in connection with or in contemplation of legal proceedings and for the purposes of such proceedings; and

(*c*) items enclosed with or referred to in such communications and made—

(i) in connection with the giving of legal advice; or

(ii) in connection with or in contemplation of legal proceedings and for the purposes of such proceedings,

when they are in the possession of a person who is entitled to possession of them.

(2) Items held with the intention of furthering a criminal purpose are not items subject to legal privilege.

Meaning of "excluded material"

11   (1) Subject to the following provisions of this section, in this Act "excluded material" means—

(a) personal records which a person has acquired or created in the course of any trade, business, profession or other occupation or for the purposes of any paid or unpaid office and which he holds in confidence;

(b) human tissue or tissue fluid which has been taken for the purposes of diagnosis or medical treatment and which a person holds in confidence;

(c) journalistic material which a person holds in confidence and which consists—

(i) of documents; or

(ii) of records other than documents.

(2) A person holds material other than journalistic material in confidence for the purposes of this section if he holds it subject—

(a) to an express or implied undertaking to hold it in confidence; or

(b) to a restriction on disclosure or an obligation of secrecy contained in any enactment, including an enactment contained in an Act passed after this Act.

(3) A person holds journalistic material in confidence for the purposes of this section if—

(a) he holds it subject to such an undertaking, restriction or obligation; and

(b) it has been continuously held (by one or more persons) subject to such an undertaking, restriction or obligation since it was first acquired or created for the purposes of journalism.

Meaning of "personal records"

12   In this Part of this Act "personal records" means documentary and other records concerning an individual (whether living or dead) who can be identified from them, and relating—

(a) to his physical or mental health;

(b) to spiritual counselling or assistance given or to be given to him;

(c) to counselling or assistance given or to be given to him, for the purposes of his personal welfare, by any voluntary organisation or by any individual who—

(i) by reason of his office or occupation has responsibilities for his personal welfare; or

(ii) by reason of an order of a court, has responsibilities for his supervision.

*   *   *   *

Search warrants—safeguards

15   (1) This section and section 16 below have effect in relation to the issue to constables under any enactment, including an enactment contained

in an Act passed after this Act, of warrants to enter and search premises, and an entry on or search of premises under a warrant is unlawful unless it complies with this section and section 16 below.

(2) Where a constable applies for any such warrant, it shall be his duty—

> (a) to state—
>> (i) the ground on which he makes the application; and
>> (ii) the enactment under which the warrant would be issued;
> (b) to specify the premises which it is desired to enter and search; and
> (c) to identify, so far as is practicable, the articles or persons to be sought.

(3) An application for such a warrant shall be made ex parte and supported by an information in writing.

(4) The constable shall answer on oath any question that the justice of the peace or judge hearing the application asks him.

(5) A warrant shall authorise an entry on one occasion only.

(6) A warrant—

> (a) shall specify—
>> (i) the name of the person who applies for it;
>> (ii) the date on which it is issued;
>> (iii) the enactment under which it is issued; and
>> (iv) the premises to be searched; and
> (b) shall identify, so far as is practicable, the articles or person to be sought.

(7) Two copies shall be made of a warrant.

(8) The copies shall be clearly certified as copies.

Execution of warrants

16   (1) A warrant to enter and search premises may be executed by any constable.

(2) Such a warrant may authorise persons to accompany any constable who is executing it.

(3) Entry and search under a warrant must be within one month from the date of its issue.

(4) Entry and search under a warrant must be at a reasonable hour unless it appears to the constable executing it that the purpose of a search may be frustrated on an entry at a reasonable hour.

(5) Where the occupier of premises which are to be entered and searched is present at the time when a constable seeks to execute a warrant to enter and search them, the constable—

> (a) shall identify himself to the occupier and, if not in uniform, shall produce to him documentary evidence that he is a constable;
> (b) shall produce the warrant to him; and
> (c) shall supply him with a copy of it.

(6) Where—

> (a) the occupier of such premises is not present at the time when a constable seeks to execute such a warrant; but

(*b*) some other person who appears to the constable to be in charge of the premises is present,

subsection (5) above shall have effect as if any reference to the occupier were a reference to that other person.

(7) If there is no person present who appears to the constable to be in charge of the premises, he shall leave a copy of the warrant in a prominent place on the premises.

(8) A search under a warrant may only be a search to the extent required for the purpose for which the warrant was issued.

(9) A constable executing a warrant shall make an endorsement on it stating—

    (*a*) whether the articles or persons sought were found; and

    (*b*) whether any articles were seized, other than articles which were sought.

(10) A warrant which—

    (*a*) has been executed; or

    (*b*) has not been executed within the time authorised for its execution, shall be returned—

        (i) if it was issued by a justice of the peace, to the clerk to the justices for the petty sessions area for which he acts; and

        (ii) if it was issued by a judge, to the appropriate officers of the court from which he issued it.

(11) A warrant which is returned under subsection (10) above shall be retained for 12 months from its return—

    (*a*) by the clerk to the justices, if it was returned under paragraph (i) of that subsection; and

    (*b*) by the appropriate officer, if it was returned under paragraph (ii).

(12) If during the period for which a warrant is to be retained the occupier of the premises to which it relates asks to inspect it, he shall be allowed to do so.

ENTRY AND SEARCH WITHOUT SEARCH WARRANT

Entry for purpose of arrest etc.

17   (1) Subject to the following provisions of this section, and without prejudice to any other enactment, a constable may enter and search any premises for the purpose—

    (*a*) of executing—

        (i) a warrant of arrest issued in connection with or arising out of criminal proceedings; or

        (ii) a warrant of commitment issued under section 76 of the Magistrates' Courts Act 1980;

    (*b*) of arresting a person for an arrestable offence;

    (*c*) of arresting a person for an offence under—

        (i) section 1 (prohibition of uniforms in connection with political objects) . . . of the Public Order Act 1936;

        (ii) any enactment contained in sections 6 to 8 or 10 of the Criminal Law Act 1977 (offences relating to entering and remaining on property);

(iii) s.4 of the Public Order Act 1986 (fear or provocation of violence);

(*d*) of recapturing a person who is unlawfully at large and whom he is pursuing; or

(*e*) of saving life or limb or preventing serious damage to property.

(2) Except for the purpose specified in paragraph (e) of subsection (1) above, the powers of entry and search conferred by this section—

(*a*) are only exercisable if the constable has reasonable grounds for believing that the person whom he is seeking is on the premises; and

(*b*) are limited, in relation to premises consisting of two or more separate dwellings, to powers to enter and search—

(i) any parts of the premises which the occupiers of any dwelling comprised in the premises use in common with the occupiers of any other such dwelling; and

(ii) any such dwelling in which the constable has reasonable grounds for believing that the person whom he is seeking may be.

(3) The powers of entry and search conferred by this section are only exercisable for the purposes specified in subsection (1)(c)(ii) above by a constable in uniform.

(4) The power of search conferred by this section is only a power to search to the extent that is reasonably required for the purpose for which the power of entry is exercised.

(5) Subject to subsection (6) below, all the rules of common law under which a constable has power to enter premises without a warrant are hereby abolished.

(6) Nothing in subsection (5) above affects any power of entry to deal with or prevent a breach of the peace.

Entry and search after arrest

18   (1) Subject to the following provisions of this section, a constable may enter and search, any premises occupied or controlled by a person who is under arrest for an arrestable offence, if he has reasonable grounds for suspecting that there is on the premises evidence other than items subject to legal privilege, that relates—

(*a*) to that offence; or

(*b*) to some other arrestable offence which is connected with or similar to that offence.

(2) A constable may seize and retain anything for which he may search under subsection (1) above.

(3) The power to search conferred by subsection (1) above is only a power to search to the extent that is reasonably required for the purpose of discovering such evidence.

(4) Subject to subsection (5) below, the powers conferred by this section may not be exercised unless an officer of the rank of inspector or above has authorised them in writing.

(5) A constable may conduct a search under subsection (1) above—

(*a*) before taking the person to a police station; and

(*b*) without obtaining an authorisation under subsection (4) above,

if the presence of that person at a place other than a police station is necessary for the effective investigation of the offence.

(6) If a constable conducts a search by virtue of subsection (5) above, he shall inform an officer of the rank of inspector or above that he has made the search as soon as practicable after he has made it.

(7) An officer who—

(*a*) authorises a search; or

(*b*) is informed of a search under subsection (6) above,

shall make a record in writing—

(i) of the grounds for the search; and

(ii) of the nature of the evidence that was sought.

(8) If the person who was in occupation or control of the premises at the time of the search is in police detention at the time the record is to be made, the officer shall make the record as part of his custody record.

SEIZURE ETC.

General power of seizure

19   (1) The powers conferred by subsections (2), (3), and (4) below are exercisable by a constable who is lawfully on any premises.

(2) The constable may seize anything which is on the premises if he has reasonable grounds for believing—

(*a*) that it has been obtained in consequence of the commission of an offence; and

(*b*) that it is necessary to seize it in order to prevent it being concealed, lost, damaged, altered or destroyed.

(3) The constable may seize anything which is on the premises if he has reasonable grounds for believing—

(*a*) that it is evidence in relation to an offence which he is investigating or any other offence; and

(*b*) that it is necessary to seize it in order to prevent the evidence being concealed, lost, altered or destroyed.

(4) The constable may require any information which is contained in a computer and is accessible from the premises to be produced in a form in which it can be taken away and in which it is visible and legible if he has reasonable grounds for believing—

(*a*) that—

(i) it is evidence in relation to an offence which he is investigating or any other offence; or

(ii) it has been obtained in consequence of the commission of an offence; and

(*b*) that it is necessary to do so in order to prevent it being concealed, lost, tampered with or destroyed.

(5) The powers conferred by this section are in addition to any power otherwise conferred.

(6) No power of seizure conferred on a constable under any enactment (including an enactment contained in an Act passed after this Act) is to

be taken to authorise the seizure of an item which the constable exercising the power has reasonable grounds for believing to be subject to legal privilege.

* * * *

Access and copying

21 (1) A constable who seizes anything in the exercise of a power conferred by any enactment, including an enactment contained in an Act passed after this Act, shall, if so requested by a person showing himself—
  (a) to be occupier of premises on which it was seized; or
  (b) to have had custody or control of it immediately before the seizure,
provide that person with a record of what he seized.

* * * *

PART III
ARREST

Arrest without warrant for arrestable and other offences

24 (1) The powers of summary arrest conferred by the following subsections shall apply—
  (a) to offences for which the sentence is fixed by law;
  (b) to offences for which a person of 21 years of age or over (not previously convicted) may be sentenced to imprisonment for a term of five years (or might be so sentenced but for the restrictions imposed by section 33 of the Magistrates' Courts Act 1980); and
  (c) to the offences to which subsection (2) below applies, and in this Act "arrestable offence" means any such offence.
  (2) The offences to which this subsection applies are—
  (a) offences for which a person may be arrested under the customs and excise Acts, as defined in section 1(1) of the Customs and Excise Management Act 1979;
  (b) offences under the Official Secrets Act 1920 that are not arrestable offences by virtue of the term of imprisonment for which a person may be sentenced in respect of them;
  (bb) offences under any provision of the Official Secrets Act 1989 except section 8(1), (4) or (5)
  (c) offences under section . . . 22 (causing prostitution of women) or 23 (procuration of girl under 21) of the Sexual Offences Act 1956;
  (d) offences under section 12(1) (taking motor vehicle or other conveyance without authority etc.) or 25(1) (going equipped for stealing, etc.) of the Theft Act 1968; and
  (e) . . . [repealed 1985]
  (3) Without prejudice to section 2 of the Criminal Attempts Act 1981,

the powers of summary arrest conferred by the following subsections shall also apply to the offences of—
  (*a*) conspiring to commit any of the offences mentioned in subsection (2) above;
  (*b*) attempting to commit any such offence [other than an offence under section 12(1) of the Theft Act 1968];
  (*c*) inciting, aiding, abetting, counselling or procuring the commission of any such offence,
any such offences are also arrestable offences for the purposes of this Act.
  (4) Any person may arrest without a warrant—
  (*a*) anyone who is in the act of committing an arrestable offence;
  (*b*) anyone whom he has reasonable grounds for suspecting to be committing such an offence.
  (5) Where an arrestable offence has been committed, any person may arrest without a warrant—
  (*a*) anyone who is guilty of the offence;
  (*b*) anyone whom he has reasonable grounds for suspecting to be guilty of it.
  (6) Where a constable has reasonable grounds for suspecting that an arrestable offence has been committed, he may arrest without a warrant anyone whom he has reasonable grounds for suspecting to be guilty of the offence.
  (7) A constable may arrest without a warrant—
  (*a*) anyone who is about to commit an arrestable offence;
  (*b*) anyone whom he has reasonable grounds for suspecting to be about to commit an arrestable offence.

General arrest conditions

25   (1) Where a constable has reasonable grounds for suspecting that any offence which is not an arrestable offence has been committed or attempted, or is being committed or attempted, he may arrest the relevant person if it appears to him that service of a summons is impracticable or inappropriate because any of the general arrest conditions is satisfied.
  (2) In this section, "the relevant person" means any person whom the constable has reasonable grounds to suspect of having committed or having attempted to commit the offence or of being in the course of committing or attempting to commit it.
  (3) The general arrest conditions are—
  (*a*) that the name of the relevant person is unknown to, and cannot be readily ascertained by, the constable;
  (*b*) that the constable has reasonable grounds for doubting whether a name furnished by the relevant person as his name is his real name;
  (*c*) that—
    (i) the relevant person has failed to furnish a satisfactory address for service; or
    (ii) the constable has reasonable grounds for doubting whether an address furnished by the relevant person is a satisfactory address for service;

(*d*) that the constable has reasonable grounds for believing that arrest is necessary to prevent the relevant person—
(i) causing physical harm to himself or any other person;
(ii) suffering physical injury;
(iii) causing loss of or damage to property;
(iv) committing an offence against public decency; or
(v) causing an unlawful obstruction of the highway;
(*e*) that the constable has reasonable grounds for believing that arrest is necessary to protect a child or other vulnerable person from the relevant person

(4) For the purposes of subsection (3) above an address is a satisfactory address for service if it appears to the constable—
(*a*) that the relevant person will be at it for a sufficiently long period for it to be possible to serve him with a summons; or
(*b*) that some other person specified by the relevant person will accept service of a summons for the relevant person at it.

(5) Nothing in subsection (3)(d) above authorises the arrest of a person under sub-paragraph (iv) of that paragraph except where members of the public going about their normal business cannot reasonably be expected to avoid the person to be arrested.

(6) This section shall not prejudice any power of arrest conferred apart from this section.

* * * *

Fingerprinting of certain offenders

27 (1) If a person—
(*a*) has been convicted of a recordable offence;
(*b*) has not at any time been in police detention for the offence; and
(*c*) has not had his fingerprints taken—
(i) in the course of the investigation of the offence by the police; or
(ii) since the conviction;
any constable may at any time not later than one month after the date of the conviction require him to attend a police station in order that his fingerprints may be taken.

(2) A requirement under subsection (1) above—
(*a*) shall give the person a period of at least 7 days within which he must so attend; and
(*b*) may direct him to so attend at a specified time of day or between specified times of day.

(3) Any constable may arrest without warrant a person who has failed to comply with a requirement under subsection (1) above.

(4) The Secretary of State may by regulations make provision for recording in national police records convictions for such offences as are specified in the regulations.

(5) Regulations under this section shall be made by statutory instrument and shall be subject to annulment in pursuance of a resolution of either House of Parliament.

Information to be given on arrest

28   (1) Subject to subsection (5) below, when a person is arrested otherwise than by being informed that he is under arrest, the arrest is not lawful unless the person arrested is informed that he is under arrest as soon as is practicable after his arrest.

(2) Where a person is arrested by a constable subsection (1) above applies regardless of whether the fact of the arrest is obvious.

(3) Subject to subsection (5) below, no arrest is lawful unless the person arrested is informed of the ground for the arrest at the time of, or as soon as is practicable after, the arrest.

(4) Where a person is arrested by a constable, subsection (3) above applies regardless of whether the ground for the arrest is obvious.

(5) Nothing in this section is to be taken to require a person to be informed—

(*a*) that he is under arrest; or

(*b*) of the ground for the arrest,

if it was not reasonably practicable for him to be so informed by reason of his having escaped from arrest before the information could be given.

Voluntary attendance at police station etc.

29   Where for the purpose of assisting with an investigation a person attends voluntarily at a police station or at any other place where a constable is present or accompanies a constable to a police station or any such other place without having been arrested—

(*a*) he shall be entitled to leave at will unless he is placed under arrest;

(*b*) he shall be informed at once that he is under arrest if a decision is taken by a constable to prevent him from leaving at will.

Arrest elsewhere than at police station

30   (1) Subject to the following provisions of this section, where a person

(*a*) is arrested by a constable for an offence; or

(*b*) is taken into custody by a constable after being arrested for an offence by a person other than a constable;

at any place other than a police station he shall be taken to a police station by a constable as soon as practicable after the arrest.

(2) Subject to subsections (3) and (4) below, the police station to which an arrested person is taken under subsection (1) above shall be a designated police station.

(3) A constable to whom this subsection applies may take an arrested person to any police station unless it appears to the constable that it may be necessary to keep the arrested person in police detention for more than six hours.

(4) Subsection (3) above applies—

(*a*) to a constable who is working in a locality covered by a police station which is not a designated police station; and

(*b*) to a constable belonging to a body of constables maintained by an authority other than a police authority.

(5) Any constable may take an arrested person to any police station if—

    (*a*) either of the following conditions is satisfied—
      (i) the constable has arrested him without the assistance of any other constable and no other constable is available to assist him;
      (ii) the constable has taken him into custody from a person other than a constable without the assistance of any other constable and no other constable is available to assist him; and
    (*b*) it appears to the constable that he will be unable to take the arrested person to a designated police station without the arrested person injuring himself, the constable or some other person.

(6) If the first police station to which an arrested person is taken after his arrest is not a designated police station he shall be taken to a designated police station not more than six hours after his arrival at the first police station unless he is released previously.

(7) A person arrested by a constable at a place other than a police station shall be released if a constable is satisfied, before the person arrested reaches a police station, that there are no grounds for keeping him under arrest.

(8) A constable who releases a person under subsection (7) above shall record the fact that he has done so.

(9) The constable shall make the record as soon as is practicable after the release.

(10) Nothing in subsection (1) above shall prevent a constable delaying taking a person who has been arrested to a police station if the presence of that person elsewhere is necessary in order to carry out such investigations as it is reasonable to carry out immediately.

(11) Where there is delay in taking a person who has been arrested to a police station after his arrest, the reasons for the delay shall be recorded when he first arrives at a police station.

* * * *

Search upon arrest

32   (1) A constable may search an arrested person, in any case where the person to be searched has been arrested at a place other than a police station, if the constable has reasonable grounds for believing that the arrested person may present a danger to himself or others.

(2) Subject to subsections (3) to (5) below, a constable shall also have power in any such case—

    (*a*) to search the arrested person for anything—
      (i) which he might use to assist him to escape from lawful custody; or
      (ii) which might be evidence relating to an offence; and
    (*b*) to enter and search any premises in which he was when arrested or immediately before he was arrested for evidence relating to the offence for which he has been arrested.

(3) The power to search conferred by subsection (2) above is only a power to search to the extent that is reasonably required for the purpose of discovering any such thing or any such evidence.

(4) The powers conferred by this section to search a person are not to be construed as authorising a constable to require a person to remove any of his clothing in public other than an outer coat, jacket or gloves.

(5) A constable may not search a person in the exercise of the power conferred by subsection (2)(a) above unless he has reasonable grounds for believing that the person to be searched may have concealed on him anything for which a search is permitted under that paragraph.

(6) A constable may not search premises in the exercise of the power conferred by subsection (2)(b) above unless he has reasonable grounds for believing that there is evidence for which a search is permitted under that paragraph on the premises.

(7) In so far as the power of search conferred by subsection (2)(b) above relates to premises consisting of two or more separate dwellings, it is limited to a power to search—

> (a) any dwelling in which the arrest took place or in which the person arrested was immediately before his arrest; and
> (b) any parts of the premises which the occupier of any such dwelling uses in common with the occupiers of any other dwellings comprised in the premises.

(8) A constable searching a person in the exercise of the power conferred by subsection (1) above may seize and retain anything he finds, if he has reasonable grounds for believing that the person searched might use it to cause physical injury to himself or to any other person.

(9) A constable searching a person in the exercise of the power conferred by subsection (2)(a) above may seize and retain anything he finds, other than an item subject to legal privilege, if he has reasonable grounds for believing—

> (a) that he might use it to assist him to escape from lawful custody; or
> (b) that it is evidence of an offence or has been obtained in consequence of the commission of an offence.

(10) Nothing in this section shall be taken to affect the power conferred by section 15(3), (4) and (5) of the Prevention of Terrorism (Temporary Provisions) Act 1989.

* * * *

PART IV
DETENTION

DETENTION—CONDITIONS AND DURATION

Limitations on police detention

34   (1) A person arrested for an offence shall not be kept in police detention except in accordance with the provisions of this Part of this Act.

(2) Subject to subsection (3) below, if at any time a custody officer—

(*a*) becomes aware, in relation to any person in police detention, that the grounds for the detention of that person have ceased to apply; and

(*b*) is not aware of any other grounds on which the continued detention of that person could be justified under the provisions of this Part of this Act,

it shall be the duty of the custody officer, subject to subsection (4) below, to order his immediate release from custody.

(3) No person in police detention shall be released except on the authority of a custody officer at the police station where his detention was authorised or, if it was authorised at more than one station, a custody officer at the station where it was last authorised.

(4) A person who appears to the custody officer to have been unlawfully at large when he was arrested is not to be released under subsection (2) above.

(5) A person whose release is ordered under subsection (2) above shall be released without bail unless it appears to the custody officer—

(*a*) that there is need for further investigation of any matter in connection with which he was detained at any time during the period of his detention; or

(*b*) that proceedings may be taken against him in respect of any such matter,

and if it so appears, he shall be released on bail.

(6) For the purposes of this Part of this Act a person arrested under section 6(5) of the Road Traffic Act 1988 is arrested for an offence.

*   *   *   *

Custody officers at police stations

36   (1) One or more custody officers shall be appointed for each designated police station.

(2) A custody officer for a designated police station shall be appointed—

(*a*) by the chief officer of police for the area in which the designated police station is situated; or

(*b*) by such other police officer as the chief officer of police for that area may direct.

(3) No officer may be appointed a custody officer unless he is of at least the rank of sergeant.

(4) An officer of any rank may perform the functions of a custody officer at a designated police station if a custody officer is not readily available to perform them.

(5) Subject to the following provisions of this section and to section 39(2) below, none of the functions of a custody officer in relation to a person shall be performed by an officer who at the time when the function falls to be performed is involved in the investigation of an offence for which that person is in police detention at that time.

*   *   *   *

Duties of custody officer before charge

37 (1) Where
  (*a*) a person is arrested for an offence—
    (i) without a warrant; or
    (ii) under a warrant not endorsed for bail, or
  (*b*) a person returns to a police station to answer to bail
the custody officer at each police station where he is detained after his arrest shall determine whether he has before him sufficient evidence to charge that person with the offence for which he was arrested and may detain him at the police station for such period as is necessary to enable him to do so.

(2) If the custody officer determines that he does not have such evidence before him, the person arrested shall be released either on bail or without bail, unless the custody officer has reasonable grounds for believing that his detention without being charged is necessary to secure or preserve evidence relating to an offence for which he is under arrest or to obtain such evidence by questioning him.

(3) If the custody officer has reasonable grounds for so believing, he may authorise the person arrested to be kept in police detention.

(4) Where a custody officer authorises a person who has not been charged to be kept in police detention, he shall, as soon as is practicable, make a written record of the grounds for the detention.

(5) Subject to subsection (6) below, the written record shall be made in the presence of the person arrested who shall at that time be informed by the custody officer of the grounds for his detention.

(6) Subsection (5) above shall not apply where the person arrested is, at the time when the written record is made—
  (*a*) incapable of understanding what is said to him;
  (*b*) violent or likely to become violent; or
  (*c*) in urgent need of medical attention.

(7) Subject to section 41(6) below, if the custody officer determines that he has before him sufficient evidence to charge the person arrested with the offence for which he was arrested, the person arrested—
  (*a*) shall be charged; or
  (*b*) shall be released without charge, either on bail or without bail.

(8) Where—
  (*a*) a person is released under subsection (7)(b) above; and
  (*b*) at the time of his release a decision whether he should be prosecuted for the offence for which he was arrested has not been taken,
it shall be the duty of the custody officer so to inform him.

(9) If the person arrested is not in a fit state to be dealt with under subsection (7) above, he may be kept in police detention until he is.

(10) The duty imposed on the custody officer under subsection (1) above shall be carried out by him as soon as practicable after the person arrested arrives at the police station or, in the case of a person arrested at the police station, as soon as practicable after the arrest.

* * * *

Responsibilities in relation to persons detained

39   (1) Subject to subsections (2) and (4) below, it shall be the duty of the custody officer at a police station to ensure—

(*a*) that all persons in police detention at that station are treated in accordance with this Act and any code of practice issued under it and relating to the treatment of persons in police detention; and

(*b*) that all matters relating to such persons which are required by this Act or by such codes of practice to be recorded are recorded in the custody records relating to such persons.

(2) If the custody officer, in accordance with any code of practice issued under this Act, transfers or permits the transfer of a person in police detention

(*a*) to the custody of a police officer investigating an offence for which that person is in police detention;

(*b*) to the custody of an officer who has charge of that person outside the police station

(i) the custody officer shall cease in relation to that person to be subject to the duty imposed on him by subsection (1)(a) above; and

(ii) it shall be the duty of the officer to whom the transfer is made to ensure that he is treated in accordance with the provisions of this Act and of any such codes of practice as are mentioned in subsection (1) above.

(3) If the person detained is subsequently returned to the custody of the custody officer, it shall be the duty of the officer investigating the offence to report to the custody officer as to the manner in which this section and the codes of practice have been complied with while that person was in his custody.

(4) If an arrested juvenile is transferred to the care of a local authority in pursuance of arrangements made under section 38(7) above, the custody officer shall cease in relation to that person to be subject to the duty imposed on him by subsection (1) above.

(5) It shall be the duty of a local authority to make available to an arrested juvenile who is in the authority's care in pursuance of such arrangements such advice and assistance as may be appropriate in the circumstances.

(6) Where—

(*a*) an officer of higher rank than the custody officer gives directions relating to a person in police detention; and

(*b*) the directions are at variance—

(i) with any decision made or action taken by the custody officer in the performance of a duty imposed on him under this Part of this Act; or

(ii) with any decision or action which would but for the directions have been made or taken by him in the performance of such a duty,

the custody officer shall refer the matter at once to an officer of the rank of superintendent or above who is responsible for the police station for which the custody officer is acting as custody officer.

Review of police detention

40   (1) Reviews of the detention of each person in police detention in connection with the investigation of an offence shall be carried out periodically in accordance with the following provisions of this section—

   (*a*) in the case of a person who has been arrested and charged, by the custody officer; and

   (*b*) in the case of a person who has been arrested but not charged, by an officer of at least the rank of inspector who has not been directly involved in the investigation.

  (2) The officer to whom it falls to carry out a review is referred to in this section as a "review officer".

  (3) Subject to subsection (4) below—

   (*a*) the first review shall be not later than six hours after the detention was first authorised;

   (*b*) the second review shall be not later than nine hours after the first;

   (*c*) subsequent reviews shall be at intervals of not more than nine hours.

  (4) A review may be postponed—

   (*a*) if, having regard to all the circumstances prevailing at the latest time for it specified in subsection (3) above, it is not practicable to carry out the review at that time;

   (*b*) without prejudice to the generality of paragraph (a) above—

    (i) if at that time the person in detention is being questioned by a police officer and the review officer is satisfied that an interruption of the questioning for the purpose of carrying out the review would prejudice the investigation in connection with which he is being questioned; or

    (ii) if at that time no review officer is readily available.

  (5) If a review is postponed under subsection (4) above it shall be carried out as soon as practicable after the latest time specified for it in subsection (3) above.

*   *   *   *

Limits on period of detention without charge

41   (1) Subject to the following provisions of this section and to sections 42 and 43 below, a person shall not be kept in police detention for more than 24 hours without being charged.

*   *   *   *

Authorisation of continued detention

42   (1) Where a police officer of the rank of superintendent or above who is responsible for the police station at which a person is detained has reasonable grounds for believing that—

   (*a*) the detention of that person without charge is necessary to secure or preserve evidence relating to an offence for which he is under arrest or to obtain such evidence by questioning him;

(*b*) an offence for which he is under arrest is a serious arrestable offence; and

(*c*) the investigation is being conducted diligently and expeditiously, he may authorise the keeping of that person in police detention for a period expiring at or before 36 hours after the relevant time.

(2) Where an officer such as is mentioned in subsection (1) above has authorised the keeping of a person in police detention for a period expiring less than 36 hours after the relevant time, such an officer may authorise the keeping of that person in police detention for a further period expiring not more than 36 hours after that time if the conditions specified in subsection (1) above are still satisfied when he gives the authorisation.

(3) If it is proposed to transfer a person in police detention to another police area, the officer determining whether or not to authorise keeping him in detention under subsection (1) above shall have regard to the distance and the time the journey would take.

(4) No authorisation under subsection (1) above shall be given in respect of any person—

(*a*) more than 24 hours after the relevant time; or

(*b*) before the second review of his detention under section 40 above has been carried out.

(5) Where an officer authorises the keeping of a person in police detention under subsection (1) above, it shall be his duty—

(*a*) to inform that person of the grounds for his continued detention; and

(*b*) to record the grounds in that person's custody record.

* * * *

Warrants of further detention

43   (1) Where, on an application on oath made by a constable and supported by an information, a magistrates' court is satisfied that there are reasonable grounds for believing that the further detention of the person to whom the application relates is justified, it may issue a warrant of further detention authorising the keeping of that person in police detention.

(2) A court may not hear an application for a warrant of further detention unless the person to whom the application relates—

(*a*) has been furnished with a copy of the information; and

(*b*) has been brought before the court for the hearing.

(3) The person to whom the application relates shall be entitled to be legally represented at the hearing and, if he is not so represented, but wishes to be so represented—

(*a*) the court shall adjourn the hearing to enable him to obtain representation; and

(*b*) he may be kept in police detention during the adjournment.

(4) A person's further detention is only justified for the purposes of this section or section 44 below if—

(*a*) his detention without charge is necessary to secure or preserve evidence relating to an offence for which he is under arrest or to obtain such evidence by questioning him;

(*b*) an offence for which he is under arrest is a serious arrestable offence; and

(*c*) the investigation is being conducted diligently and expeditiously.

(5) Subject to subsection (7) below, an application for a warrant of further detention may be made—

(*a*) at any time before the expiry of 36 hours after the relevant time; or

(*b*) in a case where—

(i) it is not practicable for the magistrates' court to which the application will be made to sit at the expiry of 36 hours after the relevant time; but

(ii) the court will sit during the 6 hours following the end of that period,

at any time before the expiry of the said 6 hours.

(6) In a case to which subsection (5)(b) above applies—

(*a*) the person to whom the application relates may be kept in police detention until the application is heard; and

(*b*) the custody officer shall make a note in that person's custody record—

(i) of the fact that he was kept in police detention for more than 36 hours after the relevant time; and

(ii) of the reason why he was so kept.

(7) If—

(*a*) an application for a warrant of further detention is made after the expiry of 36 hours after the relevant time; and

(*b*) it appears to the magistrates' court that it would have been reasonable for the police to make it before the expiry of that period,

the court shall dismiss the application.

(8) Where on an application such as is mentioned in subsection (1) above a magistrates' court is not satisfied that there are reasonable grounds for believing that the further detention of the person to whom the application relates is justified, it shall be its duty—

(*a*) to refuse the application; or

(*b*) to adjourn the hearing of it until a time not later than 36 hours after the relevant time.

(9) The person to whom the application relates may be kept in police detention during the adjournment.

(10) A warrant of further detention shall—

(*a*) state the time at which it is issued;

(*b*) authorise the keeping in police detention of the person to whom it relates for the period stated in it.

(11) Subject to subsection (12) below, the period stated in a warrant of further detention shall be such period as the magistrates' court thinks fit, having regard to the evidence before it.

(12) The period shall not be longer than 36 hours.

* * * *

Extension of warrants of further detention

44   (1) On an application on oath made by a constable and supported by an information a magistrates' court may extend a warrant of further detention issued under section 43 above if it is satisfied that there are reasonable grounds for believing that the further detention of the person to whom the application relates is justified.

(2) Subject to subsection (3) below, the period for which a warrant of further detention may be extended shall be such period as the court thinks fit, having regard to the evidence before it.

(3) The period shall not—
    (a) be longer than 36 hours; or
    (b) end later than 96 hours after the relevant time.

(4) Where a warrant of further detention has been extended under subsection (1) above, or further extended under this subsection, for a period ending before 96 hours after the relevant time, on an application such as is mentioned in that subsection a magistrates' court may further extend the warrant if it is satisfied as there mentioned; and subsections (2) and (3) above apply to such further extensions as they apply to extensions under subsection (1) above.

* * * *

PART V
QUESTIONING AND TREATMENT OF PERSONS BY POLICE

* * * *

Searches of detained persons

54   (1) The custody officer at a police station shall ascertain and record or cause to be recorded everything which a person has with him when he is—
    (a) brought to the station after being arrested elsewhere or after being committed to custody by an order or sentence of a court; or
    (b) arrested at the station or detained there under section 47(5) above.

(2) In the case of an arrested person the record shall be made as part of his custody record.

(3) Subject to subsection (4) below, a custody officer may seize and retain any such thing or cause any such thing to be seized and retained.

(4) Clothes and personal effects may only be seized if the custody officer—
    (a) believes that the person from whom they are seized may use them—
        (i) to cause physical injury to himself or any other person;
        (ii) to damage property;
        (iii) to interfere with evidence; or
        (iv) to assist him to escape; or

(*b*) has reasonable grounds for believing that they may be evidence relating to an offence.

(5) Where anything is seized, the person from whom it is seized shall be told the reason for the seizure unless he is—

(*a*) violent or likely to become violent; or

(*b*) incapable of understanding what is said to him.

* * * *

Right to have someone informed when arrested

56 (1) Where a person has been arrested and is being held in custody in a police station or other premises, he shall be entitled, if he so requests, to have one friend or relative or other person who is known to him or who is likely to take an interest in his welfare told, as soon as is practicable except to the extent that delay is permitted by this section, that he has been arrested and is being detained there.

(2) Delay is only permitted—

(*a*) in the case of a person who is in police detention for a serious arrestable offence; and

(*b*) if an officer of at least the rank of superintendent authorises it.

(3) In any case the person in custody must be permitted to exercise the right conferred by subsection (1) above within 36 hours from the relevant time, as defined in section 41(2) above.

(4) An officer may give an authorisation under subsection (2) above orally or in writing but, if he gives it orally, he shall confirm it in writing as soon as is practicable.

(5) Subject to subsection (5A) below, an officer may only authorise delay where he has reasonable grounds for believing that telling the named person of the arrest—

(*a*) will lead to interference with or harm to evidence connected with a serious arrestable offence or interference with or physical injury to other persons; or

(*b*) will lead to the alerting of other persons suspected of having committed such an offence but not yet arrested for it; or

(*c*) will hinder the recovery of any property obtained as a result of such an offence.

(5A) An officer may also authorise delay where the serious arrestable offence is a drug trafficking offence or an offence to which Part VI of the Criminal Justice Act 1988 applies (offences in respect of which confiscation orders under that Part may be made) and the officer has reasonable grounds for believing—

(*a*) where the offence is a drug trafficking offence, that the detained person has benefited from drug trafficking and that the recovery of the value of that person's proceeds of drug trafficking will be hindered by telling the named person of the arrest; and,

(*b*) where the offence is one to which Part VI of the Criminal Justice Act 1988 applies, that the detained person has benefited from the offence and that the recovery of the value of the property obtained by that person from or in connection with the offence or of the pecuniary advantage derived by him from or in connection with it will be hindered by telling the named person of the arrest.

(6) If a delay is authorised—

(*a*) the detained person shall be told the reason for it; and

(*b*) the reason shall be noted on his custody record.

* * * *

Access to legal advice

58   (1) A person who is in police detention shall be entitled, if he so requests, to consult a solicitor privately at any time.

(2) Subject to subsection (3) below, a request under subsection (1) above and the time at which it was made shall be recorded in the custody record.

(3) Such a request need not be recorded in the custody record of a person who makes it at a time while he is at a court after being charged with an offence.

(4) If a person makes such a request, he must be permitted to consult a solicitor as soon as is practicable except to the extent that delay is permitted by this section.

(5) In any case he must be permitted to consult a solicitor within 36 hours from the relevant time, as defined in section 41(2) above.

(6) Delay in compliance with a request is only permitted—

(*a*) in the case of a person who is in police detention for a serious arrestable offence; and

(*b*) if an officer of at least the rank of superintendent authorises it.

(7) An officer may give an authorisation under subsection (6) above orally or in writing but, if he gives it orally, he shall confirm it in writing as soon as is practicable.

(8) Subject to subsection (8A) below, an officer may only authorise delay where he has reasonable grounds for believing that the exercise of the right conferred by subsection (1) above at the time when the person in police detention desires to exercise it—

(*a*) will lead to interference with or harm to evidence connected with a serious arrestable offence or interference with or physical injury to other persons; or

(*b*) will lead to the alerting of other persons suspected of having committed such as offence but not yet arrested for it; or

(*c*) will hinder the recovery of any property obtained as a result of such an offence.

(8A) An officer may also authorise delay where the serious arrestable offence is a drug trafficking offence or an offence to which Part VI of the Criminal Justice Act 1988 applies and the officer has reasonable grounds for believing—

(*a*) where the offence is a drug trafficking offence, that the detained person has benefited from drug trafficking and that the recovery of the value of that person's proceeds of drug trafficking will be hindered by the exercise of the right conferred by subsection (1) above; and (*b*) where the offence is one to which Part VI of the Criminal Justice Act 1988 applies, that the detained person has benefited from the offence and that the recovery of the value of the property obtained by that person from or in connection with the offence or of the pecuniary advantage derived by him from or in connection with it will be hindered by the exercise of the right conferred by subsection (1) above.

(9) If delay is authorised—

(*a*) the person in police detention shall be told the reason for it; and

(*b*) the reason shall be noted on his custody record.

(10) The duties imposed by subsection (9) above shall be performed as soon as is practicable.

(11) There may be no further delay in permitting the exercise of the right conferred by subsection (1) above once the reason for authorising delay ceases to subsist.

(12) The reference in subsection (1) above to a person who is in police detention includes a reference to a person who has been detained under the terrorism provisions.

(13) In the application of this section to a person who has been arrested or detained under the terrorism provisions—

(*a*) subsection (5) above shall have effect as if for the words from "within" onwards there were substituted the words "before the end of the period beyond which he may no longer be detained without the authority of the Secretary of State";

(*b*) subsection (6)(a) above shall have effect as if for the words "for a serious arrestable offence" there were substituted the words "under the terrorism provisions"; and

(*c*) subsection (8) above shall have effect as if at the end there were added "or

(*d*) will lead to interference with the gathering of information about the commission, preparation or instigation of acts of terrorism; or

(*e*) by alerting any person, will make it more difficult—
(i) to prevent an act of terrorism; or
(ii) to secure the apprehension, prosecution or conviction of any person in connection with the commission, preparation or instigation of an act of terrorism."

* * * *

Tape-recording of interviews

60   (1) It shall be the duty of the Secretary of State—

(*a*) to issue a code of practice in connection with the tape-recording of interviews of persons suspected of the commission of criminal offences which are held by police officers at police stations; and

(*b*) to make an order requiring the tape-recording of interviews of persons suspected of the commission of criminal offences, or of such descriptions of criminal offences as may be specified in the order, which are so held, in accordance with the code as it has effect for the time being

(2) An order under subsection (1) above shall be made by statutory instrument and shall be subject to annulment in pursuance of a resolution of either House of Parliament.

Fingerprinting

61   (1) Except as provided by this section no person's fingerprints may be taken without the appropriate consent.

(2) Consent to the taking of a person's fingerprints must be in writing if it is given at a time when he is at a police station.

(3) The fingerprints of a person detained at a police station may be taken without the appropriate consent—

> (a) if an officer of at least the rank if superintendent authorises them to be taken; or
> (b) if—
>> (i) he has been charged with a recordable offence or informed that he will be reported for such an offence; and
>> (ii) he has not had his fingerprints taken in the course of the investigation of the offence by the police.

(4) An officer may only give an authorisation under subsection (3)(a) above if he has reasonable grounds—

> (a) for suspecting the involvement of the person whose fingerprints are to be taken in a criminal offence; and
> (b) for believing that his fingerprints will tend to confirm or disprove his involvement.

(5) An officer may give an authorisation under subsection (3)(a) above orally or in writing but, if he gives it orally, he shall confirm it in writing as soon as is practicable.

(6) Any person's fingerprints may be taken without the appropriate consent if he has been convicted of a recordable offence.

* * * *

PART VIII
EVIDENCE IN CRIMINAL PROCEEDINGS—GENERAL

* * * *

Miscellaneous

Confessions

76   (1) In any proceedings a confession made by an accused person may be given in evidence against him in so far as it is relevant to any matter in issue in the proceedings and is not excluded by the court in pursuance of this section.

(2) If, in any proceedings where the prosecution proposes to give in

evidence a confession made by an accused person, it is represented to the court that the confession was or may have been obtained—

(*a*) by oppression of the person who made it; or

(*b*) in consequence of anything said or done which was likely, in the circumstances existing at the time, to render unreliable any confession which might be made by him in consequence thereof,

the court shall not allow the confession to be given in evidence against him except in so far as the prosecution proves to the court beyond reasonable doubt that the confession (notwithstanding that it may be true) was not obtained as aforesaid.

(3) In any proceedings where the prosecution proposes to give in evidence a confession made by an accused person, the court may of its own motion require the prosecution, as a condition of allowing it to do so, to prove that the confession was not obtained as mentioned in subsection (2) above.

(4) The fact that a confession is wholly or partly excluded in pursuance of this section shall not affect the admissibility in evidence—

(*a*) of any facts discovered as a result of the confession; or

(*b*) where the confession is relevant as showing that the accused speaks, writes or expresses himself in a particular way, of so much of the confession as is necessary to show that he does so.

(5) Evidence that a fact to which this subsection applies was discovered as a result of a statement made by an accused person shall not be admissible unless evidence of how it was discovered is given by him or on his behalf.

(6) Subsection (5) above applies—

(*a*) to any fact discovered as a result of a confession which is wholly excluded in pursuance of this section; and

(*b*) to any fact discovered as a result of a confession which is partly so excluded, if that fact is discovered as a result of the excluded part of the confession.

(7) Nothing in Part VII of this Act shall prejudice the admissibility of a confession made by an accused person.

(8) In this section "oppression" includes torture, inhuman or degrading treatment, and the use or threat of violence (whether or not amounting to torture).

* * * *

Exclusion of unfair evidence

78 (1) In any proceedings the court may refuse to allow evidence on which the prosecution proposes to rely to be given if it appears to the court that, having regard to all the circumstances, including the circumstances in which the evidence was obtained, the admission of the evidence would have such an adverse effect on the fairness of the proceedings that the court ought not to admit it.

(2) Nothing in this section shall prejudice any rule of law requiring a court to exclude evidence.

* * * *

Appendix B
Excerpts from the Draft Revised Codes of Practice Under the Police and Criminal Evidence Act 1984 (Great Britain)*

CODES OF PRACTICE

*Reprinted under license from Her Majesty's Stationer's Office. Citations, sections pertaining to certain special groups or circumstances, and some documentation and notes for guidance (indicated in the Contents list by a †) are omitted. These materials are offered to illustrate the English system, not as a model for an American statutory scheme. Many provisions are duplicative of PACE or deal with administrative details that should be outside the scope of an American code.

†Not reprinted.

A. CODE OF PRACTICE FOR THE EXERCISE BY POLICE OFFICERS OF STATUTORY POWERS OF STOP AND SEARCH

1. General

1.1.   This Code of Practice must be readily available at all police stations for consultation by police officers, detained persons and members of the public.

1.2.   The notes for guidance included are not provisions of this Code, but are guidance to police officers and others about its application and interpretation. Provisions in the annexes to the Code are provisions of this Code.

1.3.   This Code governs the exercise by police officers of statutory powers to search a person without first arresting him or to search a vehicle without making an arrest.

*   *   *   *

1.5.   The exercise of the powers to which this Code applies requires reasonable grounds for suspicion that articles unlawfully obtained or possessed are being carried. Where a police officer has reasonable grounds to suspect that a person is in innocent possession of a stolen or prohibited article, the power of stop and search exists notwithstanding that there would be no power of arrest. However every effort should be made to secure the voluntary production of the article before the power is exercised.

1.6.   Whether reasonable grounds for suspicion exist will depend on the circumstances in each case, but there must be some objective basis for it. An officer will need to consider the nature of the article suspected of being carried in the context of other factors such as the time and the place, and the behaviour of the person concerned or those with him. Reasonable suspicion may exist, for example, where information has been received such as a description of an article being carried or of a suspected offender; a person is seen acting covertly or warily or attempting to hide something; or a person is carrying a certain type of article at an unusual time or in a place where a number of burglaries or thefts are known to have taken place recently. But the decision to stop and search must be based on all the facts which bear on the likelihood that an article of a certain kind will be found.

1.7.   Reasonable suspicion can never be supported on the basis of personal factors alone. For example, a person's colour, age, hairstyle or manner of dress, or the fact that he is known to have a previous conviction for possession of an unlawful article, cannot be used alone or in combination with each other as the sole basis on which to search that person. Nor may it be founded on the basis of stereotyped images of certain persons or groups as more likely to be committing offences.

Notes for guidance

1A   It is important to ensure that powers of stop and search are used responsibly and sparingly. An officer should bear in mind that he may need to be able to justify the use of the powers to a superior officer and in court, and also that misuse of the powers is likely to be harmful to the police effort in the long term. This can lead to mistrust of the police by the community. It is also particularly important to ensure that any person searched is treated courteously and considerately.

1B   This Code does not affect the ability of an officer to speak to or question a person in the ordinary course of his duties (and in the absence of reasonable suspicion) without detaining him or exercising any element of compulsion. It is not the purpose of the Code to prohibit such encounters between the police and the community with the cooperation of the person concerned and neither does it affect the principle that all citizens have a duty to help police officers to prevent crime and discover offenders.

1C   The power of search under paragraph 4(2) of Schedule 5 to the Prevention of Terrorism (Temporary Provisions) Act 1989 which does not require reasonable grounds for suspicion is not a power of stop and search as defined in paragraph 1.3 and is not covered by this Code, but searches carried out under paragraph 4(2) should follow the procedures laid down in this Code as far as practicable.

1D   Nothing in this Code affects:
(a)   the routine searching of persons entering sports grounds or other premises with their consent, or as a condition of entry; or
(b)   the ability of an officer to search a person in the street on a voluntary basis. In these circumstances, an officer should always make it clear that he is seeking the co-operation of the person concerned.

1E   If an officer acts in an improper manner this will invalidate a voluntary search. Juveniles, persons suffering from a mental handicap or mental disorder and others who appear not to be capable of giving an informed consent should not be subject to a voluntary search.

2. Action before a search is carried out

2.1.   Where an officer has the reasonable grounds for suspicion necessary to exercise a power of stop and search he may detain the person concerned for the purposes of and with a view to searching him. There is no power to stop or detain a person against his will in order to find grounds for a search.

2.2.   Before carrying out a search the officer may question the person about his behaviour or his presence in circumstances which gave rise to the suspicion, since he may have a satisfactory explanation which will make a search unnecessary. If, as a result of any questioning preparatory to a search, or other circumstances which come to the attention of the officer, there cease to be reasonable grounds for suspecting that an article is being carried of a kind for which there is a power of stop and search, no search may take place.

2.3.   The reasonable grounds for suspicion which are necessary for the exercise of the initial power to detain may be confirmed or eliminated as a result of the questioning of a person detained for the purposes of a search (or such questioning may reveal reasonable grounds to suspect the possession of a different kind of unlawful article from that originally suspected); but the reasonable grounds for suspicion without which any search or detention for the purposes of a search is unlawful cannot be retrospectively provided by such questioning during his detention or by his refusal to answer any question put to him.

2.4.   Before any search of a detained person or attended vehicle takes place the officer must take reasonable steps to give the person to be searched or in charge of the vehicle the following information:

    (i) his name (except in the case of enquiries linked to the investigation of terrorism) and the name of the police station to which he is attached;

    (ii) the object of the search; and (iii) his grounds for undertaking it.

2.5.   If the officer is not in uniform he must show his warrant card.

2.6.   Unless it appears to the officer that it will not be practicable to make a record of the search, he must also inform the person to be searched (or the owner or person in charge of a vehicle that is to be searched, as the case may be) that he is entitled to a copy of the record of the search if he asks for it within a year. If the person wishes to have a copy and is not given one on the spot, he should be advised to which police station he should apply.

2.7.   If the person to be searched, or in charge of a vehicle to be searched, does not understand what is being said, the officer must take reasonable steps to bring the information in paragraphs 2.4 to 2.6 to his attention. If the person has someone with him then the officer must try to establish whether that person can interpret.

Note for guidance
2A   In some circumstances preparatory questioning may be unnecessary, but in general a brief conversation or exchange will be desirable as a means of avoiding unsuccessful searches. Where a person is lawfully detained for the purpose of a

search, but no search in the event takes place, the detention will not thereby have been rendered unlawful.

3. Conduct of the search

3.1. Every reasonable effort must be made to reduce to the minimum the embarrassment that a person being searched may experience.

3.2. The cooperation of the person to be searched should be sought in every case, even if he initially objects to the search. A forcible search may be made only if it has been established that the person is unwilling to co-operate *e.g.* by opening a bag) or resists. Although force may only be used as a last resort, reasonable force may be used if necessary to conduct a search or to detain a person or vehicle for the purposes of a search.

3.3. The length of time for which a person or vehicle may be detained will depend on the circumstances, but must in all circumstances be reasonable and not extend beyond the time taken for the search. The thoroughness and extent of a search must depend on what is suspected of being carried, and by whom. If the suspicion relates to a particular article, which is seen to be slipped into a person's pocket, then, in the absence of other grounds for suspicion or an opportunity for the article to be moved elsewhere, the search must be confined to that pocket. In the case of a small article which can easily be concealed, such as a drug, and which might be concealed anywhere on the person, a more extensive search may be necessary. [See Note 3B]

3.4. The search must be conducted at the place where the person or vehicle was first detained or nearby.

3.5. Searches in public must be restricted to superficial examination of outer clothing. There is no power to require a person to remove any clothing in public other than an outer coat, jacket or gloves. Where on reasonable grounds it is considered necessary to conduct a more thorough search (*e.g.* by requiring a person to take off a T-shirt or headgear), this should be done out of public view (*e.g.* in a police van or nearby police station if there is one). Any search involving the removal of more than an outer coat, jacket, gloves, headgear or footwear may only be made by an officer of the same sex as the person searched and may not be made in the presence of anyone of the opposite sex unless the person being searched specifically requests it. [See Note 3A]

Notes for guidance

3A *A search in the street itself should be regarded as being in public for the purposes of paragraph 3.5 above, even though it may be empty at the time a search begins. Although there is no power to require a person to do so, there is nothing to prevent an officer from asking a person voluntarily to remove more than an outer coat, jacket or gloves in public.*

3B *As a search of a person in public should be a superficial examination of outer clothing, such searches should be completed as soon as possible.*

4. Action after a search is carried out

(a) *General*

4.1. An officer who has carried out a search must make a written record unless it is not practicable to do so, on account of the numbers to be searched or for some other operational reason, *e.g.* in situations involving public disorder.

4.2.   The record must be completed as soon as practicable—on the spot unless circumstances (*e.g.* other immediate duties or very bad weather) make this impracticable.

4.3.   The record must be made on the form provided for this purpose (the national search record).

4.4.   In order to complete the search record the officer should normally seek the name, address and date of birth of the person searched, but under the search procedures there is no obligation on a person to provide these details and no power to detain him if he is unwilling to do so.

4.5.   The following information should always be included in the record of a search even if the person does not wish to identify himself or give his date of birth:

(i)   the name of the person searched, or (if he withholds it) a description of him;

(ii)   a note of the person's ethnic origin;

(iii)   when a vehicle is searched, a description of it, including its registration number [See Note 4B];

(iv)   the object of the search;

(v)   the grounds for making it; (vi) the date and time it was made;

(vii)   the place where it was made; (viii) its results;

(ix)   a note of any injury or damage to property resulting from it;

(x)   the identity of the officer making it (except in the case of enquiries linked to the investigation of terrorism in which case the record shall state the officer's warrant number and duty station [See Note 4A]).

4.6.   A record is required for each person and each vehicle searched. However, if a person is in a vehicle and both are searched, and the object and grounds of the search are the same, only one record need be completed.

4.7.   The record of the grounds for making a search must, briefly but informatively, explain the reason for suspecting the person concerned, whether by reference to his behaviour or other circumstances.

(b)   *Unattended vehicles*

4.8.   After searching an unattended vehicle, or anything in or on it, an officer must leave a notice in it (or on it, if things in or on it have been searched without opening it) recording the fact that it has been searched.

4.9.   The notice should include the name of the police station to which the officer concerned is attached and state where a copy of the record of the search may be obtained and where any application for compensation should be directed.

4.10.   The vehicle must if practicable be left secure.

Notes for guidance

4A   *Where a search is conducted by more than one officer the identity of all the officers engaged in the search must be recorded on the search record.*

4B   *Where a vehicle has not been allocated a registration number (e.g. a rally car or a trials motorbike), that part of the requirement under 4.5(iii) does not apply.*

*   *   *   *

B. CODE OF PRACTICE FOR THE SEARCHING OF PREMISES BY POLICE OFFICERS AND THE SEIZURE OF PROPERTY FOUND BY POLICE OFFICERS ON PERSONS OR PREMISES

1. General

1.1.   This Code of Practice must be readily available at all police stations for consultation by police officers, detained persons and members of the public.

1.2.   The notes for guidance included are not provisions of this Code, but are guidance to police officers and others about its application and interpretation.

1.3.   This Code applies to the following searches of premises:

   (a) searches of premises undertaken for the purposes of an investigation into an alleged offence, with the occupier's consent, other than routine scenes of crime searches and searches following the activation of fire or burglar alarms or bomb threat calls;

   (b) searches of premises under powers conferred by sections 17, 18 and 32 of the Police and Criminal Evidence Act 1984;

   (c) searches of premises undertaken in pursuance of a search warrant issued in accordance with section 15 of, or Schedule 1 to, that Act, or Schedule 7 to the Prevention of Terrorism (Temporary Provisions) Act 1989.

"Premises" for the purposes of this Code is as defined in section 23 of the Police and Criminal Evidence Act 1984. It includes any place and, in particular, any vehicle, vessel, aircraft, hovercraft, tent or movable structure. It also includes any offshore installation as defined by section 1 of the Mineral Workings (Offshore Installation) Act 1977.

2. Search warrants and production orders

(a) *Action to be taken before an application is made*

2.1.   Where information is received which appears to justify an application, the officer concerned must take reasonable steps to check that the information is accurate, recent and has not been provided maliciously or irresponsibly. An application may not be made on the basis of information from an anonymous source where corroboration has not been sought.

2.2.   The officer shall ascertain as specifically as is possible in the circumstances the nature of the articles concerned and their location.

2.3.   The officer shall also make reasonable enquiries to establish what, if anything, is known about the likely occupier of the premises and the nature of the premises themselves; and whether they have been previously searched and if so how recently; and to obtain any other information relevant to the application.

2.4.   No application for a search warrant may be made without the authority of an officer of at least the rank of inspector (or, in a case of urgency where no officer of this rank is readily available, the senior officer on duty). No application for a production order or warrant under Schedule 1 to the Police and Criminal Evidence Act 1984, or under Schedule 7 to the Prevention of Terrorism (Temporary Provisions) Act 1989, may be made without the authority of an officer of at least the rank of superintendent.

2.5.   Except in a case of urgency, if there is reason to believe that a search might have an adverse effect on relations between the police and the community then the local police community liaison officer shall be consulted before it takes place. In urgent cases, the local police community liaison officer should be informed of the search as soon as practicable after it has been made. [See Note 2B]

(b) *Making an application*

2.6. An application for a search warrant must be supported by an information in writing, stating:

(i) the enactment under which the application is made; (ii) as specifically as is reasonably practicable the premises to be searched and the object of the search; and (iii) the grounds on which the application is made (including, where the purpose of the proposed search is to find evidence of an alleged offence, an indication of how the evidence relates to the investigation).

2.7. An application for a search warrant under paragraph 12(a) of Schedule 1 to the Police and Criminal Evidence Act 1984, or under Schedule 7 to the Prevention of Terrorism (Temporary Provisions) Act 1989, shall also, where appropriate, indicate why it is believed that service of notice of an application for a production order may seriously prejudice the investigation.

2.8. If an application is refused, no further application may be made for a warrant to search those premises unless supported by additional grounds.

Notes for guidance

2A *The identity of an informant need not be disclosed when making an application, but the officer concerned should be prepared to deal with any questions the magistrate or judge may have about the accuracy of previous information provided by that source or other related matters.*

2B *The local police/community consultative group, where it exists, or its equivalent, should be informed as soon as practicable after a search has taken place where there is reason to believe that it might have had an adverse effect on relations between the police and the community.*

3. Entry without warrant

(a) *Making an arrest etc.*

3.1. The conditions under which an officer may enter and search premises without a warrant are set out in section 17 of the Police and Criminal Evidence Act 1984.

(b) *Search after arrest of premises in which arrest takes place or in which the arrested person was immediately prior to arrest*

3.2. The powers of an officer to search premises in which he has arrested a person or where the person was immediately before he was arrested, are as set out in section 32 of the Police and Criminal Evidence Act 1984.

(c) *Search after arrest of premises in which arrest takes place*

3.3. The specific powers of an officer to search premises occupied or controlled by a person who has been arrested for an arrestable offence are as set out in Section 18 of the Police and Criminal Evidence Act 1984. They may not (unless subsection 5 of section 18 applies) be exercised unless an officer of the rank of inspector or above has given authority in writing. That authority should (unless wholly impracticable) be given on the Notice of Powers and

Rights (See paragraph 5.7(ii)). The record of the search required by section 18(7) of the Act shall be made in the custody record, where there is one.

4. Search with consent

4.1. Subject to paragraph 4.4 below, if it is proposed to search premises with the consent of a person entitled to grant entry to the premises the consent must, if practicable, be given in writing on the Notice of Powers and Rights before the search takes place. The officer must make enquiries to satisfy himself that the person is in a position to give such consent. [See Note 4B and paragraph 5.7(i)]

4.2. Before seeking consent the officer in charge of the search shall state the purpose of the proposed search and inform the person concerned that he is not obliged to consent and that anything seized may be produced in evidence. If at the time the person is not suspected of an offence, the officer shall tell him so when stating the purpose of the search.

4.3. An officer cannot enter and search premises or continue to search premises under 4.1 above if the consent has been given under duress or is subsequently withdrawn before the search is completed.

4.4. It is unnecessary to seek consent under paragraphs 4.1 and 4.2 above where in the circumstances this would cause disproportionate inconvenience to the person concerned. [Note 4C]

Notes for guidance

4A *In the case of a lodging house or similar accommodation a search should not be made on the basis solely of the landlord's consent unless the tenant is unavailable and the matter is urgent.*

4B *Where it is intended to search premises under the authority of a warrant or a power of entry and search without warrant, and the co-operation of the occupier of the premises is obtained in accordance with paragraph 5.4 below, there is no additional requirement to obtain written consent as at paragraph 4.1 above.*

4C *Paragraph 4.4 is intended in particular to apply, for example, to circumstances where police have arrested someone in the night after a pursuit and it is necessary to make a brief check of gardens along the route of the pursuit to see whether stolen or incriminating articles have been discarded.*

5. Searching of premises: general considerations

(a) *Time of searches*

5.1. Searches made under warrant must be made within one calendar month from the date of issue of the warrant.

5.2. Searches must be made at a reasonable hour unless this might frustrate the purpose of the search. [See Note 5A]

5.3. A warrant authorises an entry on one occasion only.

(b) *Entry other than with consent*

5.4. The officer in charge shall first attempt to communicate with the occupier or any other person entitled to grant access to the premises by explaining the authority under which he seeks entry to the premises and ask the occupier to allow him to do so, unless:

    (i) the premises to be searched are known to be unoccupied;

    (ii) the occupier and any other person entitled to grant access are known to be absent; or

(iii) there are reasonable grounds for believing that to alert the occupier or any other person entitled to grant access by attempting to communicate with him would frustrate the object of the search or endanger the officers concerned or other persons.

5.5. Where the premises are occupied the officer shall identify himself and, if not in uniform, show his warrant card; and state the purpose of the search and the grounds for undertaking it, before a search begins, unless sub-paragraph 5.4(iii) applies

5.6. Reasonable force may be used if necessary to enter premises if the officer in charge is satisfied that the premises are those specified in any warrant, or in exercise of the powers described in 3.1 to 3.3 above, and where:

(i) the occupier or any other person entitled to grant access has refused a request to allow entry to his premises;

(ii) it is impossible to communicate with the occupier or any other person entitled to grant access; or

(iii) any of the provisions of 5.4(i) to (iii) apply.

(c) *Notice of powers and rights*

5.7. If an officer conducts a search to which this Code applies, he shall, unless it is impracticable to do so, provide the occupier with a notice in a standard format:

(i) specifying whether the search is made under warrant, or with consent, or in the exercise of the powers described in 3.1 to 3.3 above (the format of the notice shall provide for authority or consent to be indicated where appropriate—see 3.3 and 4.1 above);

(ii) summarising the extent of the powers of search and seizure conferred in the Act;

(iii) explaining the rights of the occupier, and of the owner of property seized in accordance with the provisions of 6.1 to 6.5 below, set out in the Act and this Code;

(iv) explaining that compensation may be payable in appropriate cases for damage caused in entering and searching premises, and giving the address to which an application for compensation should be directed; and

(v) stating that a copy of this Code is available to be consulted at any police station.

5.8. If the occupier is present, copies of the notice mentioned above and a copy of the warrant (if the search is made under warrant) should, if practicable, be given to the occupier before the search begins, unless the officer in charge of the search reasonably believes that to do so would frustrate the object of the search or endanger the officers concerned or other persons. If the occupier is not present, copies of the notice, and of the warrant where appropriate, should be left in a prominent place on the premises or appropriate part of the premises and endorsed with the name of the officer in charge of the search, the name of the police station to which he is attached and the date and time of the search. The warrant itself should be endorsed to show that this has been done.

(d) *Conduct of searches*

5.9. Premises may be searched only to the extent necessary to achieve the object of the search, having regard to the size and nature of whatever is sought. A search under warrant may not continue under the authority of that warrant once all the things specified in it have been found, or the officer in charge of the search is satisfied that they are not on the premises.

5.10. Searches must be conducted with due consideration for the property and privacy of the occupier of the premises searched, and with no more disturbance than necessary. Reasonable force may be used only where this is necessary because the co-operation of the occupier cannot be obtained or is insufficient for the purpose.

5.11. If the occupier wishes to ask a friend, neighbour or other person to witness the search then he must be allowed to do so, unless the officer in charge has reasonable grounds for believing that this would seriously hinder the investigation. A search need not be delayed for this purpose unreasonably.

* * * *

6. Seizure and retention of property

(a) *Seizure*

6.1. Subject to paragraph 6.2 below, an officer who is searching any premises under any statutory power or with the consent of the occupier may seize:

(a) anything covered by a warrant; and

(b) anything which he has reasonable grounds for believing is evidence of an offence or has been obtained in consequence of the commission of an offence.

Items under (b) may only be seized where this is necessary to prevent their concealment, alteration, loss, damage or destruction.

6.2. No item may be seized which is subject to legal privilege (as defined in section 10 of the Police and Criminal Evidence Act 1984).

6.3. An officer who decides that it is not appropriate to seize property because of an explanation given by the person holding it, but who has reasonable grounds for believing that it has been obtained in consequence of the commission of an offence by some person, shall inform the holder of his suspicions and shall explain that, if he disposes of the property, he may be liable to civil or criminal proceedings.

* * * *

7. Action to be taken after searches

7.1. Where premises have been searched in circumstances to which this Code applies, other than in the circumstances covered by paragraph 4.4 above, the officer in charge of the search shall, on arrival at a police station, make or have made a record of the search. The record shall include:

(i) the address of the premises searched;

(ii) the date, time and duration of the search;

(iii) the authority under which the search was made. Where the search was made in the exercise of a statutory power to search premises without warrant, the record shall include the power under which the search was made; and where the search was made under warrant, or with written consent, a copy of the warrant or consent shall be appended to the record or kept in a place identified in the record;

(iv) the names of all the officers who conducted the search (except in the case of enquiries linked to the investigation of terrorism, in which case the record should state the warrant number and duty station of each officer concerned);

(v) the names of any persons on the premises if they are known;

(vi) either a list of any articles seized or a note of where such a list is kept and, if not covered by a warrant, the reason for their seizure;

(vii) whether force was used, and, if so, the reason why it was used;

(viii) details of any damage caused during the search, and the circumstances in which it was caused.

7.2.   Where premises have been searched under warrant, the warrant shall be endorsed to show:

(i) whether any articles specified in the warrant were found;

(ii) whether any other articles were seized;

(iii) the date and time at which it was executed;

(iv) the names of the officers who executed it (except in the case of enquiries linked to the investigation of terrorism, in which case the warrant number and duty station of each officer concerned shall be shown); and

(v) whether a copy together with the notice of powers and rights was handed to the occupier; or whether it was endorsed with the date and time of the search, and left on the premises together with the notice and, if so, where.

7.3.   Any warrant which has been executed or which has not been executed within one calendar month of its issue shall be returned, if it was issued by a justice of the peace, to the clerk to the justices for the petty sessions area concerned or, if issued by a judge, to the appropriate officer of the court from which he issued it.

* * * *

C. CODE OF PRACTICE FOR THE DETENTION, TREATMENT AND QUESTIONING OF PERSONS BY POLICE OFFICERS

* * * *

3. Initial action

(a) *Detained persons: normal procedure*

3.1.   When a person is brought to a police station under arrest or is arrested at the police station having attended there voluntarily the custody officer must inform him clearly of the following rights and of the fact that they are continuing rights which may be exercised at any stage during the period in custody.

(i) the right to have someone informed of his arrest in accordance with section 5 below;

(ii) the right to consult privately with a solicitor in accordance with section 6 below, and the fact that independent legal advice is available free of charge; and

(iii) the right to consult this and the other Codes of Practice. . . .

3.2.   The custody officer must give the person a written notice setting out the above three rights, the right to a copy of the custody record in accordance with paragraph 2.4 above and the caution in the terms prescribed in section 10 below. The notice must also explain the arrangements for obtaining legal advice. The custody officer must also give the person an additional written notice briefly setting out his entitlements while in custody. [See Note 3A] The custody officer shall ask the person to sign the custody record to acknowledge receipt of these notices and any refusal to sign must be recorded on the custody record. [See Note 3B]

3.3.   A citizen of an independent Commonwealth country or a national of a foreign country (including the Republic of Ireland) must be informed as soon as practicable of his rights of communication with his High Commission, Embassy or Consulate. . . .

3.4.   If the custody officer authorises a person's detention he must inform him of the grounds as soon as practicable and in any case before that person is then questioned about any offence.

3.5.   The person shall be asked to sign on the custody record to signify whether or not he wants legal advice at this point. The custody officer is responsible for ensuring that the person signs the custody record in the correct place to give effect to his decision. Where legal advice is requested (and unless Annex B applies) the custody officer must act without delay to secure the provision of such advice to the person concerned.

*   *   *   *

5. Right not to be held incommunicado

(a) *Action*

5.1.   Any person arrested and held in custody at a police station or other premises may on request have one person known to him or who is likely to take an interest in his welfare informed at public expense as soon as practicable of his whereabouts. If the person cannot be contacted the person who has made the request may choose up to two alternatives. If they too cannot be contacted the person in charge of detention or of the investigation has discretion to allow further attempts until the information has been conveyed. [See Notes 5C and 5D]

5.2.   The exercise of the above right in respect of each of the persons nominated may be delayed only in accordance with Annex B to this Code.

5.3.   The above right may be exercised on each occasion that a person is taken to another police station.

5.4.   The person may receive visits at the custody officer's discretion. [See Note 5B]

5.5.   Where an inquiry as to the whereabouts of the person is made by a friend, relative or person with an interest in his welfare, this information shall be given, if he agrees and if Annex B does not apply. [See Note 5D]

5.6.   Subject to the following condition, the person should be supplied with writing materials on request and allowed to speak on the telephone for a reasonable time to one person [See Note 5E]. Where an officer of the rank of Inspector or above considers that the sending of a letter or the making of a telephone call may result in any of the consequences set out in the first paragraph of Annex B, and the person is detained in connection with an arrestable or a serious arrestable offence, that officer can deny or delay the exercise of either or both these privileges. However, nothing in this section permits the restriction or denial of the rights set out in sections 5.1 and 6.1.

5.7. Before any letter or message is sent, or telephone call made, the person shall be informed that what he says in any letter, call or message (other than in the case of a communication to a solicitor) may be read or listened to as appropriate and may be given in evidence. A telephone call may be terminated if it is being abused. The costs can be at public expense at the discretion of the custody officer.

(b) *Documentation*

5.8. A record must be kept of:
   (a) any request made under this section and the action taken on it;
   (b) any letters or messages sent, calls made or visits received; and
   (c) any refusal on the part of the person to have information about himself or his whereabouts given to an outside enquirer. The person must be asked to countersign the record accordingly and any refusal to sign should be recorded.

Notes for guidance

5A   *An interpreter may make a telephone call or write a letter on a person's behalf.*

5B   *In the exercise of his discretion the custody officer should allow visits where possible in the light of the availability of sufficient manpower to supervise a visit and any possible hindrance to the investigation.*

5C   *If the person does not know of anyone to contact for advice or support or cannot contact a friend or relative, the custody officer should bear in mind any local voluntary bodies or other organisations who might be able to offer help in such cases. But if it is specifically legal advice that is wanted, then paragraph 6.1 below will apply.*

5D   *In some circumstances it may not be appropriate to use the telephone to disclose information under paragraphs 5.1 and 5.5 above.*

5E   *The telephone call at paragraph 5.7 is in addition to any communication under paragraphs 5.1 and 6.1.*

6. Right to legal advice

(a) *Action*

6.1. Subject to paragraph 6.2, any person may at any time consult and communicate privately, whether in person, in writing or on the telephone with a solicitor. [See Note 6B]

6.2. The exercise of the above right may be delayed only in accordance with Annex B to this Code. Whenever legal advice is requested (and unless Annex B applies) the custody officer must act without delay to secure the provision of such advice to the person concerned.

6.3. A poster advertising the right to have legal advice must be prominently displayed in the charging area of every police station. [See Note 6H]

6.4. No attempt should be made to dissuade the suspect from obtaining legal advice.

6.5.   Reminders of the right to legal advice must be given in accordance with paragraphs 11.2, 15.3 and section 2 of Annex A and paragraph 2.15(ii) of Code of Practice D.

6.6.   A person who wants legal advice may not be interviewed or continue to be interviewed until he has received it unless:

(a) Annex B applies; or

(b) an officer of the rank of superintendent or above has reasonable grounds for believing that:

   (i) delay will involve an immediate risk of harm to persons or serious loss of, or damage to, property; or

   (ii) where a solicitor, including a duty solicitor, has been contacted and has agreed to attend, awaiting his arrival would cause unreasonable delay to the process of investigation; or

(c) The solicitor nominated by the person, or selected by him from a list not being the duty solicitor:

   (i) cannot be contacted; or

   (ii) has previously indicated that he does not wish to be contacted; or

   (iii) having been contacted, has declined to attend

   and the person has been advised of the Duty Solicitor Scheme (where one is in operation) but has declined to ask for the duty solicitor, or the duty solicitor is unavailable. [See also Note 6B]

Where (c) applies, and the person has indicated that he does not want legal advice, the interview may be started or continued without further delay provided that the person has given his agreement in writing or on tape to being interviewed without receiving legal advice and that an officer of the rank of superintendent or above has given written agreement for the interview to proceed in those circumstances.

6.7.   Where sub-paragraph 6.6(b)(i) applies, once sufficient information to avert the risk has been obtained, questioning must cease until the person has received legal advice or sub-paragraph 6.6(a), (b)(ii), or (c) apply.

6.8.   Where a person has been permitted to consult a solicitor and the solicitor is available (*i.e.* present at the station or on his way to the station or easily contactable by telephone) at the time the interview begins or is in progress, he must be allowed to have his solicitor present while he is interviewed.

6.9.   The solicitor may only be required to leave the interview if his conduct is such that the investigating officer is unable properly to put questions to the suspect. [See Notes 6D and 6E]

6.10.   If the investigating officer considers that a solicitor is acting in such a way, he will stop the interview and consult an officer not below the rank of superintendent, if one is readily available, and otherwise an officer not below the rank of inspector who is not connected with the investigation. After speaking to the solicitor, the officer who has been consulted will decide whether or not the interview should continue in the presence of that solicitor. If he decides that it should not, the suspect will be given the opportunity to consult another solicitor before the interview continues and that solicitor will be given an opportunity to be present at the interview.

6.11.   The removal of a solicitor from an interview is a serious step and, if it occurs, the officer of superintendent rank or above who took the decision will consider whether the incident should be reported to the Law Society. If the decision to remove the solicitor has been taken by an officer below the rank of superintendent, the facts must be reported to an officer of superintendent rank or above who will similarly consider whether a report to the Law Society would be appropriate. Where the solicitor concerned is a Duty Solicitor, the report should be both to the Law Society and to the Legal Aid Board.

6.12.   In this Code "solicitor" means a solicitor qualified to practise in accordance with the Solicitors Act 1974. If a solicitor wishes to send a clerk or legal executive to provide advice on his behalf, then the clerk or legal executive shall be admitted to the police station for this purpose unless an officer of the rank of inspector or above considers that such a visit will hinder the investigation of crime and directs otherwise. Once admitted to the police station, the provisions of paragraphs 6.6 to 6.10 apply.

6.13.   In exercising his discretion under paragraph 6.12, the officer should take into account in particular whether the identity and status of the clerk or legal executive have been satisfactorily established; whether he is of suitable character to provide legal advice (a person with a criminal record is unlikely to be suitable unless the conviction was for a minor offence and is not of recent date); and any other matters in any written letter of authorisation provided by the solicitor on whose behalf the clerk or legal executive is attending the police station. [See Note 6F]

6.14.   If the inspector refuses access to a clerk or legal executive or a decision is taken that such a person should not be permitted to remain at an interview, he must forthwith notify a solicitor on whose behalf the clerk or legal executive was to have acted or was acting, and give him an opportunity of making alternative arrangements. The detained person must also be informed and the custody record noted.

6.15.   If a solicitor arrives at the station to see a particular person, that person must (unless Annex B applies) be informed of the solicitor's arrival and asked whether he would like to see him. This applies even if the person concerned has already declined legal advice. The solicitor's attendance and the detained person's decision must be noted on the custody record.

(b) *Documentation*

6.16.   Any request for legal advice and the action taken on it shall be recorded.

6.17.   If a person has asked for legal advice and an interview is begun in the absence of a solicitor or his representative (or the solicitor or his representative has been required to leave an interview), a record shall be made in the interview record.

Notes for guidance

6A   *In considering whether paragraph 6.6(b) applies, the officer should where practicable ask the solicitor for an estimate of the time that he is likely to take in coming to the station, and relate this information to the time for which detention is permitted, the time of day (i.e. whether the period of rest required by paragraph 12.2 is imminent) and the requirements of other investigations in progress. If the solicitor says that he is on his way to the station or that he will set off immediately it will not normally be appropriate to begin an interview before he arrives. If it appears that it will be necessary to begin an interview before the solicitor's arrival he should be given an indication of how long police would be able to wait before paragraph 6.6(b) applies so that he has an opportunity to make arrangements for legal advice to be provided by someone else.*

6B   *A person who asks for legal advice should be given an opportunity to consult a specific solicitor (for example, his own solicitor or one known to him) or the duty solicitor where a Duty Solicitor Scheme is in operation. If advice is not available by these means, or he does not wish to consult the duty solicitor, the person should be given an opportunity to choose a solicitor from a list of those willing to provide legal advice. If this solicitor is unavailable, he may choose up to two alternatives. If these attempts to secure legal advice are unsuccessful, the custody officer has discretion to allow further attempts until a solicitor has been contacted and agrees to provide legal advice.*

6C   *Procedures undertaken under section 7 of the Road Traffic Act 1988 do not constitute interviewing for the purposes of this Code.*

6D   *In considering whether paragraph 6.9 applies, a solicitor is not guilty of misconduct if he seeks to challenge an improper question to his client or the manner in which it is put or if he advises his client not to reply to particular questions or if he wishes to give his client further legal advice. It is the duty of a solicitor to look after the interests of his client and to advise him without obstructing the interview. He should not be required to leave an interview unless his interference with its conduct clearly goes beyond this. Examples of misconduct may include answering questions on the client's behalf, or providing written replies for the client to quote.*

6E   *In a case where an officer takes the decision to exclude a solicitor, he must be in a position to satisfy the court that the decision was properly made. In order to do this he may need to witness what is happening himself.*

6F   *If an officer of at least the rank of inspector considers that a particular solicitor or firm of solicitors is persistently sending as clerks or legal executives persons who are unsuited to provide legal advice, he should inform an officer of at least the rank of superintendent, who may wish to take the matter up with the Law Society.*

6G   *Subject to the constraints of Annex B, a solicitor may advise more than one client in an investigation if he wishes. Any question of a conflict of interest is for the solicitor under his professional code of conduct. If, however, waiting for a solicitor to give advice to one client may lead to unreasonable delay to the interview with another, the provisions of paragraph 6.6(b) may apply.*

6H   *In addition to the poster in English, the poster containing translations into the main ethnic minority languages and the principal EC languages should be displayed wherever they are likely to be helpful and it is practicable to do so.*

* * * *

10. Cautions

(a) *When a caution must be given*

10.1.   A person whom there are grounds to suspect of an offence must be cautioned before any questions about it (or further questions if it is his answers to previous questions that provide grounds for suspicion) are put to him for the purpose of obtaining evidence which may be given to a court in a prosecution. He therefore need not be cautioned if questions are put for other purposes, for example, to establish his identity or his ownership of any vehicle or the need to search him in the exercise of powers of stop and search.

10.2.   Whenever a person who is not under arrest is initially cautioned before or during an interview he must at the same time be told that he is not under arrest and is not obliged to remain with the officer. . . .

10.3.   A person must be cautioned upon arrest for an offence unless:
(a) it is impracticable to do so by reason of his condition or behaviour at the time; or
(b) he has already been cautioned immediately prior to arrest in accordance with paragraph 10.1 above.

(b) *Action: general*
10.4.   The caution shall be in the following terms:

"You do not have to say anything unless you wish to do so, but what you say may be given in evidence."

Minor deviations do not constitute a breach of this requirement provided that the sense of the caution is preserved. [See Notes 10C and 10D]
10.5.   When there is a break in questioning under caution the interviewing officer must ensure that the person being questioned is aware that he remains under caution. If there is any doubt the caution should be given again in full when the interview resumes. [See Note 10A]

(c) *Juveniles, the mentally disordered and the mentally handicapped*
10.6.   If a juvenile or a person who is mentally ill or mentally disordered is cautioned in the absence of the appropriate adult, the caution must be repeated in the adult's presence.

(d) *Documentation*
10.7.   A record shall be made when a caution is given under this section, either in the officer's pocket book or in the interview record as appropriate.

Notes for guidance
10A   *In considering whether or not to caution again after a break, the officer should bear in mind that he may have to satisfy a court that the person understood that he was still under caution when the interview resumed.*

10B   *It is not necessary to give or repeat a caution when informing a person who is not under arrest that he may be prosecuted for an offence.*

10C   *If it appears that a person does not understand what the caution means, the officer who has given it should go on to explain it in his own words.*

10D   *In case anyone who is given a caution is unclear about its significance, the officer concerned should explain that the caution is given in pursuance of the general principle of English law that a person need not answer any questions or provide any information which might tend to incriminate him, and that no adverse inferences from this silence may be drawn at any trial that takes place. The person should not, however, be left with a false impression that non-cooperation will have no effect on his immediate treatment as, for example, his refusal to provide his name and address when charged with an offence may render him liable to detention.*

11. Interviews: general

(a) *Action*
11.1.   Following a decision to arrest a suspect he must not be interviewed about the relevant offence except at a police station (or other authorised place of detention) unless the consequent delay would be likely:
(a) to lead to interference with or harm to evidence connected with

an offence or interference with or physical harm to other persons; or

(b) to lead to the alerting of other persons suspected of having committed an offence but not yet arrested for it; or

(c) to hinder the recovery of property obtained in consequence of the commission of such an offence.

Interviewing in any of these circumstances should cease once the relevant risk has been averted or the necessary questions have been put in order to attempt to avert that risk. For the definition of an interview see Note 11A.

11.2.　Immediately prior to the commencement or re-commencement of any interview at a police station or other authorised place of detention, the interviewing officer should remind the suspect of his entitlement to free legal advice. It is the responsibility of the interviewing officer to ensure that all such reminders are noted in the record of interview.

11.3.　No police officer may try to obtain answers to questions or to elicit a statement by the use of oppression or shall indicate, except in answer to a direct question, what action will be taken on the part of the police if the person being interviewed answers questions, makes a statement or refuses to do either. If the person asks the officer directly what action will be taken in the event of his answering questions, making a statement or refusing to do either, then the officer may inform the person what action the police propose to take in that event, provided that that action is itself proper and warranted.

11.4.　As soon as a police officer who is making enquiries of any person about an offence believes that a prosecution should be brought against him and that there is sufficient evidence for it to succeed, he should ask the person if he has anything else to say. If the person indicates that he has nothing more to say the officer shall without delay cease to question him. This should not, however, be taken to prevent officers in revenue cases or acting under the confiscation provisions of the Criminal Justice Act 1988 or the Drug Trafficking Offences Act 1986 from inviting suspects to complete a formal question and answer record after the interview is concluded.

(b) *Interview records*

11.5　(a) An accurate record must be made of each interview with a person suspected of an offence, whether or not the interview takes place at a police station.

(b) The record must state the place of the interview, the time it begins and ends, the time the record is made (if different), any breaks in the interview and the names of all those present; and must be made on the forms provided for this purpose or in the officer's pocketbook or in accordance with the code of practice for the tape-recording of police interview with suspects.

(c) The record must be made during the course of the interview, unless in the investigating officer's view this would not be practicable or would interfere with the conduct of the interview, and must constitute either a verbatim record of what has been said or, failing this, an account of the interview which adequately and accurately summarises it.

* * * *

Notes for guidance
*11A   An interview is the questioning of a person regarding his involvement or sus-
pected involvement in a criminal offence or offences. Questioning a person
simply to obtain information or his explanation of the facts or in the ordinary
course of the officer's duties, does not constitute an interview for the purpose of
this Code. Neither does questioning which is strictly confined to the proper and
effective conduct of a search.*

*   *   *   *

12. Interviews in police stations

(a) *Action*

12.1.   If a police officer wishes to interview, or conduct enquiries which
require the presence of, a detained person the custody officer is responsible
for deciding whether to deliver him into his custody.

12.2.   In any period of 24 hours a detained person must be allowed a
continuous period of at least 8 hours for rest, free from questioning, travel
or any interruption arising out of the investigation concerned. This period
should normally be at night. The period of rest may not be interrupted or
delayed unless there are reasonable grounds for believing that it would:

(i) involve a risk of harm to persons or serious loss of, or damage
to, property;

(ii) delay unnecessarily the person's release from custody; or

(iii) otherwise prejudice the outcome of the investigation.

If a person is arrested at a police station after going there voluntarily, the
period of 24 hours runs from the time of his arrest and not the time of arrival
at the police station.

12.3.   A detained person may not be supplied with intoxicating liquor except on medical directions. No person who is unfit through drink or drugs to
the extent that he is unable to appreciate the significance of questions put to
him and his answers may be questioned about an alleged offence in that condition except in accordance with Annex C. [See Note 12B]

12.4.   As far as practicable interviews shall take place in interview rooms
which must be adequately heated, lit and ventilated.

12.5.   Persons being questioned or making statements shall not be required to stand.

12.6.   Before the commencement of an interview each interviewing officer
shall identify himself and any other officers present by name and rank to the
person being interviewed, except in the case of persons detained under the
Prevention of Terrorism (Temporary Provisions) Act 1989 when each officer
shall identify himself by his warrant number and rank rather than his name.

12.7.   Breaks from interviewing shall be made at recognised meal times.
Short breaks for refreshment shall also be provided at intervals of approxi-
mately two hours, subject to the interviewing officer's discretion to delay a
break if there are reasonable grounds for believing that it would:

(i) involve a risk of harm to persons of serious loss of, or damage
to, property;

(ii) delay unnecessarily the person's release from custody; or

(iii) otherwise prejudice the outcome of the investigation.

12.8.   If in the course of the interview a complaint is made by the person being questioned or on his behalf concerning the provisions of this Code then the interviewing officer shall:

  (i) record it in the interview record; and

  (ii) inform the custody officer, who is then responsible for dealing with it in accordance with section 9 of this Code.

(b) *Documentation*

12.9.   A record must be made of the times at which a detained person is not in the custody of the custody officer, and why; and of the reason for any refusal to deliver him out of that custody.

12.10.   A record must be made of any intoxicating liquor supplied to a detained person, in accordance with paragraph 12.3 above.

12.11.   Any decision to delay a break in an interview must be recorded, with grounds, in the interview record.

12.12.   All written statements made at police stations under caution shall be written on the forms provided for the purpose.

12.13.   All written statements made under caution shall be taken in accordance with Annex D to this Code.

Notes for guidance

12A   *If the interview has been contemporaneously recorded and the record signed by the person interviewed in accordance with paragraph 11.10 above, or has been tape recorded, it is normally unnecessary to ask for a written statement. Statements under caution should normally be taken in these circumstances only at the person's express wish. An officer may, however, ask him whether or not he wants to make such a statement.*

12B   *The police surgeon can give advice about whether or not a person is fit to be interviewed in accordance with paragraph 12.3 above.*

* * * *

16. Charging of detained persons

(a) *Action*

16.1.   When an officer considers that there is sufficient evidence to prosecute a detained person, and that there is sufficient evidence for a prosecution to succeed, and that the person has said all that he wishes to say about the offence, he should without delay and subject to the following qualification bring him before the custody officer who shall then be responsible for considering whether or not he should be charged. Where a detained person is suspected of more than one offence it is permissible to delay bringing him before the custody officer until the above conditions are satisfied in respect of all the offences (but see paragraph 11.4). Any resulting action should be taken in the presence of the appropriate adult if the person is a juvenile or mentally disordered or mentally handicapped.

16.2.   When a detained person is charged with or informed that he may be prosecuted for an offence he shall be cautioned in the terms of paragraph 10.4 above.

16.3.   At the time a person is charged he shall be given a written notice showing particulars of the offence with which he is charged and including the name of the officer in the case (in terrorist cases, the officer's warrant number instead), his police station and the reference number for the case. So far as possible the particulars of the charge shall be stated in simple terms, but they shall also show the precise offence in law with which he is charged. The notice shall begin with the following words:

> "You are charged with the offence(s) shown below. You do not have to say anything unless you wish to do so, but what you say may be given in evidence."

If the person is a juvenile or is mentally disordered or mentally handicapped the notice shall be given to the appropriate adult.

16.4. If at any time after a person has been charged with or informed he may be prosecuted for an offence a police officer wishes to bring to the notice of that person any written statement made by another person or the content of an interview with another person, he shall hand to that person a true copy of any such written statement or bring to his attention the content of the interview record, but shall say or do nothing to invite any reply or comment save to caution him in the terms of paragraph 10.4 above. If the person cannot read then the officer may read it to him. If the person is a juvenile or mentally disordered or mentally handicapped the copy shall also be given to, or the interview record brought to the attention of, the appropriate adult.

16.5. Questions relating to an offence may not be put to a person after he has been charged with that offence, or informed that he may be prosecuted for it, unless they are necessary for the purpose of preventing or minimising harm or loss to some other person or to the public or for clearing up an ambiguity in a previous answer or statement, or where it is in the interests of justice that the person should have put to him and have an opportunity to comment on information concerning the offence which has come to light since he was charged or informed that he might be prosecuted. Before any such questions are put he shall be cautioned in the terms of paragraph 10.4 above. . . .

* * * *

ANNEX A (SEE PARAGRAPH 4.1)

Intimate and strip searches

(a) *Action*

1. Body orifices may be searched only if an officer of the rank of superintendent or above has reasonable grounds for believing:

(a) that an article which could cause physical injury to a detained person or others at the police station has been concealed; or

(b) that the person has concealed a Class A drug which he intended to supply to another or to export; and

(c) that in either case an intimate search is the only practicable means of removing it.

The reasons why an intimate search is considered necessary shall be explained to the person before the search takes place.

2. Before any intimate search takes place, the person to be searched

must be reminded of his entitlement to legal advice and the reminder must be noted in the custody record.

3.   An intimate search may only be carried out by a registered medical practitioner or registered nurse, unless an officer of at least the rank of superintendent considers that this is not practicable and the search is to take place under sub-paragraph 1(a) above.

4.   An intimate search under sub-paragraph 1(a) above may take place only at a hospital, surgery, other medical premises or police station. A search under sub-paragraph 1(b) may take place only at a hospital, surgery or other medical premises.

5.   An intimate search at a police station of a juvenile or a mentally disordered or mentally handicapped person may take place only in the presence of the appropriate adult of the same sex (unless the person specifically requests the presence of a particular adult of the opposite sex who is readily available). In the case of a juvenile the search may take place in the absence of the appropriate adult only if the juvenile signifies in the presence of the appropriate adult that he prefers the search to be done in his absence and the appropriate adult agrees. A record should be made of the juvenile's decision and signed by the appropriate adult.

6.   A strip search (that is a search involving the removal of more than outer clothing) may take place only if the custody officer considers it to be necessary to remove an article which the detained person would not be allowed to keep.

7.   Where an intimate search under sub-paragraph 1(a) above or a strip search is carried out by a police officer, the officer must be of the same sex as the person searched. Subject to paragraph 5 above, no person of the opposite sex who is not a medical practitioner or nurse shall be present, nor shall anyone whose presence is unnecessary.

(b) *Documentation*

8.   In the case of an intimate search the custody officer shall as soon as practicable record which parts of the person's body were searched, who carried out the search, who was present, the reasons for the search and its result.

9.   In the case of a strip search he shall record the reasons for the search and its result.

10.   If an intimate search is carried out by a police officer, the reason why it is impracticable for a suitably qualified person to conduct it must be recorded.

Annex B

Delay in notifying arrest or allowing access to legal advice

(A) Persons detained under the Police and Criminal Evidence Act 1984

(a) *Action*

1.   The rights set out in sections 5 or 6 of the Code or both may be delayed if the person is in police detention in connection with a serious arrestable offence, has not yet been charged with an offence and an officer of the

rank of superintendent or above has reasonable grounds for believing that the exercise of either right:
  (i) will lead to interference with or harm to evidence connected with a serious arrestable offence or interference with or physical injury to other persons; or
  (ii) will lead to the alerting of other persons suspected of having committed such an offence but not yet arrested for it; or
  (iii) will hinder the recovery of property obtained as a result of such an offence. . . .
  2. These rights may also be delayed where the serious arrestable offence is either:
  (i) a drug trafficking offence and the officer has reasonable grounds for believing that the detained person has benefited from drug trafficking, and that the recovery of the value of that person's proceeds of drug trafficking will be hindered by the exercise of either right; or
  (ii) an offence to which Part VI of the Criminal Justice Act 1988 (covering confiscation orders) applies and the officer has reasonable grounds for believing that the detained person has benefited from the offence, and that the recovery of the value of the property obtained by that person from or in connection with the offence or of the pecuniary advantage derived by him from or in connection with it will be hindered by the exercise of either right.
  3. Access to a solicitor may not be delayed on the grounds that he might advise the person not to answer any questions or that the solicitor was initially asked to attend the police station by someone else, provided that the person himself then wishes to see the solicitor. In the latter case the detained person must be told that the solicitor has come to the police station at another person's request, and must be asked to sign the custody record to signify whether or not he wishes to see the solicitor.
  4. These rights may be delayed only for as long as is necessary and, subject to paragraph 8 [on terrorism, not reprinted—CMB], in no case beyond 36 hours after the relevant time as defined in section 41 of the Police and Criminal Evidence Act 1984. If the above grounds cease to apply within this time, the person must as soon as practicable be asked if he wishes to exercise either right, the custody record must be noted accordingly, and action must be taken in accordance with the relevant section of the Code.
  5. A detained person must be permitted to consult a solicitor for a reasonable time before any court hearing.

(b) *Documentation*
  6. The grounds for action under this Annex shall be recorded and the person informed of them as soon as practicable.
  7. Any reply given by a person under paragraphs 4 and 9 must be recorded and the person asked to endorse the record in relation to whether he wishes to receive legal advice at this point.

(B) Persons detained under the Prevention of Terrorism (Temporary Provisions) Act 1984

*   *   *   *

9.   These rights may be delayed only for as long as is necessary and in no case beyond 48 hours from the time of arrest. If the above grounds cease to apply within this time, the person must as soon as practicable be asked if he wishes to exercise either right, the custody record must be noted accordingly, and action must be taken in accordance with the relevant section of this Code.

* * * *

ANNEX C

Urgent interviews

1.   If, and only if, an officer of the rank of superintendent or above considers that delay will involve an immediate risk of harm to persons or serious loss of or serious damage to property:
   (a) a person heavily under the influence of drink or drugs may be interviewed in that state; or
   (b) an arrested juvenile or a person who is mentally disordered or mentally handicapped may be interviewed in the absence of the appropriate adult; or
   (c) a person who has difficulty in understanding English or who has a hearing disability may be interviewed in the absence of an interpreter.

2.   Questioning in these circumstances may not continue once sufficient information to avert the immediate risk has been obtained.

3.   A record shall be made of the grounds for any decision to interview a person under paragraph 1 above.

Note for guidance
C1   The special groups referred to in Annex C are all particularly vulnerable. The provisions of the annex, which override safeguards designed to protect them and to minimise the risk of interviews producing unreliable evidence, should be applied only in exceptional cases of need.

ANNEX D

Written statements under caution (See paragraph 12.13)

(a) *Written by a person under caution*
1.   A person shall always be invited to write down himself what he wants to say.

2.   Where the person wishes to write it himself, he shall be asked to write out and sign before writing what he wants to say, the following:

"I make this statement of my own free will. I understand that I need not say anything unless I wish to do so and that what I say may be given in evidence."

3.   Any person writing his own statement shall be allowed to do so without any prompting except that a police officer may indicate to him which matters are material or question any ambiguity in the statement.

(b) *Written by a police officer*
4.   If a person says that he would like someone to write it for him, a police officer shall write the statement, but, before starting, he must ask him to sign, or make his mark, to the following:

> "I, ..., wish to make a statement. I want someone to write down what I say. I understand that I need not say anything unless I wish to do so and that what I say may be given in evidence."

5.   Where a police officer writes the statement, he must take down the exact words spoken by the person making it and he must not edit or paraphrase it. Any questions that are necessary (*e.g.* to make it more intelligible) and the answers given must be recorded contemporaneously on the statement form.

6.   When the writing of a statement by a police officer is finished the person making it shall be asked to read it and to make any corrections, alterations or additions he wishes. When he has finished reading it he shall be asked to write and sign or make his mark on the following certificate at the end of the statement:

> "I have read the above statement, and I have been able to correct, alter or add anything I wish. This statement is true. I have made it of my own free will."

7.   If the person making the statement cannot read, or refuses to read it, or to write the above mentioned certificate at the end of it or to sign it, the senior police officer present shall read it over to him and ask him whether he would like to correct, alter or add anything and to put his signature or make his mark at the end. The police officer shall then certify on the statement itself what has occurred.

*   *   *   *

D. CODE OF PRACTICE FOR THE IDENTIFICATION OF PERSONS BY POLICE OFFICERS

1. General [material analogous to that for other codes, not reprinted— CMB]

*   *   *   *

2. Identification by witnesses

(a) *Cases where the suspect is known*
2.1.   In a case which involves disputed identification evidence, and where the identity of the suspect is known to the police, the methods of identification by witnesses which may be used are:
(i)   a parade;
(ii)   a group identification;

(iii) a video film; or
(iv) a confrontation.
2.2.   The arrangements for, and conduct of, these types of identification shall be the responsibility of an officer in uniform not below the rank of inspector who is not involved with the investigation ("the identification officer"). No officer involved with the investigation of the case against the suspect may take any part in these procedures.

Identification Parade
2.3.   In a case which involves disputed identification evidence a parade must be held if the suspect asks for one and it is practicable to hold one. A parade may also be held if the officer in charge of the investigation considers that it would be useful, and the suspect consents.
2.4.   A parade need not be held if the identification officer considers that, whether by reason of the unusual appearance of the suspect or for some other reason, it would not be practicable to assemble sufficient people who resembled him to make a parade fair.
2.5.   Any parade must be carried out in accordance with Annex A.

Group Identification
2.6.   If a suspect refuses or, having agreed, fails to attend an identification parade or the holding of a parade is impracticable, arrangements must if practicable be made to allow the witness an opportunity of seeing him in a group of people.
2.7.   A group identification may also be arranged if the officer in charge of the investigation considers, whether because of fear on the part of the witness or for some other reason, that it is, in the circumstances, more satisfactory than a parade, and if the suspect consents.
2.8.   The suspect should be asked for his consent to "group identification" and advised in accordance with paragraphs 2.15 and 2.16. However, where consent is refused the identification officer has the discretion to proceed with a group identification if it is practicable to do so.
2.9.   A group identification should, if practicable, be held in a place other than a police station (for example, in an underground station or a shopping centre). It may be held in a police station if the identification officer considers, whether for security reasons or on other grounds, that it would not be practicable to hold it elsewhere. In either case the group identification should, as far as possible, follow the principles and procedures for a parade as set out in Annex A.

Video Film Identification
2.10.   The identification officer may show a witness a video film of a suspect if the investigating officer considers, whether because of the refusal of the suspect to take part in an identification parade or group identification or other reasons, that this would in the circumstances be the most satisfactory course of action.
2.11.   The suspect should be asked for his consent to a video identification and advised in accordance with paragraphs 2.15 and 2.16. However, where such consent is refused the identification officer has the discretion to proceed with a video identification if it is practicable to do so.
2.12.   A video identification must be carried out in accordance with Annex B.

Confrontation

2.13. If neither a parade nor a video identification nor a group identification procedure is arranged, the suspect may be confronted by the witness. Such a confrontation does not require the suspect's consent, but may not take place unless none of the other procedures are practicable.

2.14. A confrontation must be carried out in accordance with Annex C.

Notice to Suspect

2.15. Before a parade takes place or group identification or a video identification is arranged, the identification officer shall explain to the suspect:

(i) the purposes of the parade or group identification or video identification;

(ii) the fact that he is entitled to free legal advice;

(iii) the procedures for holding it (including his right to have a solicitor or friend present);

(iv) where appropriate the special arrangements for juveniles;

(v) where appropriate the special arrangements for mentally disordered and mentally handicapped persons;

(vi) the fact that he does not have to take part in a parade, or group identification or cooperate with the making of a video film and, if it is proposed to hold a group identification or video identification, his entitlement to a parade if this can practicably be arranged;

(vii) the fact that, if he does not consent to take part in a parade or group identification or video identification, his refusal may be given in evidence in any subsequent trial, and police may proceed covertly without his consent or make other arrangements to test whether a witness identifies him;

(viii) whether the witness had been shown photographs, photofit, identikit or similar pictures by the police during the investigation before the identity of the suspect became known.

2.16. This information must also be contained in a written notice which must be handed to the suspect. The identification officer shall give the suspect a reasonable opportunity to read the notice, after which he shall be asked to sign a second copy of the notice to indicate whether or not he is willing to attend the parade or group identification or cooperate with the making of a video film. The signed copy shall be retained by the identification officer.

(b) *Cases where the identity of the suspect is not known*

2.17. A police officer may take a witness to a particular neighbourhood or place to see whether he can identify the person whom he said he saw on the relevant occasion. Care should be taken, however, not to direct the witness's attention to any individual.

2.18. A witness must not be shown photographs or photofit, identikit or similar pictures if the identity of the suspect is known to the police and he is available to stand on an identification parade. If the identity of the suspect is not known, the showing of such pictures to a witness must be done in accordance with Annex D. (See paragraph 2.15 (viii))

(c) *Documentation*

2.19. The identification officer shall make a record of the parade, group identification or video identification on the forms provided.

2.20.   If the identification officer considers that it is not practicable to hold a parade, he shall tell the suspect why and record the reason.

2.21.   A record shall be made of a person's refusal to cooperate in a parade, group identification or video identification.

Note for guidance

2A   *Except for the provisions of Annex D, paragraph 1, a police officer who is a witness for the purposes of this part of the Code is subject to the same principles and procedures as a civilian witness.*

* * * *

4. Identification by photographs

(a) *Action*

4.1.   The photograph of a person who has been arrested may be taken at a police station only with his written consent or if paragraph 4.2 applies. In either case he must be informed of the reason for taking it and that the photograph will be destroyed if paragraph 4.4 applies. He must be told that he may witness the destruction of the photograph or be provided with a certificate confirming its destruction if he applies within five days of being cleared or informed that he will not be prosecuted.

4.2.   The photograph of a person who has been arrested may be taken without consent if:

  (i) he is arrested at the same time as other persons, or at a time when it is likely that other persons will be arrested, and a photograph is necessary to establish who was arrested, at what time and at what place;

  (ii) he has been charged with, or reported for a recordable offence and has not yet been released or brought before a court [see Note 3A]; or

  (iii) he is convicted of such an offence and his photograph is not already on record as a result of (i) or (ii). There is no power of arrest to take a photograph in pursuance of this provision which applies only where the person is in custody as a result of the exercise of another power (*e.g.* arrest for fingerprinting under section 27 of the Police and Criminal Evidence Act 1984).

4.3.   Force may not be used to take a photograph.

4.4.   Where a person's photograph has been taken in accordance with this section, the photograph, negatives and all copies taken in that particular case must be destroyed if:

  (a) he is prosecuted for the offence and cleared; or

  (b) he is not prosecuted (unless he admits the offence and is cautioned for it).

An opportunity of witnessing the destruction or a certificate confirming the destruction must be given to him if he so requests, provided that, in accordance with paragraph 4.1, he applies within five days of being cleared or informed that he will not be prosecuted. [See Note 4B]

(b) *Documentation*

4.5.   A record must be made as soon as possible of the reason for taking a person's photograph under this section without consent and of the destruction of any photographs.

Note for guidance
4A   *All references to photographs include computer images.*
4B   *This paragraph is not intended to require the destruction of copies of a police gazette in cases where, for example, a remand prisoner has escaped from custody, or a person in custody is suspected of having committed offences in other force areas, and a photograph of the person concerned is circulated in a police gazette for information.*

5. Identification by body samples, swabs and impressions

(a) *Action*

5.1.   Dental impressions and intimate samples may be taken from a person in police detention only:
  (i)   if an officer of the rank of superintendent or above considers that the offence concerned is a serious arrestable offence; and
  (ii) if that officer has reasonable grounds to believe that such an impression or sample will tend to confirm or disprove the suspect's involvement in it; and
  (iii) with the suspect's written consent.

5.2.   Before a person is asked to provide an intimate sample, he must be warned that a refusal may be treated, in any proceedings against him, as corroborating relevant prosecution evidence. [See Note 5A]

5.3.   Except for samples of urine or saliva, intimate samples may be taken only by a registered medical or dental practitioner as appropriate.

5.4.   A non-intimate sample, as defined in paragraph 5.11, may be taken from a detained suspect only with his written consent or if paragraph 5.5 applies. Even if he consents, an officer of the rank of inspector or above must have reasonable grounds for believing that such a sample will tend to confirm or disprove the suspect's involvement in a particular offence.

5.5.   A non-intimate sample may be taken without consent if an officer of the rank of superintendent or above has reasonable grounds for suspecting that the offence in connection with which the suspect is detained is a serious arrestable offence and for believing that the sample will tend to confirm or disprove his involvement in it.

5.6.   Where paragraph 5.5 applies, reasonable force may be used if necessary to take non-intimate samples.

5.7.   The suspect must be informed, before the intimate or non-intimate sample or dental impression is taken, of the grounds on which the relevant authority has been given, including the nature of the suspected offence, and that the sample will be destroyed if paragraph 5.8 applies.

5.8.   Where a sample or impression has been taken in accordance with this section, it and all copies of it taken in the particular case must be destroyed as soon as practicable if:
  (a) the suspect is prosecuted for the offence concerned and cleared; or
  (b) he is not prosecuted (unless he admits the offence and is cautioned for it).

(b) *Documentation*

5.9.   A record must be made as soon as practicable of the reasons for taking a sample or impression and of its destruction. If force is used a record shall be made of the circumstances and those present. If written consent is given to the taking of a sample or impression, the fact must be recorded in writing.

5.10.   A record must be made of the giving of a warning required by paragraph 5.2 above.

(c) *General*

5.11.   The following terms are defined in section 65 of the Police and Criminal Evidence Act 1984 as follows:

>   (a) "intimate sample" means a sample of blood, semen or any other tissue fluid, urine, saliva or pubic hair, or a swab taken from a person's body orifice;
>   (b) "non-intimate sample" means:
>   (i) a sample of hair other than pubic hair;
>   (ii) a sample taken from a nail or from under a nail;
>   (iii) a swab taken from any part of a person's body other than a body orifice;
>   (iv) a footprint or similar impression of any part of a person's body other than a part of his hand.

5.12.   Where clothing needs to be removed in circumstances likely to cause embarrassment to the person, no person of the opposite sex who is not a medical practitioner or nurse shall be present (unless, in the case of a juvenile, that juvenile specifically requests the presence of a particular adult of the opposite sex who is readily available), nor shall anyone whose presence is unnecessary. However, in the case of a juvenile this is subject to the overriding proviso that such a removal of clothing may take place in the absence of the appropriate adult only if the juvenile signifies in the presence of the appropriate adult that he prefers the search to be done in his absence and the appropriate adult agrees.

Note for guidance

5A   *In warning a person who refuses to provide an intimate sample or swab in accordance with paragraph 5.2, the following form of words may be helpful:*

>   *"You do not have to [provide this sample] [allow this swab to be taken], but I must warn you that if you do not do so, a court may treat such a refusal as supporting any relevant evidence against you."*

ANNEX A

Identification parades

(a) *General*

1.   A suspect must be given a reasonable opportunity to have a solicitor or friend present, and the identification officer shall ask him to indicate on a second copy of the notice whether or not he so wishes.

2.   A parade may take place either in a normal room or in one equipped with a screen permitting witnesses to see members of the parade without being seen. The procedures for the composition and conduct of the parade are the same in both cases, subject to paragraph 7 below (except that a parade

involving a screen may take place only when the suspect's solicitor, friend or appropriate adult is present or the parade is recorded on video).

* * * *

(c) *Conduct of the parade*

5.   Immediately before the parade, the identification officer must remind the suspect of the procedures governing its conduct and caution him in the terms of paragraph 10.4 of the Code of Practice for the detention, treatment and questioning of persons by police officers.

6.   All unauthorised persons must be excluded from the place where the parade is held.

7.   Once the parade has been formed, everything afterwards in respect of it shall take place in the presence and hearing of the suspect and of any interpreter, solicitor, friend or appropriate adult who is present (unless the parade involves a screen, in which case everything said to or by any witness at the place where the parade is held must be said in the hearing and presence of the suspect's solicitor, friend or appropriate adult or be recorded on video).

8.   The parade shall consist of at least eight persons (in addition to the suspect) who so far as possible resemble the suspect in age, height, general appearance and position in life. One suspect only shall be included in a parade unless there are two suspects of roughly similar appearance in which case they may be paraded together with at least 12 other persons. In no circumstances shall more than two suspects be included in one parade and where there are separate parades they shall be made up of different persons.

9.   Where all members of a similar group are possible suspects, separate parades shall be held for each member of the group unless there are two suspects of similar appearance when they may appear on the same parade with at least 12 other members of the group who are not suspects. Where police officers in uniform form an identification parade, any numerals or other identifying badge shall be concealed.

10.   When the suspect is brought to the place where the parade is to be held, he shall be asked by the identification officer whether he has any objection to the arrangements for the parade or to any of the other participants in it. The suspect may obtain advice from his solicitor or friend, if present, before the parade proceeds. Where practicable, steps shall be taken to remove the grounds for objection. Where it is not practicable to do so, the officer shall explain to the suspect why his objections cannot be met.

11.   The suspect may select his own position in the line. Where there is more than one witness, the identification officer must tell the suspect, after each witness has left the room, that he can if he wishes change position in the line. Each position in the line must be clearly numbered, whether by means of a numeral laid on the floor in front of each parade member or by other means.

12.   The identification officer is responsible for ensuring that, before they attend the parade, witnesses are not able to:

   (i) communicate with each other about the case or overhear a witness who has already seen the parade;
   (ii) see any member of the parade;
   (iii) on that occasion see or be reminded of any photograph or de-

scription of the suspect or be given any other indication of his identity; or

(iv) see the suspect either before or after the parade.

13.   The officer conducting a witness to a parade must not discuss with him the composition of the parade, and in particular he must not disclose whether a previous witness has made any identification.

* * * *

ANNEX C

Confrontation by a witness

1.   The identification officer is responsible for the conduct of any confrontation of a suspect by a witness.

2.   Before the confrontation takes place, the identification officer must tell the witness that the person he saw may or may not be the person he is to confront and that if he cannot make a positive identification he should say so.

3.   The suspect shall be confronted independently by each witness, who shall be asked "Is this the person?" Confrontation must take place in the presence of the suspect's solicitor, interpreter or friend, unless this would cause unreasonable delay.

4.   The confrontation should normally take place in the police station, either in a normal room or in one equipped with a screen permitting a witness to see the suspect without being seen. In both cases the procedures are the same except that a room equipped with a screen may be used only when the suspect's solicitor, friend or appropriate adult is present or the confrontation is recorded on video.

* * * *

E. CODE OF PRACTICE ON TAPE RECORDING

* * * *

3. Interviews to be tape recorded

3.1.   Subject to paragraph 3.2 below, tape recording shall be used at police stations for any interview:

(a) with a person who has been cautioned in accordance with section 10 of Code C in respect of an indictable offence (including an offence triable either way) [See Notes 3A and 3B];

(b) which take place as a result of a police officer exceptionally putting further questions to a suspect about an offence described in sub-paragraph (a) above after he has been charged with, or informed he may be prosecuted for, that offence [See Note 3C]; or

(c) in which a police officer wishes to bring to the notice of a person, after he has been charged with, or informed he may be prosecuted for an offence described in sub-paragraph (a) above, any written statement made by another person, or the content of an interview with another person. [See Note 3D]

3.2. Tape recording is not required in respect of the following:
(a) an interview with a person arrested under section 12(1)(a) of the Prevention of Terrorism (Temporary Provisions) Act 1984 or an interview with a person being questioned in respect of an offence where there are reasonable grounds for suspecting that it is connected to terrorism or was committed in furtherance of the objectives of an organisation engaged in terrorism. This sub-paragraph applies only where the terrorism is connected with the affairs of Northern Ireland or is terrorism of any other description except terrorism connected solely with the affairs of the United Kingdom or any part of the United Kingdom other than Northern Ireland. "Terrorism" has the meaning given by section 14(1) of the Prevention of Terrorism (Temporary Provisions) Act 1984. [See Notes 3E, 3F, 3G and 3H];
(b) an interview with a person suspected on reasonable grounds of an offence under section 1 of the Official Secrets Act 1911. [See Note 3H]

3.3. The custody officer may authorise the interviewing officer not to tape record the interview:
(a) where it is not reasonably practicable to do so because of failure of the equipment or the non-availability of a suitable interview room or recorder and the authorising officer considers on reasonable grounds that the interview should not be delayed until the failure has been rectified or a suitable room or recorder becomes available [See Note 3J]; or
(b) where it is clear from the outset that no prosecution will ensue.

In all cases the custody officer shall make a note in specific terms of the reasons for not tape recording. [See Note 3K]

3.4. Where an interview takes place with a person voluntarily attending the police station and the police officer has grounds to believe that person has become a suspect (*i.e.* the point at which he should be cautioned in accordance with paragraph 10.1 of Code C) the continuation of the interview shall be tape recorded, unless the custody officer gives authority in accordance with the provisions of paragraph 3.3 above for the continuation of the interview not to be recorded.

3.5. The whole of each interview shall be tape recorded, including the taking and reading back of any statement.

Notes for guidance

3A *Nothing in this Code is intended to preclude tape recording at police discretion of interviews at police stations with persons cautioned in respect of offences not covered by paragraph 3.1, or responses made by interviewees after they have been charged with, or informed they may be prosecuted for, an offence, provided that this Code is complied with.*

3B *Attention is drawn to the restrictions in paragraph 12.3 of Code C on the questioning of persons unfit through drink or drugs to the extent that they are unable to appreciate the significance of questions put to them or of their answers.*

* * * *

3K   A decision not to tape record an interview for any reason may be the subject of comment in court. The authorising officer should therefore be prepared to justify his decision in each case.

4. The interview

(a) *Commencement of interviews*

4.1.   When the suspect is brought into the interview room the police officer shall without delay, but in the sight of the suspect, load the tape recorder with previously unused tapes and set it to record. The tapes must be unwrapped or otherwise opened in the presence of the suspect. [See Note 4A]

4.2.   The police officer shall then tell the suspect formally about the tape recording. He shall say:

(a) that the interview is being tape recorded;

(b) his name and rank and the name and rank of any other police officer present;

(c) the name of the suspect and any other party present (*e.g.* a solicitor);

(d) the date, time of commencement and place of the interview; and

(e) that the suspect will be given a notice about what will happen to the tapes. [See Note 4B]

4.3.   The police officer shall then caution the suspect in the following terms:

"You do not have to say anything unless you wish to do so, but what you say may be given in evidence."

Minor deviations do not constitute a breach of this requirement provided that the sense of the caution is preserved. [See Notes 4C and 4D].

*   *   *   *

(c) *Objections and complaints by the suspect*

4.5.   If the suspect raises objections to the interview being tape recorded either at the outset or during the interview or during a break in the interview, the police officer shall explain the fact that the interview is being tape recorded and that the provisions of this Code require that the suspect's objections should be recorded on tape. When any objections have been recorded on tape or the suspect has refused to have his objections recorded, the police officer may turn off the recorder. In this eventuality he shall say that he is turning off the recorder and 'give his reasons for doing so and then turn it off. The police officer shall then make a written record of the interview in accordance with section 11 of Code C. If, however, the police officer reasonably considers that he may proceed to put questions to the suspect with the tape recorder still on, he may do so. [See Note 4G]

4.6.   If in the course of an interview a complaint is made by the person being questioned, or on his behalf, concerning the provisions of this Code or of Code C, then the officer shall act in accordance with paragraph 12.8 of Code C. [See Notes 4H and 4J]]

4.7.   If the suspect indicates that he wishes to tell the police officer about matters not directly connected with the offence of which he is suspected and that he is unwilling for these matters to be recorded on tape, he shall be given the opportunity to tell the police officer about these matters after the conclusion of the formal interview.

Notes for guidance

4A   *The police officer should attempt to estimate the likely length of the interview and ensure that the appropriate number of unused tapes and labels with which to seal the master copies are available in the interview room.*

4B   *It will be helpful for the purpose of voice identification if the officer asks the suspect and any other persons present to identify themselves.*

4C   *If it appears that a person does not understand what the caution means, the officer who has given it should go on to explain it in his own words.*

4D   *In case anyone who is given a caution is unclear about its significance, the officer concerned should explain that the caution is given in pursuance of the general principles of English law that a person need not answer any questions or provide any information which might tend to incriminate him, and that no adverse inferences from this silence may be drawn at any trial that takes place. The person should not, however, be left with a false impression that non-co-operation will have no effect on his immediate treatment as, for example, his refusal to provide his name and address may render him liable to detention.*

*   *   *   *

4G   *The officer should bear in mind that a decision to continue recording against the wishes of the suspect may be the subject of comment in court.*

4H   *Where the custody officer is called immediately to deal with the complaint, wherever possible the tape recorder should be left to run until the custody officer has entered the interview room and spoken to the person being interviewed. Continuation or termination of the interview should be at the discretion of the interviewing officer pending action by an inspector under paragraph 9.1 of Code C.*

4J   *Where the complaint is about a matter not connected with this Code of Practice or Code C, the decision to continue with the interview is at the discretion of the interviewing officer. Where the interviewing officer decides to continue with the interview the person being interviewed shall be told that the complaint will be brought to the attention of the custody officer at the conclusion of the interview. When the interview is concluded the interviewing officer must, as soon as practicable, inform the custody officer of the existence and nature of the complaint made.*

*   *   *   *

Table of Cases*

*German cases not included as they have no names.

Bibliography

Allen, Francis A. "The Judicial Quest for Penal Justice: The Warren Court and the Criminal Cases." *University of Illinois Law Review* (1975): 518–42.

Alschuler, Albert W. "Failed Pragmatism: Reflections on the Burger Court." *Harvard Law Review* 100 (1987): 1436–56.

American Bar Association. Special Committee on Criminal Justice in a Free Society. *Criminal Justice in Crisis*. Washington, DC: American Bar Association, 1988.

American Law Institute. *Code of Criminal Procedure*: Official Draft. Philadelphia: The Institute, 1930.

———. *Model Code of Pre-Arraignment Procedure*. Proposed Official Draft. Philadelphia: The Institute, 1975.

American Series of Penal Codes. *The German Code of Criminal Procedure* (*Strafprozessordnung*) (StPO). Translated by Horst Niebler. S. Hackensack, NJ: Fred B. Rothman and Co., 1965.

Amodio, Ennio and Eugenio Selvaggi. "An Accusatorial System in a Civil Law Country: The 1988 Italian Code of Criminal Procedure." *Temple Law Review* 62 (1989): 1211–24.

Amsterdam, Anthony G. "Perspectives on the Fourth Amendment." *Minnesota Law Review* 58 (1974): 349–477.

Ashby, David. "Safeguarding the Suspect." In *The Police: Powers, Procedures, and Proprieties*, edited by John Benyon and Colin Bourn, 183–93. New York: Pergamon Press, 1986.

Australian Law Reform Commission. *Report No. 2* (interim): *Criminal Investigation*. Sydney: The Commission, 1975.

Baker, Liva. *Miranda: Crime, Law and Politics*. New York: Atheneum, 1983.

Bator, Paul M. and James Vorenberg. "Arrest, Detention, Interrogation, and the Right to Counsel: Basic Problems and Possible Legislative Solutions." *Columbia Law Review* 66 (1966): 62–78.

Beale, Sara Sun. "Reconsidering Supervisory Power in Criminal Cases: Constitutional and Statutory Limits on the Authority of the Federal Courts." *Columbia Law Review* 84 (1984): 1433–522.

Beling, Ernst Ludwig von. *Die Beweisverbote als Grenzen der Wahrheitserforschung im Strafprozess in Strafrechtlichen Abhandlungen* (*The Exclusionary Rules as the Borders of the Search for Truth in Criminal Procedure*). Darmstadt: Wissenschaftliche Buchgesellschaft, 1968.

Berger, Mark. "Legislating Confession Law in Great Britain: A Statutory Approach to Police Interrogations." *University of Michigan Journal of Law Reform* 24 (1990): 1–64.

Bevan, Vaughan and Ken Lidstone. *A Guide to the Police and Criminal Evidence Act 1984*. London: Butterworths, 1985.

———. *The Investigation of Crime: A Guide to Police Powers*. London: Butterworths, 1991.

Birch, Di. "The PACE Hots Up: Confessions and Confusions Under the 1984 Act." *Criminal Law Review* (1989): 95–116.

Bookspan, Phyllis T. "Reworking the Warrant Requirement: Resuscitating the Fourth Amendment." *Vanderbilt Law Review* 44 (1991): 473–530.

Bradley, Craig. "Are State Courts Enforcing the Fourth Amendment? A Preliminary Study." *Georgetown Law Journal* 77 (1988): 251–86.

———. "Constitutional Protection for Private Papers." *Harvard Civil Rights-Civil Liberties Law Review* 16 (1981): 461–494.

———. "Criminal Procedure in the Land of Oz: Lessons for America." *Journal of Criminal Law and Criminology* (Spring 1990): 99–135.

———. "The Exclusionary Rule in Germany." *Harvard Law Review* 96 (1983): 1032–66.

———. "Murray v United States: The Bell Tolls for the Search Warrant Requirement." *Indiana Law Journal* 64 (1989): 907–23.

———. "Two Models of the Fourth Amendment." *Michigan Law Review* 83 (1985): 1468–1501.

———. "The Uncertainty Principle in the Supreme Court." *Duke Law Journal* (1986): 1–64.

Bradley, Craig, Yale Kamisar, Joseph D. Grano; and James Brian Haddad. *Sum and Substance: Criminal Procedure*. 2d ed. Santa Monica, CA: Herbert Legal Series, 1988.

Brennan, William J. Jr. "State Constitutions and the Protection of Individual Rights." *Harvard Law Review* 90 (1977): 489–504.

Brewer's Dictionary of Phrase and Fable. 14th ed. New York: Harper & Row, 1989.

Brilmayer, R. Lea. "The Jurisprudence of Article III: Perspectives on the 'Case or Controversy' Requirement." *Harvard Law Review* 93 (1979): 297–321.

Brown, Winifred R. *Federal Rulemaking: Problems and Possibilities*. Washington, DC: Federal Judicial Center, 1981.

Bureau of National Affairs. *The Criminal Law Revolution and its Aftermath, 1960–1977*. Washington, D.C.: U.S. Government Printing Office, 1978.

Burt, Robert A. "Miranda and Title II: A Morganatic Marriage." *Supreme Court Review* (1969): 81–134.

Caplan, Gerald M. "Questioning Miranda." *Vanderbilt Law Review* 93 (1985): 1417–76.

Cardozo, Benjamin N. *The Nature of the Judicial Process*. New Haven, CT: Yale University Press, 1921. Reprint 1974.

Carr, James G. "Wiretapping in West Germany." *American Journal of Comparative Law* 29 (1981): 607–645.

Choper, Jesse H., Yale Kamisar, Laurence H. Tribe, and Dorothy Oppermar. *The Supreme Court: Trends and Developments 1981–82*. Minneapolis, MN: National Practice Institute, 1983.

———. *The Supreme Court: Trends and Developments 1982–83*. Minneapolis, MN: National Practice Institute, 1984.

Code of Practice for the Detention, Treatment, and Questioning of Persons by the Police. London: British Home Office, 1990.

Code of Practice for the Exercise By Police Officers of Statutory Powers of Stop and Search. London: British Home Office, 1990.

Code of Practice for the Searching of Premises by Police Officers. London: British Home Office, 1990.

Code of Practice on Tape Recording. London: British Home Office, 1990.

Curtis, Leslie. "Policing the Streets." In *The Police: Powers, Procedures and Proprieties,* edited by John Benyon and Colin Bourn, 95–102. New York: Pergamon Press, 1986.

Dahl, Robert A. "Decision Making in a Democracy." In *Judicial Review and the Supreme Court: Selected Essays,* edited by Leonard Levy, 105–23. New York: Harper & Row, 1967.

Davies, Thomas Y. "A Hard Look at What We Know (and Still Need to Learn) About the Costs of the Exclusionary Rule: The NIJ Study and Other Studies of Lost Arrests." *American Bar Foundation Research Journal* (Summer 1983): 611–90.

Dencker, Friedrich. *Verwertungsverbote im Strafprozess.* Köln: Heymann, 1977.

Dershowitz, Alan M. and John Hart Ely. "*Harris v. New York*: Some Anxious Observations on the Candor and Logic of the Emerging Nixon Majority." *Yale Law Journal* 80 (1971): 1198–227.

Dowling, Donald C. "Escobedo and Beyond: The Need for a Fourteenth Amendment Code of Criminal Procedure." *Journal of Criminal Law, Criminology and Police Science* 56 (1965): 143–58.

Dripps, Donald A. "Beyond the Warren Court and Its Conservative Critics: Toward a Unified Theory of Constitutional Criminal Procedure." *University of Michigan Journal of Law Reform* 23 (1989): 591–640.

Ely, John Hart. *Democracy and Distrust: A Theory of Judicial Review.* Cambridge: Harvard University Press, 1980.

Fassler, Lawrence J. "The Italian Penal Procedure Code: An Adversial System of Criminal Procedure in Continental Europe." *Columbia Journal of Transnational Law* 29 (1991): 245–278.

Feldman, David. "Regulating Treatment of Suspects in Police Stations: Judicial Interpretation of Detention Provision in the Police and Criminal Act 1984." *Criminal Law Review* (1990): 452–471.

Frase, Richard S. "Comparative Criminal Justice as a Guide to American Law Reform: How Do the French Do It, How Can We Find Out and Why Should We Care?" *California Law Review* 78 (1990): 539–683.

———. "Criminal Procedure in a Conservative Age: A Time to Rediscover the Critical Nonconstitutional Issues." *Journal of Legal Education* 35 (1986): 79–92.

———. *The French Code of Criminal Procedure.* Littleton, CO: F. B. Rothman, 1988.

Friendly, Henry J. "The Bill of Rights as a Code of Criminal Procedure." *California Law Review* 53 (1965): 929–56.

Gainer, Ronald. "Report to the Attorney General on Federal Criminal Code Reform." Reprinted in *Criminal Law Forum* 1 (1989): 99–183.

Goldberg, Arthur J. *Equal Justice: The Warren Era of the Supreme Court.* Evanston, IL: Northwestern University Press, 1971.

Goldsmith, Michael. "The Supreme Court and Title III: Rewriting the Law of Electronic Surveillance." *Journal of Criminal Law and Criminology* 74 (1983): 1–171.

Gordon, Irving A. "The Nature and Uses of Congressional Power Under Section Five of the Fourteenth Amendment to Overcome Decisions of the Supreme Court." *Northwestern Law Review* 72 (1977): 656–705.

Gössel, Karl. "Kritische Bemerkungen zum gegenwartigen Stand der Lehre von den Beweisverboten im Strafverfahren." *Neue Juristische Wochenschrift* 34 (1981): 649.

Gowran. "How Supreme Court Ruling Puts Straightjacket [sic] on Police." *Chicago Tribune*, August 11, 1964: 27.

Graham, Fred P. *The Self-Inflicted Wound*. New York: Macmillan, 1970.

Grano, Joseph D. "The Changed and Changing World of Constitutional Criminal Procedure: The Contribution of the Department of Justice's Office of Legal Policy." *University of Michigan Journal of Law Reform* 22 (1989): 395–424.

Greenhouse, Linda. "High Court Votes to Further Limit Prisoner Appeals." *New York Times*, May 5, 1992: 1.

Haddad, James B. "Well-Delineated Exceptions, Claims of Sham, and Four-fold Probable Cause." *Journal of Criminal Law and Criminology* 68 (1977): 198–225.

Harvie, Robert and Hamar Foster. "Ties that Bind? The Supreme Court of Canada, American Jurisprudence and the Revision of the Canadian Criminal Law Under the Charter." *Osgoode Hall Law Journal* 28 (1990): 729–88.

Heffernan, William C., and Richard W. Lovely. "Evaluating the Fourth Amendment Exclusionary Rule: The Problem of Police Compliance with the Law." *University of Michigan Journal of Law Reform* 24 (1991): 311–69.

Hesse, Konrad. *Gründzuge des Verfassungsrechts der Bundesrepublik Deutschland*. 12th ed. Karlsruhe: Müller, Juristischer Verl., 1980.

Hutchinson, Scott and James Cooper Morton. *Search and Seizure Law in Canada*. Toronto: Carswell, 1991.

Israel, Jerold H. "Criminal Procedure, the Burger Court, and the Legacy of the Warren Court." *Michigan Law Review* 75 (1977): 1319–425.

Jenkins, John A. "The Partisan." *New York Times* (magazine) March 3, 1985: 35.

Kadish, Sanford H. "Methodology and Criteria in Due Process Adjudication—A Survey and Criticism." *Yale Law Journal* 66 (1957): 319–63.

Kamisar, Yale. "Remembering the 'Old World' of Criminal Procedure: A Reply to Professor Grano." *University of Michigan Journal of Law Reform* 23 (1990): 537–89.

———. "The Warren Court (Was It Really So Defense-Minded?), the Burger Court (Is It Really So Prosecution-Oriented?) and Police Investigatory Practices." In *The Burger Court: The Counter-Revolution That Wasn't*, edited by Vincent Blasi, 62–91. New Haven: Yale University Press, 1983.

Kamisar, Yale, Wayne R. LaFave and Jerold H. Israel. *Modern Criminal Procedure: Cases, Comments, and Questions*. 7th ed. St. Paul, MN: West Publishing Co., 1989. Supplement 1990.

Kitch, Edmund W. "The Supreme Court's Code of Criminal Procedure: 1958–1969 Edition." *Supreme Court Review* (1969): 155–202.

Kleinknecht, Theodor. *Strafprozessordnung*. 40th ed. München: Beck, 1991. (Abbrev. as StPO)

LaFave, Wayne. "'Case-by-Case Adjudication' Versus 'Standardized Procedures': The Robinson Dilemma." *Supreme Court Review* (1974): 127–163.
———. *Search and Seizure: A Treatise on the Fourth Amendment*. 2nd edition plus 1990 supplements. 4 vols. St. Paul, MN: West Publishing Co., 1987.
LaFave, Wayne and Jerold H. Israel. *Criminal Procedure*. 3 vols. St. Paul, MN: West Publishing Co., 1984.
Latzer, Barry. *State Constitutions and Criminal Justice*. New York: Greenwood Press, 1991.
Law Reform Commission. *Criminal Investigation*. Ottawa: Law Reform Commission of Canada, 1991.
Löwe, Ewald and Werner Rosenberg. *Die Strafprozessordnung und das Gerichtsverfassungsgesetz mit Nebengensetzemi: Grosskommentar*. 23rd ed. Berlin: De Gruyter, 1976.
Lusky, Louis. "Minority Rights and the Public Interest." *Yale Law Journal* 52 (1942): 1–41.
Markman, Stephen J. "The Fifth Amendment and Custodial Questioning: A Response to Reconsidering *Miranda*." *University of Chicago Law Review* 54 (1987): 938–49.
Martin's Annual Criminal Code. Toronto: Canada Law Books, Inc., 1991.
McCormick, Charles T. "Some Problems and Developments in the Admissibility of Confessions." *Texas Law Review* 24 (1946): 239–78.
McKeon, Marion. "Lawyers Urge Interim Criminal Procedure Reform." *Law Society's Gazette* 7 (March 20, 1991).
Moreland, Roy. *Modern Criminal Procedure*. Indianapolis: Bobbs-Merrill, 1959.
Morissette, Yves-Marie. "The Exclusion of Evidence Under the Canadian Charter of Rights and Freedoms: What to Do and What Not to Do." *McGill Law Journal* 29 (1984): 521–56.
Nardulli, Peter F. "The Societal Costs of the Exclusionary Rule Revisited." *University of Illinois Law Review* (1987): 223–39.
National Commission of Law Observance and Enforcement (Wickersham Commission). Report No. 8. *Criminal Procedure*. Washington, DC: U.S. Government Printing Office, 1931.
———. Report No. 11. *Report on Lawlessness in Law Enforcement*. Washington, DC: U.S. Government Printing Office, 1931.
Nowak, John E. "Due Process Methodology in the Postincorporation World." *Journal of Criminal Law and Criminology* 70 (1979): 397–423.
Nutting, Charles B. "The Supreme Court, the Fourteenth Amendment and State Criminal Cases." *University of Chicago Law Review* 3 (1935): 244–60.
Oade, K. Preston. "The High Court Sows Confusion." *Wall Street Journal*, July 13, 1984: 18.
Orfield, Myron W., Jr. "The Exclusionary Rule and Deterrence: An Empirical Study of Chicago Narcotics Officers." *University of Chicago Law Review* 54 (1987): 1016–55.
Packer, Herbert L. "The Courts, the Police, and the Rest of Us." *Journal of Criminal Law, Criminology and Police Science* 57 (1966): 238.
Pakter, Walter. "Exclusionary Rules in France, Germany and Italy." *Hastings International and Comparative Law Review* 9 (1985): 1–57.
Parliamentary Research Service. Digest of Crimes (Investigation of Commonwealth Offenses) Amendment Bill 1990 (Now "Act 1991"). Canberra: Parliamentary Research Service, 1991.

Paulsen, Monrad G. "The Fourteenth Amendment and the Third Degree." *Stanford Law Review* 6 (1954): 411–37.

"Plea Bargaining and its Analogues Under the New Italian Criminal Procedure Code and In the United States: Towards a New Understanding of Comparative Criminal Procedure." Student Editorial Note. *New York University Journal of International Law and Politics* 22 (1990): 215–251.

Polsky, Leon B., H. Richard Uviller, Vincent A. Ziccordi, and Alan J. Davis. "The Role of the Defense Counsel at a Lineup in Light of the *Wade, Gilbert,* and *Stovall* Decisions." *Criminal Law Bulletin* 4 (1968): 273–96.

Prosser, William Lloyd. *Handbook of the Law of Torts.* 4th ed. St. Paul, MN: West Publishing Co., 1971.

Rehnquist, William H. *The Supreme Court: How It Was, How It Is.* New York: Morrow, 1987.

Remington, Frank J. "A Quarter of a Century of Rulemaking with Particular Attention to the Federal Rules of Criminal Procedure." *Maine Law Review* 36 (1984): 219–251.

Report of the Board of Inquiry into the Enforcement of Criminal Law in Queensland. Australian Law Reform Commission, 1977. Cited as Lucas Report.

Report of the Royal Commission on Criminal Procedure. (Cmnd. 8092) London: Her Majesty's Stationer's Office, 1981.

Rogall, Klaus. "Gegenwärtiger Stand und Entwicklungstendenzen der Lehre von den Strafprozessualen Beweisverboten." *Zeitschrift für die Gesamte Strafrechtswissenschaft* [ZSTW] 91 (1979): 1–44.

Salhany, Roger E. *Canadian Criminal Procedure.* 5th ed. Aurora, Ont.: Canada Law Book, 1989.

Sallman, Peter and John Willis. *Criminal Justice in Australia.* New York: Oxford University Press, 1984.

Saltzburg, Stephen A. "Foreword: The Flow and Ebb of Constitutional Criminal Procedure in the Warren and Burger Courts." *Georgetown Law Journal* 69 (1980): 151–209.

Schulhofer, Stephen. "Reconsidering Miranda." *University of Chicago Law Review* 54 (1987): 435–461.

Shreve, Gene R. and Peter Raven-Hansen. *Understanding Civil Procedure.* New York: M. Bender, 1989.

Stephens, Otis H. Jr. *The Supreme Court and Confessions of Guilt.* Knoxville: University of Tennessee Press, 1973.

Stevens, John Paul. "The Life-Span of a Judge-Made Rule." *New York University Law Review* 58 (1983): 1–21.

Stewart, Potter. "The Road to *Mapp v Ohio* and Beyond: The Origins, Development and Future of the Exclusionary Rule in Search and Seizure Cases." *Columbia Law Review* 83 (1983): 1365–1404.

Stone, Geoffrey R. "The Miranda Doctrine in the Burger Court." *Supreme Court Review* (1977): 99–169.

Stone, Richard. "Police Powers after the Act." In *The Police: Powers, Procedures and Proprieties,* edited by John Benyon and Colin Bourn, 53–61. New York: Pergamon Press, 1986.

Uchida, Craig D. and Timothy S. Bynum. "Search Warrants, Motions to Suppress and 'Lost Cases': The Effects of the Exclusionary Rule in Seven Jurisdictions." *Journal of Criminal Law and Criminology* 81 (1991): 1034–66.

United States Department of Justice. Federal Bureau of Investigation. *Uni-*

form Crime Report for the United States. Washington, DC: U.S. Government Printing Office, annual.

——. National Institute of Justice. *Criminal Justice Research Report: The Effects of the Exclusionary Rule: A Study in California*. Washington, DC: U.S. Government Printing Office, 1982.

——. Office of Legal Policy. Truth in Criminal Justice Series, reprinted in *University of Michigan Journal of Law Reform* 22 (1989). "Report to the Attorney General on the Law of Pretrial Interrogation" (Report No. 1, February 12, 1986) (437–572); "Report to the Attorney General on the Search and Seizure Exclusionary Rule" (Report No. 2, February 26, 1986) (573–659).

Untitled article. *Reform* 26 (1982): 63.

Wasserstrom, Silas J. "The Incredible Shrinking Fourth Amendment." *American Criminology Law Review* 21 (1984): 257–401.

Weaver, John Dowling. *Warren: The Man, the Court, the Era*. Boston: Little, Brown & Co., 1967.

Weigand, Thomas. "Continental Cures for American Ailments: European Criminal Procedure as a Model for Law Reform." In *Crime and Justice: An Annual Review of Research*, Vol. 2, edited by Norval Morris and Michael Tonry, 381–428. Chicago: University of Chicago Press, 1980.

Weinreb, Lloyd L. *Denial of Justice: Criminal Process in the United States*. New York: Free Press, 1977.

——. "Generalities of the Fourth Amendment." *University of Chicago Law Review* 42 (1974): 47–85.

Weinstein, Jack B. "Reform of Federal Court Rulemaking Procedures." *Columbia Law Review* 76 (1976): 905–64.

Whitebread, Charles H. "The Burger Court's Counter-Revolution in Criminal Procedure: The Recent Criminal Decisions of the United States Supreme Court." *Washburn Law Journal* 24 (1985): 471–98.

Wolchover, David and Anthony Heaton-Armstrong. "The Questioning Code Revamped." *Criminal Law Review* (1991): 232–251.

Wright, Charles Alan. *Federal Practice and Procedure*. 2d ed. St. Paul, MN: West Publishing Co., 1982.

Zander, Michael. "The Act in the Station." In *The Police: Powers, Procedures and Proprieties*, edited by John Benyon and Colin Bourn, 123–35. New York: Pergamon Press, 1986.

——. *The Police and Criminal Evidence Act: 1984*. 2d ed. London: Sweet & Maxwell, 1990.

Index

This book was set in Baskerville and Eras typefaces. Baskerville was designed by John Baskerville at his private press in Birmingham, England, in the eighteenth century. The first typeface to depart from oldstyle typeface design, Baskerville has more variation between thick and thin strokes. In an effort to insure that the thick and thin strokes of his typeface reproduced well on paper, John Baskerville developed the first wove paper, the surface of which was much smoother than the laid paper of the time. The development of wove paper was partly responsible for the introduction of typefaces classified as modern, which have even more contrast between thick and thin strokes.

Eras was designed in 1969 by Studio Hollenstein in Paris for the Wagner Typefoundry. A contemporary script-like version of a sans-serif typeface, the letters of Eras have a monotone stroke and are slightly inclined.

Printed on acid-free paper.